NAVIGATING ECONOMIC DEVELOPMENT IN CAMEROON

Policy Trajectories from Independence to the Heavily Indebted Poor Countries (HIPC) Initiative Completion

1960-2006

ÉMERGENCES AFRICAINES
Dirigée par Magloire KEDE ONANA

La collection « ÉMERGENCES AFRICAINES » se propose de renverser des certitudes faciles. Nous sommes convaincus que l'Afrique, longtemps considérée comme en retrait, s'ouvre au monde, et est plus que jamais au cœur des enjeux. Son Histoire ne doit plus s'écrire ailleurs, par des continents eux-mêmes en crise de modèles à proposer/imposer.

Une nouvelle génération très entreprenante d'Africains et d'Africanistes existe aujourd'hui, qui problématise et réécrit l'Histoire du continent dans toutes ses facettes, et par une approche multidisciplinaire. Il s'agit de dévoiler une Afrique des « Bonnes Nouvelles » : celle qui, parce que plus ouverte au monde, présente tous ses atouts d'émergence.

Dernière arrivée dans la compétition mondiale, l'Afrique est capable d'apporter un élan différent à la mondialisation grâce à son devenir, qui est subordonné à son être.

Dernières parutions

Guy MVELLE, *Intégration en Afrique centrale : Réformes, projets prioritaires et rationalisation des Communautés économiques régionales*, 2024
Georges-Giresse MONDO, *Terre d'errance*, Roman, juin 2023
Sarah Anyang AGBOR, Edward Oben AKO, Manyaka Toko DJOCKOUA, *American literature, Periods, Trends and Themes*, janvier 2023
Jacques Didier LAVENIR MVOM, *Cameroun 1962 le train de la mort, Un épisode tragique oublié de la guerre d'indépendance*, janvier 2023
Abel MINKO MINKO, *Les voies d'exécution dans l'espace OHADA, Le cas du Cameroun*, décembre 2022
Eric Bertrand LEKINI, *L'intelligence artificielle, Le nouvel art de la guerre hybride au Cameroun*, septembre 2022
Marcelline DJEUMENI TCHAMABE, *La pédagogie des urgences à l'ère du numérique en de Covid-19*, septembre 2022
Rémy MBIDA MBIDA, *L'Union Africaine dans le maintien de la paix et sa coopération avec les Nations unies*, septembre 2022
Magloire Bienvenu MBA, *La responsabilité catéchétique des missionnaires. Analyse théologique des archives missionnaires du Sud-Cameroun 1890-1965*, 2022.
Victor-Joseph BELLA, *L'Ultime mort du Ressuscité*, 2022.
Guy David MBARA A BETSEM, *La chose constatée devant le Comité des droits de l'Homme des Nations Unies. Contribution à la théorie de l'expertise internationale*, 2021.

George Fuh Kum

NAVIGATING ECONOMIC DEVELOPMENT IN CAMEROON

Policy Trajectories from Independence to the Heavily Indebted Poor Countries (HIPC) Initiative Completion

1960-2006

Foreword by Verkijika G. Fanso

L'Harmattan

5-7, rue de l'Ecole-Polytechnique, 75005 Paris
http://www.editions-harmattan.fr
ISBN : 978-2-336-50538-1
EAN : 9782336505381

To
My wife, Felicity FUH KUM and children
for the love and togetherness

TABLE OF CONTENTS

ILLUSTRATIONS

ABBREVIATIONS AND ACRONYMS

ACADA	Aghem Cultural Development Association
ADB	African Development Bank
AfDBG	African Development Bank Group
ADI	Agricultural Development Institute
ALCAM	*Assemblée Législative du Cameroun*
ARCAM	*Assemblée Répresentative Camerounaise*
ASAP	Agricultural Sector Adjustment Plan
ATCAM	*Assemblée Territoriale Camerounaise*
BEAC	*Banque des Etats de l'Afrique Centrale*
BEF	Bloc Extension Farming
BICEC	*Banque Internationale du Cameroun pour l'Epargne et le Crédit*
CAMAIR	Cameroon Airlines
CAMSHIP	Cameroon Shipping Lines
CAMSUCO	Cameroon Sugar Company
CAMTEL	Cameroon Telecommunications
CCFOM	Central Fund for Overseas Territories
CDB	Cameroon Development Bank
CDC	Cameroon Development Corporation
CELLUCAM	*Cellulose du Cameroun*
CENADEC	*Centre National de Développement des Entreprises Coopératives*
CENEEMA	*Centre National d'Etudes et D'Expérimentation du Machinisme Agricole*
CFA	*Communauté Financière Africaine*
CHB	*Compte Hors-Budget*
CNF	Cameroon National Federation
CNU	Cameroon National Union
CPDM	Cameroon People's Democratic Movement
CTUF	Cameroon Trade Union Federation
ECUDA	Esu Cultural Development Association
EEC	European Economic Community
EITI	Extractive Industries' Transparency Initiative
ENSA	*Ecole Nationale Supérieure d'Agronomie et des Sciences Agronomiques*
EU	European Union
FAC	*Fonds d'Aide et de Coopération*
FAO	Food and Agriculture Organization

FASA	*Faculté d'Agronomie et des Sciences Agricoles*
FIDES	*Fonds d'Investissement pour le Développement Economique et Social*
FONADER	*Fonds National pour le Développement Rural*
FRC	Federal Republic of Cameroon
GDP	Gross Domestic Product
GFP	Group Farming Programme
HEVECAM	Hévéa Cameroun
HIPC	Heavily Indebted Poor Countries Initiatives
IDA	International Development Association
IMF	International Monetary Fund
INADER	*Institut National pour le Développement Rural*
INTELCAM	*Société des Télécommunications Internationale du Cameroun*
IRAD	*Institut de Recherche Agricole pour le Développement*
IRZ	*Institut de Recherche Zoologique*
KNDP	Kamerun National Democratic Party
MACUDA	Mankon Cultural and Development Association
MDGs	Millennium Development Goals
MDRI	Multilateral Debt Relief Initiative
MIDO	*Mission de Développement d'Ombessa*
MINADER	*Ministère de l'Agriculture et du Développement Rural*
MINEPAT	*Ministère de l'Economie, de la Planification et de l'Aménagement du Territoire*
MINFIB	Ministry of Finance and Budget
NADA	Njinikom Area Development Association
NAERP	National Agricultural Extension and Research Program
NAO	National Anti-Corruption Observatory
NAP	New Agricultural Policy
NCC	National Credit Council
NEF	National Employment Fund
NFSP	National Food Security Program
NGAP	National Governance and Anti-Corruption Programme
NGOs	Non-Governmental Organisations
NPDP	National Participative Development Program
NPMB	National Produce Marketing Board

OECD	Organisation for Economic Cooperation and Development
ONCPB	*Office National de Commercialisation des Produits de Base*
OTFP	Oxen Training and Farming Programme
PRGF	Poverty Reduction and Growth Facility
PRSD	Poverty Reduction Strategy Document
PWD	Public Works Department
REGIFERCAM	*Régie des Chemins de Fer du Cameroun*
RSDSD	Rural Sector Development Strategy Document
SAID	Swiss Association for International Development
SACIII	Third Structural Adjustment Credit
SAP	Structural Ajustement Programme
SEMRY	*Société d'Expansion et de Modernisation de la Riziculture de Yagoua*
SIB	*Société Internationale des Brasseries*
SITABAC	*Société Industrielle des Tabacs du Cameroun*
SNEC	*Société National des Eaux du Cameroun*
SNI	*Société Nationale d'Investissement*
SNI	*Société Nationale des Hydrocarbures*
SOCAPALM	*Société Camerounaise de Palmeraies*
SOCAR	*Crédit Société Camerounaise d'Assurance et de Réassurance*
SODECAO	*Société de Développement du Cacao*
SODECOTON	*Société de Développement du Coton*
SODENKAM	*Société de Développement du Nkam*
SODERIM	*Société de Développement de la Riziculture dans la plaine Mbo*
SONARA	*Société Nationale de Raffinage*
SONEL	*Société Nationale d'Electricité*
SOTUC	*Société des Transports Urbains du Cameroun*
UC	*Union Camerounaise*
UNDP	United Nations Development Programme
UNDVA	Upper Noun Valley Development Authority
UNO	United Nations Organisation
UPC	*Union des Populations Camerounaises*
URC	United Republic of Cameroon
USA	United States of America

USAID	United States Agency for International Development
VAT	Value Added Tax
VCPs	Village Community Projects
VDAs	Village Development Associations
WADA	Wum Area Development Authority
WW II	World War II
ZAPI	*Zones d'Actions Prioritaires Intégrées*

FOREWORD

Not much is known about Cameroon's economic development trends during the post-independence era. It is generally argued that a people without knowledge of their past might never know where they are coming from or where they are heading to. It is of utmost importance that every Cameroonian should have some knowledge of their country's history, most especially its economic development trends. This book is thus a welcome companion not only to students and researchers of economic history, but also to Cameroonians in general, especially those in positions of responsibility. That is why I wholeheartedly appreciate Professor Kum's effort, for meticulously and insightfully establishing the basic trajectories that characterised Cameroon's economic development strategies, from the time of independence to the completion point of the Heavily Indebted Poor Countries (HIPC) Initiative in 2006.

Knowledge of the basis from which Cameroon's early economic development ideas emerged is very essential and Professor Kum has done well in laying much emphasis on the country's colonial economic experiences under the Germans, the French and the British administrations, demonstrating how these influenced the post-colonial economy. He contends that like the colonial regimes, Cameroon's post-independent state played a central role in the country's economic development process during the study period. This is to say that Cameroon's foundational economic values were essentially influenced by externally imposed factors. The book further outlines the country's initial economic development guidelines, fundamentally based on the (regional) development planning and planned liberalism. These were based on promoting development, growth and curbing economic disparities among all the regions and intimates that it was from the foregoing principles that others gestated.

The book informs that Cameroon's early political economy was centred on her dire need for industrialisation, agricultural development and transport, although immense emphasis was placed on the foremost. Later it was deduced that it was too costly and slow at spurring growth and development. These main goals were guided through the Five Years Development Plans, which paid attention to providing public utilities through parastatals. Professor Kum has argued that these initiatives were less productive because Cameroon's economic development was purposefully funded through foreign sources due to purported inadequate domestic resources.

The study also delineates why policy makers endorsed agriculture in the early 1970s to replace industrialisation as the primary base for boosting real development in Cameroon. For Professor Kum, philosophies such as the operation green revolution, agro-pastoral shows, agro-industry, self-reliance development and food self-sufficiency were instituted to materialise the country's agricultural development drive and the various parastatals that had been, or were put in place. Unlike the initial policies that depended almost entirely on external financing, the author argues that most of those established in the 1970s depended more on domestic sources, accrued from Cameroon's oil revenues. Although these policies enhanced the country's early agricultural development vision, they nevertheless nose-dived due to inadequate financial resources, lack of proper functioning mechanisms and the advent of economic crisis in the mid-1980s.

The book further sketches the different measures, undertaken by the Cameroon government, the International Monetary Fund (IMF), the World Bank and other stakeholders to restore and sustain the country's economy, drained by the economic crisis. It is maintained that even before the crisis, many state-sponsored structures and projects, within the planned development framework, had become huge drain pipes to Cameroon's resources. These, combined with poor management of the oil boom of the late 1970s, greatly weakened the country's economy towards the period of the economic crisis. It was due to the slow progress in the structural and sustainable measures, imposed by the Bretton Woods institutions, that Cameroon got admitted into the HIPC initiative in 1994 and was able to record significant results, leading it through to the decision and eventual completion points in 2002 and 2006 respectively. I conclude that the completion point was not a means to an end of Cameroon's economic constraints, but an occasion for more sacrifices to be made by the country, for a more sustained economy.

Verkijika G. Fanso
Emeritus Professor
University of Yaoundé I

PREFACE

Navigating Economic Development in Cameroon: Policy Trajectories from Independence to the Heavily Indebted Poor Countries (HIPC) Initiative Completion, 1960-2006, is a fruit of several years of my interest on the country's economic development history. In fact, very little has been written on this sphere of Cameroon's history. Existing literature is difficult to grasp, because it is rare and appears in inadequate and incomplete forms. Some aspects of this history have been written, reason why this analytical compendium, presents a logical evolution of the country's economic development strides within the period earmarked. It has therefore ventured into establishing the different trajectories of the country's economic development systems, demonstrating that its economy was an affluent and flaggy one. This economy was systematically based on core values such as economic sovereignty, Capitalist-socialism, planned liberalism, regional planning, balanced development, self-reliance development, self-sufficiency, agro-industry, operation green revolution, agropastoral shows and others. These were all aimed at promoting growth, reducing poverty and improving social welfare in Cameroon.

Again, complaints from some of my third year and post graduate students about the difficulty of coming across specialised books on the economic history of post-independent Cameroon equally ignited my inspiration to write the book. Encouraged by their persistence and finding their worries adequately appealing, I embarked on crafting the book. This, because I thought it would be the best way through which such an important part of Cameroon history could be preserved for generations to come. The book is intended therefore to guide students initiated into this domain of history, researchers and Cameroonians' understanding of the country's economic development strides and influences that shaped its evolution. Most importantly, it would be useful to policy makers, enabling them to make informed decisions about the process of the country's economic development drive for its growth.

The best way to study, understand and draw valuable conclusions about Cameroon's post-independence economic history is by laying deep emphasis on its colonial experiences (Germans, French and British) and the influences they had on the economy. Not claiming to have answered all the questions that have been raised about Cameroon's economic development trends, it is essential that while reading through the book, close attention should be paid to important milestones, such as the development planning scheme, exhibited through a series of Five Years Economic and Social Development Plans. These laid emphasis on three basic domains: industrialisation, agriculture and infrastructural development; planned liberalism, regional planning, post-1970s agricultural policies, parastatal boom, the economic crises and the role the state; Bretton Wood institutions and other stake holders that played a role in refitting the country's economic sustainability, both before and after its admission into the HIPC initiative.

Finally, I will state that the production of this book was made possible by many people, all of whom am unable to mention by name. I humbly thank them all for their contributions, either directly or indirectly. I wish to thank the students and some of my supervisors who raised concerns about the scarcity of text books on the economic history of Cameroon, especially within the period earmarked for the project. Special thanks go to my academic father, Professor Verkijika G. Fanso, who was there from conceptualization through the development and conclusion of the book; taking time off to read, orientate and encourage its progress. I am also immensely indebted to Professors Canute Ngwa, Tassou Andre, Virginie Wanyaka, Raymond Ebale, Willibroad Dze-Ngwa, Maxime Dong Mougnol, Faustin Kenne, Alexis Tague, Nixon Takor, Edouard Bokagne, Anafak Japhet, Rene Ngek Monteh, Abena Etoundi and Chamberlain Nenkam, whose, ideas, invaluable suggestions, encouragements, criticisms and corrections, gave me the impetus to enrich my analysis. I thank Roger Che in the same light. I also thank all the authors (most especially those that focused on Cameroon's early independence economic) history and informants whose works and information were of great inspiration in the realisation of the project.

In all I wish to sincerely thank my wife Felicity, who showed much interest in the book and encouraged me time and again to progress, notwithstanding our kids, who provided a delightful working and resting environment. Nevertheless, I remain responsible for any shortcomings that appear in the book.

George Fuh Kum
University of Yaoundé I

INTRODUCTION

Cameroon's post-independence and reunification economic guidelines were inbred from the German, French and British colonial capitalist economies. These colonial administrations played dominant roles in upholding the then economic and social development orientations of their distinctive territories. This was inherited by the new born Republic and later Federal Republic of Cameroon for its quest of rapid national development, in the absence and or limited appropriate institutions for the task.[1] Development efforts were thus championed by public rather than private agencies, even in fields where the state had neither the requisite expertise nor comparative advantage over the latter sector.[2] Blending political and economic practices was assumed, would result to a fairer distribution of power and wealth to sustain and transform the newfound reunion between the British Southern Cameroons and French Cameroon (West and East Cameroon respectively). The aftermath was nevertheless that the state became more of a liability than an asset, with development infrastructures becoming incapable of discharging the duties for which they were established.

The foundations of Cameroon's political economy was initiated in its vision of a united East and Southern Cameroons, in spite the former, gaining its independence earlier on January 1st, 1960 and introducing the development planning machinery.[3] A plan was elaborated in 1960 to run for a period of 20 years and initial efforts on its achievement were framed in two medium phases: First and Second Five Year Development Plans.[4] The first plan (July 1960 to June 1965) was produced and in some haste by a French research and planning group, without adequate preliminary studies. It was equally put together before reunification and did not take into account the entering of West Cameroon into the total economy of the Federation.[5] It was therefore

[1] A. Ahidjo, *As Told by Ahmadou Ahidjo*, Paul Bory, Monaco, 1968, p.54.

[2] A. C. Ngwa and C. M. Lambi, "An Evaluation of the Upper Nun Valley Authority's Agricultural Innovation in the Ndop Plain (Cameroon) since 1970", Epassa Moto vol. 4, No. 1, 2009, p.51.

[3] T. Eyongetah and R. Brain, *A History of the Cameroons,* London, Longman, 1974. p.146.

[4] H.Philippe, *Analyse du sous-développement en Afrique noire: l'exemple de l'économie du Cameroun,* Paris presses universitaires de France, 1968, pp. 249-254.

[5] V.G. Fanso, *Cameroon History for Secondary Schools and Colleges, vol.2, The Colonial and Post-Colonial Periods*, London, Macmillan Publishers, 1989, p. 170.

without any comprehensive feasibility studies for possible development projects in former West Cameroon at the time, which made it difficult to extend the plan immediately there. This plan was unrealistic in that its results, only partially corresponded in domains such as infrastructure (railways), public education, health and housing, with very little met in the field of agriculture, one of the plan's key points of emphasis.[6]

It is worthy of note that Southern Cameroons (later West Cameroon) was relatively much underdeveloped than East Cameroon at reunification in such vital economic structures and basic social amenities like industries, rural infrastructure, schools, hospitals and recreational facilities.[7] This was in spite the general spatial imbalanced development and infrastructural distribution throughout the country that resulted in undesirable socio-economic relationships between rural and urban settings within and between both states in particular. This situation urged many youths to drift to towns for greener pastures.[8] The government of the Federal Republic of Cameroon (hereafter, FRC) took upon itself the challenge of providing solutions to this trend, in order to enable a compatible development of all the regions of the country.[9] The national development planning machinery that had been earmarked for the country before reunification, got transformed by its precursor President Ahmadou Ahidjo, still within its framework to what was termed regional economic development planning, to meet the country's development needs, ensuing from its independence and reunification.

This idea of a regional economic planning began in 1966, during the period of the second Five Years plan to harmonize development in the country. Its central aim was to fill the gaps that had been created by the first plan, thereby, working towards eliminating the economic and social disparities that were between the various regions and integrating their economies.[10] Still in connection to this was the need to doubling the real per capital income of the country by 1980.[11] In this plan, the

---

[6] W. A. Ndongko, *Planning for Economic Development in a Federal State: The Case of Cameroon, 1960-1971*, Munchen, Welt Form Verlage, 1975, p. 132.
[7] Ndongko, "A Comparative Analysis of French and British Investment Policies in Cameroon", *Pan African Journal,* Vol. VII, No.2, summer, 1974.
[8] G. F. Kum, "The Socio-Economic Impact of the Liquidation of the Wum Area Development Authority (WADA) on Wum Central Sub-Division 1989- 2004" Maîtrise Dissertation, Department of History, University of Yaoundé I, 2004, p.20.
[9] Ibid.
[10] Fanso, *Cameroon History for Secondary Schools and Colleges,* p.170.
[11] Ndongko, *Planning for Economic Development in a Federal State*, pp. 130-131.

Cameroon Government elaborated strategies aimed at tackling rural development with emphasis on self-reliance and regional development. This was not only because 85 percent of its population lived in rural areas, but also because regional and national development could not go that far without a wider examination, planning, management, and utilisation of rural areas.[12] The principles for a rapid and balanced economic development of Cameroon were embedded in president Ahidjo's principles of economic sovereignty, capitalist socialism, planned liberalism, self-reliant development, planning and others.[13]

To Ahidjo, development was not necessary without complete national sovereignty.[14] He intimated that national sovereignty was not complete so long as the economic dependence characteristic of under-development remained. Therefore, complete sovereignty entailed economic sovereignty, which to him could only be achieved through the influence of African Socialism. African Socialism was social justice to be obtained through modern technical means by concerting internal effort and foreign aid together in a coherent and realistic plan.[15] Its ultimate intension was to ensure balanced development in the necessary stability. Applying African socialism was undertaking reconversion, adaptation and not systematic destruction of existing structures. African socialism was a combination of realities as it borrowed its techniques from abroad and did graft them on African heritage.[16] It was therefore characterised by Africa's community spirit, respect for spiritual values and the central place of man.

This philosophy was nevertheless replaced by Cameroon's economic doctrine of planned liberalism, which was a conciliation of both the capitalist and socialist economic orientations. Under it, the state permitted a free market, managed natural resources and oriented foreign investment towards the common interest. It also partnered with foreign entities to set up various parastatals providing jobs to the population, especially the youths.[17] By self-reliance, economic

---

[12] Ahidjo, *As told by Ahmadou Ahidjo*, p.55.

[13] Ibid.

[14] Ahidjo, *The Political Philosophy of Ahmadou Ahidjo,* Paul Bory, Monte Carlo, 1968, p.87.

[15] Ahidjo, *As Told by Ahmadou Ahidjo*, p.53.

[16] Ibid.

[17] C. Dongmo, "The Green Revolution and Food Self-sufficiency: Cameroon's Land Theory of Economic Development", *Cameroon Link,* June 2008. Retrieved on 7th February 2011,

development depended largely on the natural, human and financial resources available within the country, while through development plans, special projects were targeted in various aspects of socio-economic life under three main spheres: agriculture, industry and transport.[18] Government set out to achieve this by increased funding of rural development projects.

During its early stages, precisely the period of the first and second five years development plans the development planning strategy emphasised on industrialisation, trusting this was going to quickly attain Cameroon's development goals, despite its financial constraints. In fact, the dominant political sentiment at the time was one of optimism, that the country would attain self-sustained growth.[19] It is argued that some political leaders at the time did virtually equate development with industrialisation.[20] This was nevertheless so costly and slow in reducing poverty and stimulating Cameroon's socio-economic development.[21] It did not work and in crafting a third plan in the early 1970s, agriculture was reconsidered as the crucial and most important stage to real development, especially as food insecurity became a major concern at the time. The country's Gros Domestic Product (GDP) fell from 8 percent in 1970, to 4 percent in 1971 and 3 percent in 1972.[22]

This continuous drop urged the government of Cameroon to adopt alternative measures other than those during the early independence era, to elevate the living standards of its masses. Hence, rather than depend solely on industrialisation initially perceived as the most practical way out for the country's development needs, agriculture was merged to the former, with the later taking precedence. Hence, agricultural frameworks like the *Sahel Vert* operation, operation Green Revolution, agro-pastoral shows, agro-industry and others were conceived and implemented to meet Cameroon's food sufficiency and self-reliant development goals. Ndongko acknowledges this when he opines that one of the most remarkable events in the country's political economy

---

http://www.camerounlink.net/?bnid=83&SessionID=&wid=&tid=&nid=38660&id

[18] Ibid.

[19] V. T. LeVine, *The Cameroon Federal Republic*, Cornell University Press, Ithaca and London, 1971, p.161.

[20] C. Zuvekas, Economic Development: An Introduction. London, Macmillan, 1979, p. 209.

[21] J. Seitz, The Politics of Development. New York, Basil Blackwell Inc, 1988, p. 15.

[22] Ibid.

in the 1970s was the promotion of agriculture, based on the forgoing patterns. [23] All these developments culminated in the country's discovery of immense oil reserves towards the late 1970s.

The year 1977 saw the start of Cameroon's oil boom. That year farmers were offered a large increase in real producer prices for cocoa, coffee, and cotton. [24] Prior to the oil boom, an extreme centralization of decision-making had resulted in heavy red tape and fragmentation of responsibilities in the bureaucracy and extension service.[25] This resulted in poor policy implementation, and misallocations as little expenditure was allotted to smallholder agriculture during the boom.[26] Three distinct kinds of resource misallocations became increasingly severe. The classic Dutch Disease was the first, due to unsustainable price incentives, which limited investment in smallholder agriculture. Another misallocation occurred within government institutions, due to unsustainable management structures. The third kind of misallocation was under-investment in new technology.[27] All these strictly worked down on Cameroon's most desired agricultural economy at the time.

The institution of five years development plans and petroleum boom of the 1970s introduced Cameroon into a period of economic triumphs. This period ensued to a serious economic crisis in 1986, as the country's economy shrivelled dramatically due to world market price instabilities on raw materials and fall in oil production. This plunged the country into serious hysteria.[28] A policy of internal adjustments was put in place, where salaries of civil servants and other costs of production were slashed. The condition got morose, due to the incessant decrease in revenue and over 40 percent drop in consumption per Cameroonian.[29] External debts increased during that same period. The government tried

---

[23] Ndongko, *Regional Development Policy in Cameroon*, the Faculty of Law and Economics, University of Yaoundé, 1975.

[24] E. Bamou and W. A. "Masters, Distortions to Agricultural Incentives in Cameroon", Paper 42, December 2007 https://www.researchgate.net/publication/228618483

[25] Ibid.

[26] Ibid.

[27] Ibid.

[28] W. J., Awung and M., Atanga, "Economic Crisis and Multi-Party Politics in Cameroon, Cameroon *Journal on Democracy and Human Rights*, Vol.5 No. 1, 2011, pp 94-124.

[29] M. D., Tambi, "Economic Growth, Crisis, and Recovery in Cameroon: A Literature Review", *International Journal of Industrial Distribution & Business* 6-1, 2015, pp. 5-15.

to survive on its saving programs for two years.[30] This did not work as the situation got worst and the country's letter of intent was accepted by the International Monetary Fund (IMF) in 1988.[31]

With the foregoing matter, a series of measures (internal and external) were instituted in deterring the economic crisis in Cameroon. These essentially constitute in the country's two years emergency plan, financial contributions from the IMF and Structural Adjustment Policies (SAP) of the World Bank. Emphasis shall equally be laid on the efforts made by the Cameroon government in accomplishing the completion point in 2006, under the IMF and World Bank's HIPC initiative. In its development process, Cameroon adopted models that were neither endocentric, appropriate, nor based on the needs of the plurality of its population. Consequently, the most blatant remnants of her experiments were abandoned projects, dysfunctional machinery and a visibly disenchanted population.

I- Geographical Setting

Cameroon is located in Central Africa in the heart of the Gulf of Guinea, with a surface area of about 475,000 km². Its population is about 25 million with high densities recorded in the cities and grassfields' area, where much of the population is constituted of rural dwellers.[32] It consists of highlands and steppes, savannahs and forests, located at the bottom of the Gulf of Guinea, in the shape of a triangle open to the Atlantic. It is bordered by Nigeria to the west, Chad to the north and northeast, the Central African Republic to the east and Gabon and Equatorial Guinea to the south.[33] It is the natural access and evacuation route for Central Africa. It is marked by diversity in unity with more than 250 national languages spoken by populations of its 10 regions.[34]

---

[30] S., Bertelsmann, *Cameroon Country Report, BTI*, 2012, in http://www.bti-project.org, retrieved on 20/07/2013.
[31]Ibid.
[32] C. C. Fonchingong and L. N. Fonjong, "The Concept of Self-Reliance in Community Development Initiatives in the Cameroon Grassfields," *Nordic Journal of African Studies* 12(2),2003, p. 197.
[33] P. Chauleur, «Un « libéralisme planifié » pour associer le secteur privé aux efforts de développement », https://www.monde-diplomatique.fr/1976/08/CHAULEUR/33871, Retrieved on 03, November 2023.
[34] Ibid.

Cameroon's population growth rate rose from less than 2 percent in 1950 to 2.9 percent per year between 1976 and 1987; this means that it doubled in less than 24 years. In 1976, Cameroon had 7,663,246 inhabitants and by 1987, the population was 10,493,655. [35] In 2005, the final results of the 3rd General Census of the Human Population indicated 17,463,836 inhabitants.[36] This demographic evolution confirms the maintenance of a strong human potential in the country, with an average annual population growth rate of approximately 2.8 percent during the period 1987-2005. This trend was downward in terms of the proportion of undernourished people and remained low in relation to the reality of sub-Saharan Africa.[37]

Before its independence, Cameroon was geographically divided between France and Britain, gained its independence through a two-stage process in 1960 and 1961 to become the Federal Republic of Cameroon.[38] It was renamed United Republic of Cameroon in 1972 and later Republic of Cameroon in 1984. Its first president, Ahmadou Ahidjo, ruled for over 20 years. Agriculture, education, health care and transport services were improved during his tenure of office. It was equally during this period that agro-pastoral shows were introduced under the policy of planning for development to boost agricultural development.[39] This continued shortly after President Paul Biya, but terminated due to the outbreak of the economic crisis in 1986.

Cameroon is a considerable potential, with varied resources, whose economic development was delayed due to a rebellion in the Bamileke region of the country.[40] It took all the political shrewdness of President Amadou Ahidjo to restore a difficult situation, harmonize ethnic relations, organize national unity, and establish the framework for a new economy.[41] It is heavily dependent on revenues generated from oil, timber and agricultural products.[42] Most of its regions are branded by

---

[35] J. M. Moudio, "The Dynamics of Food security policy in Cameroon (2008-2019)", *American Journal of Public Policy and Administration,* Vol.6, Issue 1, 2021, pp 12-43.

[36] Ibid.

[37] Ibid.

[38] Ibid.

[39] Bertelsmann Stiftung, "Cameroon Country Report", p.3.

[40] Chauleur, «Un « libéralisme planifié ».

[41] Ibid.

[42] G. Norrington-Davies, Climate Change Financing and Aid Effectiveness: Cameroon Case Study, OECD, March 2011, p.1.

shared cultural and traditional qualities, socialisation methods and other distinct physical and economic features. Very few countries in Africa possess such enormous human and natural resources as Cameroon.[43] Due to its socio-economically diverse nature, Cameroon's policy makers decided to opt for a regional development planning in 1966 during the period of the second five years development plan, aimed at harmonising development in the country thereby eliminating the various economic and social disparities between the various regions and integrating their economies.

It should be pointed out that as a result of the foregoing, the second development plan (1966-1971), became the first regionalized one, formulated for the six economic regions within the federal set-up: the Littoral, North, East, West, Center-south and West Cameroon.[44] For the first time, the planning process considered the spatial dimension of national development. This plan was therefore strategically aimed at integrating the federated states of East and West Cameroons economically, notwithstanding its diverse cultural, linguistic and ethnic backgrounds with a view of ensuring a balanced distribution of investment resources and fruits of economic progress. The essence of regional planning was equally to "assert, symbolise and strengthen national unity.[45]

II- Analytical Framework

The analytical framework of the study builds on a number of development theories. This choice was made for the fact that factors influencing the establishment of economic development policies in Africa and Cameroon in particular were innate in the history of development and economic development in particular. Economic development policies are government strategies that have an economic impact or determine how political forces shape national and global economic interactions, being the result of interaction between politics

---

[43] A. A. Amin (ed.), *Developing a Sustainable Economy in Cameroon*, https://books.google.cm/books/about/Developing_a_Sustainable_Economy_in_Came.html?id=0yewbFW06aYC&redir_esc=y, consulted on the 30th January 2023.

[44] Ndongko, "The Political Economy of Regional Economic Development in Cameroon", N. Kofele-Kale, *An African Experiment in Nation Building: The Bilingual Cameroon Republic since Reunification*, Westview Press, Boulder, Colorado, 1980, p.227-228.

[45] Ndongko, Regional Economic Planning in Cameroon, Research Report No. 21, the Scandinavian institute of African Studies, Uppsala, 1974, p. 6.

and the economy. Among types of economic development policies are socialism, whereby any production and wealth are regulated and distributed by society; capitalism, where private owners control the nation's industry and trade for profit, and communism, where all property is publicly owned and everyone works based on their needs and strengths. Cameroons economic development drive was based on capitalism, just like India did in 1947.[46]

India's economic growth however languished due to a number of economic policies and approaches it embraced that proved ineffective, including: a heavily statist approach of government intervention which gave rise to a "license raj" imposing strict controls on the economy; import substitution industrialization (ISI) policies that sought to see the development of indigenous industries by restricting foreign imports, but which often proved counterproductive; and a "small is beautiful" mentality that spurred higher productivity for fear it would destroy jobs.[47] Unfortunately, these policies significantly constrained the country's growth (especially compared to that achieved by peer countries) through to the 1980s. Though their impact was significantly mollified by the liberalizing reforms of the 1990s that enhanced its economic growth and contributed to the "Indian Economic Miracle". Economic theories of the time continued to animate policy thinking, leading to the trade-distorting policies Indian policy makers re-embraced in the 2010s.

Worthy of note is that the factors influencing the economic development choices of developing economies and Cameroon in particular, were diverse and controversial. Cameroon's economic development policies did not however record satisfactory results. In the same light, Albert Hirschman, writing about the experiences of Latin American countries in the 1960s, opines that many which pursued similarly ineffectual economic policies as India failed: "the blame for the economic disasters in these countries lay not in the use of policies considered by economic theorists to be wrong, but in the blind pursuit of policies considered by theorists to be right."[48] This could be understood in the arguments that follow, characterized by the Modern, Dependence, World Systems and State theories.

[46] S. Ezell and R. Atkinson, *The Indian Economy at a Crossroads*, The Information Technology & Innovation Foundation (ITI F), 2014, p.214.

[47] Ibid.

[48] Ibid., p.18.

The Modern Theory is a theory of economic development, which states that development can only be achieved through following the processes that were used by currently developed countries.[49] This theory emerged based on the continuing rise in the income levels in Western countries (since the Industrial Revolution). It was also due to the desire for developed countries to embark on a campaign of massive transfer of capital and technology to developing countries in order to enable a rapid industrialization intended to result to an economic take-off.[50] According to this model, technology was going to play a great role in the development of developing countries because it was believed that as soon as it was developed and introduced to the less developed countries, it would spur growth. Mier[51] buttresses this view and advances further that the greatest benefit of this to the recipient country is the access to foreign knowledge that could help overcome managerial and technical gaps. Nevertheless, as Piel[52] argues, the availability of modern industrial technology from the rich nations is indeed a matter of great importance, but the greatest problem is putting it into use, as it requires the recipient country to maintain sustained economic, political as well as cultural relations with the lending country.

It was further believed that if this is done, less developed countries would develop and grow faster than developed countries. The theory was built upon the argument that it is possible for equal development to be reached between the developed and less developed countries. One key factor of the modern theory was the belief that developed countries had to aid developing countries learn from their experiences in order to develop, with the state being at the centre. Whatsoever, although it did effect some changes, the technologies transferred to Cameroon from the West for economic development purposes, did not work as expected, but reflected Jequier's view which states that: "... by the late 1960s, it was becoming clear that this development method did not work as expected ... became a potential cause of increasing poverty and income

[49] A. B. Djeudo, *Advanced Human, Economic and Regional Geography (Area Studies): Concepts and case studies in a World of Development Contrast A4 in I Volume,* Success Education Publishers Limbe, Cameroon, 2008, p.5.

[50] S. Jackson and P.K. Ghosh (eds), *Appropriate Technology in Third World Development,* London, Greenwood Press, 1984, p.76.

[51] G.M. Meier, *Problems of Cooperation for Development*, New York, Oxford University Press, 1974, p.98.

[52] G. Piel, *Technology and Economic Development,* USA, Alfred A. Knofe, 1963, p.182.

inequality in developing countries".[53] Thus, unlike classical liberalism the modern theory viewed the state as a vital actor in modernising developing societies.

However, the modern theory was highly contradicted by the dependency model, which propounded that the effects of colonialism on developing countries must be considered when creating future development endeavours. This theory grew out of Latin America, especially when scholars like Raul Presbisch observed that the modern theory was failing to address the consequences of colonialism, such as trade inequities in which the colonial trade patterns of exporting raw materials, agriculture and importing the processed and manufactured goods continued to persist.[54] Krause further connotes the modern theory as the process in which developing countries became more and more entrenched and dependent on the developed world.[55] The dependency theory therefore categorizes countries into two levels of development: centre and periphery. The centre is the colonising and developed countries, while the periphery consists of the colonized and developing countries.[56] In the theory, the structural change models stress the transformation from a traditional agriculture to a modern industrial economy.

Brunel opines that the dependency ideology that did preoccupy African states at independence, insisted on an anti-centre development against international exchanges, viewed as a source of alienation and underdevelopment because of unequal exchange.[57] She demonstrates this through the sale of manufactured goods at high cost by the rich to the poor countries in exchange of lowly paid primary products and thus concludes that it was through colonial and post-colonial exploitation that centre countries were able to develop. For her, since exploitation allowed the centre countries to develop, it is difficult for the same process to lead to development in the previously exploited countries. Albeit important for attracting attention to linkages between traditional agriculture and modern industry, the dependency theory is criticised for

---

[53] N. Jequier, *Appropriate Technology: Problems and Promises*, Paris, OECD, 1976, p.16.

[54] Djeudo, *Advanced Human, Economic and Regional Geography,* p.5.

[55] Krause, *The Underdeveloped World and American Interest*, p.27.

[56] Ibid.

[57] S. Brunel, *La Cooperation Nord-Sud,* Paris, Presses Universitaires de France, 1997.p.94.

not providing any feasible development solution.[58] This is because Cameroon's economic development policies were tilted towards the production of raw materials to furnish European economies.

The World Systems model initiated by Wallesein[59] discredits the dependency argument by furthering the gap between the periphery and centre into a trimodal system consisting of the core, semi-periphery and periphery. In this theory, the semi-periphery lies between the core and periphery and is exploited by the core and exploits the periphery. One distinguishing feature of the World Systems is the distrust for the state, that is seen as a group of elites and also the fact that industrialisation cannot be equated with development.[60] The World Systems focuses on inequality as a separate entity from growth in development and examines change in the capitalist system. This distrust on the state by the world systems urged Cameroon into accepting the IMF and World Bank conditionality that stressed on the private sector and privatisation. This theory provoked the introduction of the state system.

In response to the distrust of the state in the World Systems theory, is the State theory. The State theory is based on the notion that the economy is intertwined with politics and therefore the take-off period in development is unique to each country. It emphasises the effects of class relations and the strength and autonomy of the state on historical outcomes. According to it, development is dependent upon state stability and its influence both externally as well as internally. State theorists believe that a developmental state is required for development by taking control of the development process in the country. This view of the state as the main actor in development endeavours is commensurate with what obtained in most independent African countries, as revealed by Ahidjo during the first congress of the CNU party, held on the 10th March 1969:

> We have always remained faithful to our policy of planned Liberalism, consequently, while we have always strongly encouraged foreign investments, we have never made it a secret that we will not allow our foreign partners to set up autonomous industrial and commercial enterprise which operate outside the scope of the state constitution as if it were states in states, that is why we advocate a participation of some state organs, like the *Société Nationale d'Invetissement*

[58] Djeudo, *Advanced Human, Economic and Regional Geography,* p.5.

[59] I. Wallstein, *World Systems Analysis*, Durtham NC, Duke University Press, 2004. Cited in Djeudo, *Advanced Human, Economic and Regional Geography,* p.6.

[60] Djeudo, *Advanced Human, Economic and Regional Geography,* p.6.

(SNI) and the Cameroon Development Bank (CDB), in these enterprises, assuring a Cameroonian share in the management.[61]

The theories raised shall enable us to better enhance the centrality of our book based on the evolution of Cameroon's economic development policies from independence to the completion point of the Heavily Indebted Poor Countries' Initiative. From the analytical outline of the study, we realise that although these theories effected some constructive changes in Cameroon's economy and social values, politics and statism remained decisive features in the process, which did not however augur well for its development. This section introduces us to chapter one which examines the organisation of colonial economies and how they influenced post-independence development policies in Cameroon.

[61] Ahidjo, *Anthologies des discours du Président Ahidjo, 1973-1978,* (II), Dakar, NEA, 1980, p.212.

CHAPTER ONE
BACKGROUND STUDY

Introduction

Chapter one examines the background to Cameroon's economic development trends It lays deep emphasis on the organisation of colonial economies in the territory, stressing on the different patterns European countries employed for their economic gains. It begins by generally examining the motives of European colonisation especially the Germans and their economic development patterns in Cameroon. It continues with both the mandates and trusteeships periods in British and French Cameroons, emphasizing on their economic development policies in the territory, during these periods. It argues that because of pressure on the United Nations (UN), from political events in British and French Cameroons geared towards finding a solution to the question of the status of both trust territories. The chapter finally presents the circumstances that led to the independence and reunification of both territories.

I- German Cameroon (1884-1914)

The colonization of Africa was largely motivated by economic exploitation. This was in itself a way to monopolise the control of colonized territories' economies. The role of colonial offices in Europe and governors in Africa was to exploit colonies for the development of colonial mother countries. Hence, European economic policies during this period consisted of the large-scale production of raw materials for European industries; large-scale control of mining activities in the colonies; building of railway networks to connect production areas to seaports; introduction of European currencies and establishment of banks to facilitate trade and enable Africans to buy finished products, brought in from Europe. These economic policies also consisted of trade monopoly for European companies, to prevent competition by Africans and the establishment of Marketing Boards to fix prices for African export commodities.[1]

The onset of the process of European economic exploitation of Africa was when explorers, scientists, missionaries and traders, of the

[1] B. Barkindo, M. Omolewa and G. Babalola, *Colonial Economy and underdevelopment of Africa and the Wider world 3: Africa since the scramble*, Longman Nigeria, 1994, p. 62.

19th century made Europeans understand that tropical and sub-tropical Africa possessed enormous wealth that could be tapped to satisfy European economies. The Industrial Revolution had begun in Europe, brought about a production boom and need for raw materials and markets for its sustenance.[2] This urged economic colonialists to embark on promoting trade, agriculture and most importantly the production of cash crops on secured territories in Africa. They began setting up agricultural stations in many parts of the continent where cash crops like cocoa, cotton, groundnuts, tobacco, palm trees, rubber and others could be experimented.[3] Improved seeds and seedlings were equally produced and distributed to farmers in areas that were suitable for the cultivation of particular experimented crops. It was mandatory for farmers to grow these crops.[4] Europeans never had the intension of developing the agricultural sector in the interest of the colonised, but rather for the production of crops needed to feed their economies.

As far as Germany was concerned, it became one of the most powerful nations in the world due to her unification in 1871.[5] During this period, she was flourishing with nationalism and patriotism and there was every need to expand this great energy to other parts of the world. It was in this light that great proponents like Treitschke, advocated colonialism as a means of projecting German nationalism. He and other great German minds like Franz Mauer strongly believed that Germany's most pressing need was the acquisition of colonies as summarized following:

> People from elder states who have been disciplined, go out and found new states...Every virile people have established colonial power... All great nations in the fullness of their strength have desired to set their mark upon barbarian lands and those who fail to participate in this great rivalry will play a pitiable role in the time to come. The colonizing impulse has become a vital question for every great nation.[6]

Apart from the question of projecting German nationalism to the outside world, there was equally the need to spread the gospel to the barbaric people of the uncivilized world and most especially to the Dark

---

[2] P. Agbor-Tabi, "German Colonialism in Africa: Domestic Pressure or Governmental Policy?" in *Cameroon Review of International Studies*, Vol 2, No. 1, 1985, p.12.

[2] Ibid., p. 13.

[3] Barkindo, Omolewa and Babalola, *Colonial Economy and underdevelopment,* p.63.

[4] J.F. M. Kibaya, *L'information stratégique agricole en Afrique : L'échec de la vulgarisation*, Harmattan, Paris, 2006, p.21.

[5] Agbor-Tabi, "German Colonialism in Africa: Domestic Pressure or Governmental Policy?" p.15.

[6] Ibid., p. 13.

Continent. This role was played by missionary societies. In this group, the Basel and the Bremen Rhine missions advocated colonialism, as a means to spread the word of God in the 1870s. As time went by, their interest went beyond the spread of Christianity to include trade and exploration. These missions were eager to see the flag follow the gospel. One of the most prominent of the missionaries, Doctor Fabri, Inspector of the Rhine Mission requested the German government to protect his works in the Negro land. To him, colonies were to serve as markets, new fields of investment and outlets for surplus population. It is argued that though he went to Africa under religious guise, his propaganda converted more Germans to imperialism, than the heathen Africans to Christianity.[7]

Other forces were from scientists and explorers. To this group, Africa was a curiosity and they wanted to discover the myth that kept it away from the civilized world. Their efforts led to the International Congress at Brussels called by king Leopold of Belgium in 1876, which resulted in the creation of the African International Society.[8] Again, the journeys of Stanley, Gustave Natchtigal and Heinrich Barth in the hinterlands of Cameroon awakened new interest in Africa and acted as impetus to exploration.[9] These explorers through their writings and public pronouncements, depicted very geographically marvelous economic potentialities of the areas they visited in their efforts to arouse a colonialist attitude in the German people.

Commercial colonialists played a very vital role in pressurizing the government to expand overseas. They found ready arguments to support their views from within the domestic arena. The Industrial Revolution had begun in Germany and there was a production boom. Raw materials were needed in order to sustain the revolution. Such arguments were pronounced by industrialists and commercial classes, aided by financiers like Bleichroder and Von Hansemann, friends and advisers to Bismarck, who tended to influence him.[10]

External forces were also capital in influencing Germany into acquiring territories in Africa. The prevailing economic theory that

---

[7] T.P. Moon, *Imperialism and World Politics*, New York, 1940, p.64.
[8] Tabi, “German Colonialism in Africa: Domestic Pressure or Governmental Policy?”, pp. 14 -15
[9] Ibid.
[10] Ibid., pp.15-16.

existed before the 1870s was free trade.[11] This policy rendered the acquisition of colonies anachronistic, especially as all European powers had equal access to markets. Influenced by this dominant economic thought at the time, Bismarck said that: "the desire for colonies should be considered chimerical. They are an anachronism; the advantages of colonialism are very few and the expense very great. Beyond our frontiers, we wish to seek nothing than peace.''[12]

By 1874, activities of the English in the Fiji Islands proved that free trade was slowly being replaced by protective tariffs and the British were playing the unfair game which advocated such an economic policy only when it was in their interest to do so. Bismarck felt that if he had to maintain supremacy in Europe, he had to join the game played by great powers and play according to the new rule. Although Otto Von Bismarck claimed that: "No country should engage upon colonial activity unless a strong public opinion supports it",[13] he later on changed his mind. As a matter of fact, he was so opposed to colonial expansion, especially as he turned down several opportunities to acquire colonies during the preliminary Frankfort talks in 1870 and 1876. He rejected requests to extend protection to Zanzibar and other territories in South West Africa, where German traders and missionaries were very present.[14]

Bismarck's negative rejoinder to colonialism was because he wanted a German hegemony and to maintain the balance of power in Europe. For him, indulging in the colonial race would cause friction with other European powers that could end up affecting the different groups in Germany.[15] Again, Bismarck knew that Germany lacked a strong navy to back up her colonial activities. For instance, when Luderitz contacted Bismarck about founding a colony in South Africa as a result of the request from the Boers, he rejected the offer and said the time was not propitious politically. Bismarck equally suspected a war of vengeance from the French who had just suffered defeat and the loss of Alsace and Lorraine. Thus, he needed to maintain friendly ties with England in

---

[11] A. Cheradame, *La colonisation et les colonies Allemands,* Paris, 1905, p. 28. Cited in Cameroon *Review of International Studies*, p.18.

[12] Ibid.

[13] M. E. Townsend, *The Origins of Modern German Colonialism,* 1871-1885, New York, 1921, p.20., Cited in *Cameroon Review of International Studies*, p.19.

[14] Ibid.

[15] Tabi, "German Colonialism in Africa: Domestic Pressure or Governmental Policy?", p. 20.

order to isolate France in the 1870s, but things changed in the 1880s as Bismarck through his alliance system reversed the balance, thereby enabling Britain to depend on the goodwill of Germany especially on the Egyptian issue.[16]

Despite numerous calls from his nationals, Otto Von Bismarck remained disinterested in the acquisition of territories in Africa. This was not only due to fears on the heavy costs involved, but also because of his desire to maintain a German hegemony and balance of power in Europe. Germany felt much secured in Europe by 1883 after the conclusion of the Triple Alliance. This was however not long as by 1874, England's activities in the Fiji Islands proved that the prevailing economic theory: "Free Trade", propounded by the Manchester School at the time was slowly, but steadily giving way for protective tariffs. England had begun to play this unfair game of advocating this theory only when it was to her advantage.[17] This diplomacy made Bismarck to reconsider his stance by joining the colonial race. His stance was further buttressed by German traders both at home and abroad, who pointed out that possessing territories would assure markets for Germany's surplus goods and control over them would produce the raw materials they needed.[18] There was equally an abundance of cheap labour and natural water transport facilities in the territories they had secured, as added values.[19]

One of the Germans, who did enormous in territorial acquisition in Africa was, Aldolf Woermann, president of a firm that bore his name. This firm had been in West Africa since 1849, but opened its first trading station in Cameroon in 1868.[20] Increasing trade plus fears of British and French imperial ambitions, made Woermann to become an active person in the steps leading to the German occupation of Cameroon in 1884.[21] For preventive motives, he urged Bismarck to protect trade in Cameroon. The chiefs in Cameroon owed German businessmen huge sums of money and were unable to pay these debts. The Germans equally feared that if the British annexed Cameroon, obstacles would be placed on German commerce. It was in this

---

[16] Ibid., p. 21.

[17] Ibid.

[18] H.H. Rudin, *Germans in the Cameroons 1884-1914*, New York, 1969, p.34.

[19] B.S.Takang, *An Illustrated History of Cameroon Since 1800: A Digest for Advance Level Students*, Book House, Yaounde, 2013, p.88.

[20] Eyongetah and. Brain, *A History of the Cameroons,* p.79.

[21] Ibid.

perspective that Woermann projected five motivating reasons for the need of a German protectorate stemming from: Increased German Trade; English opposition to German traders generally; the need for protecting trade against the indigenes; the fear of the French and their high duties; and the fear of the Congo treaty made by England and Portugal.[22]

As far as the German annexation of Cameroon was concerned, Nachtigal was in many ways, personal emissary of the two great German commercial houses, Woermann and Jantzen Und Thormahlen, since he was tutored by both to claim for Germany whatever land the two had acquired or would acquire by treaty in places that they named. In Cameroon, two documents were signed at the time. The first was an expression of the wishes of the local chiefs, in which it was clear that the Europeans accepted to keep out of the markets in the interior and to continue providing credit facilities to carry on with trade.[23]

The chiefs also stipulated that no land should be taken from them. This document was very important as far as later developments were concerned in the territory as they were all bypassed. The second one was a treaty between German traders and the kings. This was signed on the part of Germany by Edouard Schmidt representing the Carl Woermann firm and by Johannes Voss, for the Jantzen Und Thormahlen firm; all two were from Hamburg and merchants for years on the rivers. Sovereignty over the land was given to the Germans under certain conditions: rights of third parties to be respected, treaties of commerce and friendship were to remain in force.

Kumi (a gift to the indigenes) for the right of trade was to be paid as in the past. Indigenous land was to remain the property of the present owners.[24] Mveng holds another view that before the signing of the 12th July 1884 treaty, some others had been signed with quarter heads, like Deido, on the 11th July 1884. It was in relation to this that on the 14th July 1884; Doctor Nachtigal hoisted the German flag in the three signatory quarters.[25] When the Germans colonised Cameroon, they decided to despise the terms of the treaties, as they immediately placed their relations with the interior of Cameroon, in order to trade with it directly and make more profits. It can be argued that this abrogation

[22] Ibid., p. 62.
[23] Ibid., p. 63.
[24] Ibid.
[25] E. Mveng, *Histoire du Cameroun*, Paris, Présence Africaine, 1963, p.293.

was linked to the outcomes of the Berlin West African Conference that met between the 15th November 1884 and 25th February 1885.

As soon as the territory was annexed, Bismarck held discussions with Karl Woermann and Jantzen Und Thormalen on how the newly acquired territory would be administered. The outcome was that matters concerning war, foreign affairs and justice would be the responsibility of the government, while the ministries of interior and commerce were to be under the special care and responsibility of the traders. Woermann's spokesman then worked out a detailed scheme and was sent to Bismarck on October 15th 1884 in which he asked for a governor, secretaries, courts, schools and others.[26]

Initially, Bismarck did not accept due to the heavy costs involved, but was eventually pressured and convinced to bear the cost of administration. The Chancellor's colonial system was one run by traders in the interest of trade. He wanted the colonial beneficiaries of the colonial enterprise to have a greater responsibility than the Government thereby averting too much expenditure. This placed German firms at the centre of the colonial enterprise. The Germans moved inland over the years, extending their control and claims to lands far beyond Cameroon, where they opened up trade and secured monopolies in particular areas.[27]

The economic exploitation of Cameroon was affected by trade and plantations. Bismarck's desire to protect trade led to placing the Cameroons under the German flag. Bismarck's utmost purpose of acquiring colonies was simply to protect German trade.[28] Just as the tariff of 1879 protected the German domestic market from competition, so too was the acquisition of territories beyond the seas to protect distant markets. Initially, Germans' major trade dealings were with African traders, mainly Duala, along the coast. But they did not enjoy dealing with these "middlemen," for direct trade with the interior due to the limited profits incurred thereby using colonial power to break this monopoly.[29]

At the time of annexation, mention was made on the possibility of plantation agriculture in the Cameroons, but that was purely secondary and suggested merely as an additional reason to make the territory's

[26] Fanso, *Cameroon History for Secondary Schools and Colleges,* p.177.

[27]M. D. Delancey, et al., *Historical Dictionary of the Republic of Cameroon*, Fourth Edition, the Scarecrow Press, Inc. Lanham, Maryland, 2010, p.4.

[28] Fanso, *Cameroon History for Secondary Schools and Colleges,* pp.152-153.

[29] S. G. Ardener, *Eye-Witnesses to the Annexation of Cameroon, 1883-1889,* Ministry of Primary Education and West Cameroon antiquities Commission, Buea, 1968, p. 24.

occupation more meaningful to likely objectors back home. Interest in this activity developed rather slowly, but gained strength when the Germans came to the conviction that there was a chance of acquiring through plantations such commodities as tobacco which Germany had to import from other countries or produce near the coast. These were equally items that trader bought from the interior at great expense and danger.

Plantation agriculture was the second major economic activity during the German colonial era. Large estates were established, especially in the southwest of Cameroon, to provide a variety of tropical crops like cocoa, bananas, tea, rubber and others, to Germany[30]. All this was only possible as from 1895 after the defeat of Bakwerians and expropriation of their lands where the first German plantation was opened by the newly founded Victoria Plantations Company.[31] By 1902, about fourteen German plantations existed in the territory. The Germans took some 120,000 hectares of land for plantations where coffee, tobacco, cocoa, rubber, palm oil and bananas were cultivated.[32] Traders, plantation owners, and government officials competed for scarce labour, and force was necessary for the Germans to break the Africans away from their homes and farms.[33] The labour system established was harsh and cruel, and many labourers died while serving German interests. Apart from existing basic labour force in the territory, there was need for increased skilled labour to help meet Germans' needs. It was this that urged them to embark on vocational education.

The Germans succeeded in Cameroon due to their insistence on the schooling allocative function. In other words, they were less interested in making Africans quassi-Germans, but concentrated on crafting those who were capable of understanding and implementing their definition of work. These were equally thanks to the German Colonial Society (*Deutsche Kolonial Gesellschaft*), a propaganda organisation that was founded in 1884, to win popular support for colonial ventures and encourage research on tropical agriculture enabled excessive economic

---

[30] DeLancey et al., *Historical Dictionary of the Republic of Cameroon,* p. 5.
[31] Ibid.
[32] Kum, "Drives and Prospects of Agriculture in Vocational Training During the period of the Germans in Cameroon", I. S. Njock Nyobe and J. P. Nzogue (eds.) *Le Cameroun sous Domination Européen: Entre Rencontre, Partages et Conflictualités,* 1884-1914, Editions Ifrikaya, 2018, p.163.
[33] DeLancey, *Historical Dictionary of the Republic of Cameroon,* p. 5.

attainments.[34] It was it that urged German traders to penetrate and establish control of the interior so that they could increase the cultivation of the much needed tropical crops and that by 1913, there were altogether 58 German plantations in the territory with a total of 195 European employees and 17827 African workers.[35]

Germans' economic exploitation policy came to a swift halt in the territory in 1916, when they were defeated in the First World War by Britain and France. After their defeat, the administration of Cameroon was temporarily passed over to both powers in a Condominium. This ran up to 1919 after the signing of the Versailles treaty.[36] Worthy of note is the fact that the Germans were not admitted at the peace talks. According to articles 118 and 158 of the treaty, Germany was deprived of all her lawfully acquired colonies, which were very valuable parts of her national capital.[37] The German National House of Assembly was generally disgruntled by the conditions imposed on Germany by the victorious powers.

According to Scheidemann, president of the German National Assembly, these conditions were intolerable for Germany and in contradiction with the basis of peace on justice.[38] The Germans said the seizure of colonies was unjustified and thus vowed that these were territories to be recuperated. In justifying their position, allied powers invoked the permanent attitude of German force labour in West Africa, Cameroon and the Heroros in South Africa.[39] Again, the German colonial administration was presented as cruel and oppressive.[40] German resistance to the terms of peace yielded no fruits, as victorious powers went ahead to implement their rules in the various territories they had seized from Germany.

German colonial demands started after the peace treaty. As soon as this treaty was made known, the Weiman Republic's constitution

---

[34] Eyongetah, Brain and Palmer, *A History of the Cameroon*, p.68.

[35] Fanso, *Cameroon History for Secondary Schools and Colleges.*

[36] D. Oyono, "L'Allemagne et le statut international du Cameroun 1919-1939 », *Revue Camerounaise des Relations Internationales,* Vol. 2, No 1, Berlin, 1985, p.85.

[37] V. J. Ngoh, *The World since 1919: A Short History,* Pioneer Publishers, Yaoundé, 1989, p.5.

[38] P. Renonim, *Le Traite de paix de Versailles,* Paris, Flammarion, 1969, p. 85. Cited in *Revue Camerounaise des Relations Internationales Vol2,* No.1, Berlin, 1985, p.109.

[39] Oyono, « L'Allemagne et le statut international du Cameroun », p.105.

[40] R. Cornevin, *Histoire de la Colonisation Allemande*, Paris, PUF, 1969, p. 102. Cited in *Revue Camerounaise des Relations Internationales Vol2,* No.1, Berlin, 1985, p.109.

stipulated in its article six that the "Reich has a legislative competence in the colonial domain", which meant that if by law Germany had lost her colonies, in reality she considered them territories to be recuperated.[41] The foregone developments explain why the Germans came back to the territory, most especially in British Southern Cameroons. This was in spite the partition and introduction of two distinct economic policies in British and French Cameroons by the victorious powers. This arrangement, ran from 1922 to 1961 under the League of Nations mandates and United Nations Trusteeship.

II- British Southern Cameroons

The British Cameroon (Southern and Northern Cameroons) was ruled as an integral part of Nigeria, after the defeat of the Germans in the territory. Our point of focus in this section shall be on Southern Cameroons, which reunified with the Republic of Cameroon in 1961. The economic history of Southern Cameroons was characterised by two distinct periods (Mandates and trusteeship) as shall be seen in the sub-sections that follow.

A) Mandate Period

Key economic activities in Southern Cameroons after the official departure of the Germans were plantation and subsistence agriculture. The Germans had set up many plantations in the territory, constructed roads and railways, established ports and airstrips as well as putting in place modern buildings, which made the territory comparable to none in colonial Africa.[42] One of the foremost concerns of the British upon assuming control of the territory in 1916 was to have the economy of the territory re-established, after WWI and the expulsion of German economic operators. Again, the Anglo-French partition of the territory that same year had left about 90 per cent of the total plantation acreage in the former German protectorate in the hands of the British.[43]

---

[41] Oyono, « L'Allemagne et le statut international du Cameroun », p. 111.

[42] J. N. Mokake, *Basic Facts on Cameroon History*, Cure Series Publishers, Limbe, 2008, p.93.

[43] Fanso, *Cameroon History for Secondary Schools and Colleges, from prehistoric Times to the twenty-first century (revised and updated combined edition),* Team Work Press, Bamkika'ay, Kumbo, p.241.

As soon as the British took over, they appointed an agricultural expert to supervise all the plantations. The major problem facing these plantations and other properties of enemy nationals was to maintain their pre-war productive capacity. A series of efforts were employed by the British to improve on this. Medical officers were appointed to ensure proper sanitation and health of plantation workers and also made sure that the estates had civil police to bring about law and order in the area.[44] But no sooner did the British encounter difficulties in running the plantations and other German infrastructures.[45] The roads and railways were neglected, with the old ones totally abandoned, without maintenance or replacement.[46] German plantations were confiscated and handed over to the custodian of Enemy Property to be administered during the War.

After the war, the possibility of returning the land to the original inhabitants was considered, but the Lieutenant Governor of the southern provinces of Nigeria, said it would be impracticable to split the plantations into small plots for Cameroonian owners, since without capital backing the buildings, machinery would fall into ruins.[47] Moreover, it was feared that Cameroonians' lack of experience in plantation agriculture meant that disease would spread among the crops and cocoa plants would be destroyed. Consequently, in 1922, the custodian of Enemy Property was directed to sell the estates to anyone except ex-enemy nationals. When the estates were put up on sale in London in 1923, almost all of them failed to find buyers as security of titles and large amounts of money were needed to put the plantations back into operation.[48] The low level of prices obtaining for raw products at that time must have been a determining factor.

Another auction was held in London in November 1924 with the restrictions against ex-enemy nationals withdrawn. As a result, all the plantations apart from small lots were bought by their original German owners.[49] Within the space of two years after this, the plantations were in full production. This was such that by 1936 for instance, 120 000 hectares of land were in German hands and less than 8,000 in British

[44] Mokake, *Basic Facts on Cameroon History,* pp.93-94.
[45] Ibid., p.94.
[46] Ibid.
[47] Eyongetah and Brain, *A History of the Cameroons*, p. 103.
[48] Fanso, *Cameroon History for Secondary Schools and Colleges,* p.241.
[49] Ibid.

ownership.[50] The auction sale included properties like buildings, houses, factories, rolling stock, bridges, wharves and railways, and the prices were less than those offered in 1922. The situation in British Southern Cameroons after 1924 was that although the territory was under British rule, there were three times as many German expatriates than British.[51] In fact, the British did little or nothing when compared to the Germans in promoting plantation agriculture in the territory as it was only the return of the later that helped to have them revitalised.[52]

This made the pattern of trade in the territory at the time to be more German than British, as the bulk of plantation produce was shipped and one-half of the territory's imports came.[53] Trade relations with Great Britain were quite limited, since most of the plantations expropriated were sold back to their former owners, who in turn traded largely with Germany. In 1931 for example, Germany received about 109,603 pounds of Cameroonian products, Great Britain 6 341 pounds of the total exports of 155 432 pounds.[54] In 1937, about 47,57 percent of the imports of British Cameroons came from Germany, 11.9 per cent from Great Britain; 79,75 percent of the exports went to Germany, only 6,5 per cent to Britain.[55]

Throughout the period preceding the Second World War, plantations flourished, proving to be the main financial and economic support of the territory. Port facilities were also instituted at Tiko and Victoria; shops, ware houses and offices accompanied. Plantations attracted a lot of people from the grassland areas of the territory, Nigeria, and French Cameroon. Except for German agitation in the southern section of the territory, life there was relatively uneventful during the inter-war period. These were people who played an important role in the economic and political development of the territory. The neglect on plantations during and immediately after WWI, the slump in world prices for primary products during the depression and reluctance of the British government to finance new under-takings helped account for the

[50] Eyongetah, Brain and R. Palmer, *A History of Cameroon (New Edition)*, Longman Group, UK, 1987, p. 89.
[51] Fanso, *Cameroon History for Secondary Schools and Colleges*, p.242.
[52] Mokake, *Basic Facts on Cameroon History*, p.95.
[53] Fanso, *Cameroon History for Secondary Schools and Colleges*, p. 242.
[54] Ibid.
[55] Ibid.

stagnation. There were also uncertainties related to Germany's claims for the return of her former colonies. [56]

British Cameroons was joined to Nigeria in an administrative union, with it generally considered as a backwash in the mainstream of Nigerian development. Most Africans and Europeans in British Cameroons were concerned more with economic than political problems. The most important influence on the economic development of the British mandate was the group of German plantations in Southern Cameroons that had been repurchased by their former owners after 1924.[57] Within two years after their return, the Germans, comprising the largest European population group in the territory, had begun to make their plantations viable. The expansion of these plantations introduced many economic changes in the Southern Cameroons. The planters expanded the port facilities at Tiko and Victoria and a new wharf for loading bananas was constructed. They also constructed comfortable workers' Camps, numerous shops, warehouses and office buildings.

A 1929 report on Cameroon shows that Germany bought all the territory's bananas and most of its cocoa, palm products and rubber and shipped almost all produce in German bottoms.[58] At the same time Germany supplied the majority of the imports, mostly equipment for plantations and consumers in the territory. The Nigerian government which was fully aware of the economic potential of the province, feared investing in it because the territory's political future had been made uncertain by the mandate system. As a consequence of their activity, trade with Germany between 1925 and 1938 comprised the territory's principal source of revenue.[59] Enough acreage had been brought into cultivation and employment rose from 11000 workers in 1924 to 13500 in 1928, 15500 in 1935 and 25000 in 1938.[60]

The number of German planters in the territory in the 1930s was between 200 and 250, and they were almost virtually in control of economic life in the British mandate.[61] Plantations provided about

[56] Mokake, *Basic Facts on Cameroon History*, p.95.
[57] V. T. Le Vine, "The Cameroon Federal Republic", G. M. Carter (ed.), *Five African States, Responses to Diversity,* Cornell University Press, Ithaca, New York,1963, p. 269.
[58] Ibid.
[59] Ibid.
[60] Ibid, p.242.
[61] Ibid.

25000 jobs to indigenes by 1938.[62] They equally led to the construction of roads, railways, shops, new camps, health centres to cater for labourers etc. Nevertheless, the British created the Cameroon Development Corporation (CDC) in 1946 to take over and manage most of the German plantations, even though it effectively went operational in 1947.[63] This was so because during the Second World War, the German community in British Southern Cameroons was repatriated and its plantations once more expropriated.

The CDC was the biggest agro-industrial company in the Central African region at the time and largest statutory organization in the territory, created in December 1946 by an ordinance of the British colonial authorities to manage and develop former German plantations. Its activities were initially concentrated in the South West but later expanded to the North West with a tea estate at Ndu, the West with a tea estate at Djuttitsa, and the Littoral Region with a rubber estate at Kompina.[64] It also had to struggle with indeterminate financial subsidies from Great Britain, Nigeria, and the Commonwealth in the early period for its survival.

An aspect of the economy that was neglected by the British administration in Cameroon was the development of roads. Throughout the mandate period, there was only one road in the territory, from Tiko and Victoria through Mutengene, Muyuka, Kumba and Mamfe. By the outbreak of the Second World War, some 67kms of this road remained uncompleted, between Mamfe and Bamenda.[65] A motor ring road built during the period circled the Bamenda grassfields, joining the Bamenda township of Abakwa, the Ndop plain, Nso, Nkambe and Wum.[66] To encourage the building of roads, the British sustained compulsory labour for public works in labourers' own districts. Another aspect of the economy was the traditional long-distance trade that developed among peoples within the territory and across borders with Nigeria and French Cameroon.

Generally, the British did very little to develop their own sphere of Cameroon during the mandate period. The territory was considered and treated as unimportant within the development of the Nigerian

---

[62] Mokake, *Basic Facts on Cameroon History*, p.94.
[63] Ibid.
[64] DeLancey, et al., *Historical Dictionary of the Republic of Cameroon*, pp.83-84.
[65] Ibid.
[66] Ibid.

economy. Very little government revenue was used for this purpose and every opportunity was exploited, especially the territory's resources. The British failed to grant an autonomous separate budget for Southern Cameroons and administered the territory as an integral part of first the S13428-709outhern Province of Nigeria and later, the Eastern Region of Nigeria and little was done to promote its development.[67] There was never at any time during the period, a separate budget for British Cameroon.

The foregoing was unlike in Congo Kinshasa, where the Belgians were justifiably proud of their economic achievements and sometimes contended that their tardiness in the sphere of political development was more than compensated by their remarkable accomplishments in the economic and social fields.[68] The British saw Cameroon as a territory which Germany might later reacquire and so did not treat it as a significant part of their colony. The British administration's economic policy ruled out most types of government action and only attempted to influence private concerns: German planters.[69]

The British refusal to manage Southern Cameroons separately, made it difficult for them to protect them against Nigerians' harassments. This neglect especially within the development sphere was because of their fear that the Germans, would one day return for its recovery.[70] British belief was also that since the territory was administered as part of Nigeria, Nigerians would assist them for its development.[71] Compulsory labour, even though paid meagre salaries, was to ensure the construction of roads, bridges and public buildings, in Southern Cameroons.[72] This was mostly in areas that proved resourceful to them. It however, helped in constructing small and narrow roads linking Victoria and Tiko, Muyuka, Kumba and Mamfe, notwithstanding the ring road in the Bamenda grassfields, linking Bamenda, Ndop plain,

---

67 Mokake, *Basic Facts on Cameroon History*, p.95.

68 E. Bustin, "The Congo", G. M. Carter, *Five African States, Responses to Diversity: the Congo, Dahomey, the Cameroon Federal Republic, the Rhodesians and Nyasaland South Africa*, Cornell University Press, Ithaca, New York,1963, p. 60.

69 Fanso, *Cameroon History for Secondary Schools and Colleges*, p.242.

70 Mokake, *Basic Facts on Cameroon History*, p.96.

71 Ibid.

72 Kum, "Wum Area Development Authority (WADA), 1965-1994, Implantation, Economic and Social Conversions in Menchum Division", Doctorat/PhD in History, University of Yaounde I, Cameroon, p. 66.

Nso, Nkambe and Wum.[73] There were also roads that linked Kumba in Southern Cameroons and Loum in French Cameroon as well as Bamenda and Mbouda, respectively. Finally, the port facilities in Victoria and Tiko were expanded.[74]

In terms of trade, the British allowed the sale of salt which left Mamfe to the Bamenda grassfields, French Cameroon and even Nigeria in Southern Cameroons.[75] The Nso region was noted for its heavy supply of kolanuts to both French Cameroon and Nigeria, while the Ndop plain remained a major supplier of farm and hunting implements in the Bamenda central region as well as to the coastal region.[76] Plantation crops such as banana, rubber, cocoa, and palm products were exported to Britain and Germany. Smuggling was also another important aspect of trade as lots of coffee and cocoa were smuggled from the Bakossi area into French Cameroon. Trade created jobs for the indigenes, raised their incomes and consequently improved on their standard of living.[77] This particularly encouraged peasant agriculture to develop in the territory, especially in the latter years of British rule.[78] Cocoa became important in the 1930s; coffee and bananas, both for export, saw rapid growth after World War II as a result of Cameroonian initiatives often with British opposition or reluctance.[79]

In another dimension, the Igbos dominated the economy of Southern Cameroons and exploited it at the expense of its inhabitants. These incomers monopolised vital trade in the territory. They owned most of the shops and sold at very high prices.[80] In most cases, they imposed goods on Southern Cameroonians to buy. The Igbos also dominated the educational sphere of Southern Cameroons, enjoyed most British scholarships and important places in schools. Igbo teachers were equally very rude and brutal towards Southern Cameroonians. They disrespected the people's tradition and customs and molested the people to the extent of committing adultery, raping and looting. The Igbos dominated the administration of Southern Cameroons, making it difficult for them to enjoy social justice. Most important professions

---

[73] Ibid.

[74] Mokake, *Basic Facts on Cameroon History*, p.94.

[75] Ibid., p.95.

[76] Kum, "Wum Area Development Authority (WADA), p. 67.

[77] Ibid.

[78] DeLancey et al., *Historical Dictionary of the Republic of Cameroon,* p.6.

[79] Ibid.

[80] Mokake, *Basic Facts on Cameroon History*, p.98.

were hogged by them such as driving, law and teaching. Igbo activities influenced most Southern Cameroonians to favour reunification with French Cameroon.[81]

B) Trusteeship Period

British Cameroons remained a neglected backwater in many aspects.[82] The British declared in 1946 that their general economic objective in the Southern Cameroons was to do everything to work towards the economic advancement of the territory.[83] This was in order to raise the general standards of living and encourage every form of economic development among the indigenous populations. Nevertheless, the economic record of the British in Cameroon throughout its tenure of administration showed that neither of these goals was meticulously pursued in the territory. There was no separate budget for Southern Cameroons until 1954, when it ceased to be part of the Eastern Region of Nigeria.[84] Hence, the economic development of the territory during that period was one sided as the territory depended solely on CDC plantations, with very little or no other substantial economic activity in the territory.

The CDC was created in 1946 as a legal corporation to take over and run most of the plantations that the British confiscated from the Germans in 1939 for the benefit of Southern Cameroons.[85] This was the largest agro-industrial company in Cameroon and Central Africa. Its activities were initially centered in the South West of the territory, but later extended into the North West with a tea estate at Ndu, the West with a tea estate at Djuttitsa, and the Littoral with a rubber estate at Kompina.[86] These plantations were acquired by the Governor General of Nigeria on behalf of the British Government at the end of the war from the Custodian of Enemy property for 850, 000 pounds and leased to the CDC for 60 years at a nominal rent.[87] Among its many functions spelt out in the ordinance setting it up, the CDC was to cultivate

---

[81] Ibid., p.120.

[82] Eyongetah, Brain and Palmer, *A History of Cameroon (New Edition)*, p. 87.

[83] Fanso, *Cameroon History for Secondary Schools and Colleges vol. 2*, p.133.

[84] Eyongetah, Brain and Palmer, *A History of Cameroon (New Edition)*, p. 89.

[85] E. Ardener, et al. *Plantation and Village in the Cameroons: Some Economic and Social Studies*, Oxford University Press, United Kingdom, 1960, p. 12.

[86] Ibid.

[87] Kum, "Wum Area Development Authority (WADA), 1965-1994," p. 65.

economic crops, raise stock and deal in the production and sale of all kinds as producer, manufacturer, exporter or importer.[88] Its major economic crops were the palm tree for oil and kernels, banana, rubber, cocoa, and eventually tea.[89]

The CDC heavily depended on the Nigerian Government for capital after 1947 and increasingly on Britain for its export and import markets. It was the main employer of labour in Southern Cameroons; it also played a crucial role in the remainder of the economy. During its heyday, it contributed about two-thirds of the territory's export tonnage and more than half of its earnings.[90] It made important contributions to the ports and transport systems through the taxes it paid to the government. The Corporation's net profit after taxes and payment of certain charges, was paid to the Governor-General of Nigeria for the benefit of the Trust-territory's inhabitants. In 1948 for example, the corporation allocated 54,352 pounds for expenditure on the people of British Cameroons and of this sum, 22,352 pounds was allocated to British Northern Cameroons and 32,000 pounds to the Southern Cameroons.[91] Of the Southern Cameroons allocation, 5,000 pounds was spent on reading rooms, 2000 pounds on secondary school education and health care.[92]

However, when the Southern Cameroons became a quasi-federal territory with its own government in 1954, the Corporation's net profits were paid to it directly.[93] The valuable contribution of the CDC to the Southern Cameroons financial structure was adversely affected by its irregular record of profitability, sinking from a maximum of 60,000 pounds in 1953 to less than one-third of that sum in 1954. This worsened during the remainder period up to 1961 as it exceeded 25,000 pounds only three times.[94] As a result, from 1954, the Southern Cameroons government decided to seek direct budgetary assistance from Nigeria. The extent to which the Southern Cameroons could be self-supporting was only given attention immediately it became a

[88] Fanso, *Cameroon History for Secondary Schools and Colleges vol. 2,* p.134
[89] S. B. Takang, "The Cameroon Development Corporation, 1946-2020: Political and Socio-Economic Mutations, PhD thesis, Department of History and Archaeology, University of Bamenda, 2023, p.43.
[90] Ibid.
[91] Fanso, *Cameroon History for Secondary Schools and Colleges vol. 2,* p.134
[92] Ibid.
[93] Ibid.
[94] Ibid.

separate administrative unit within Nigeria.[95] Before then, it was only covered in the budgetary allocation for Eastern Nigeria with which it was administratively integrated and its public accounts kept for the region.

Revenues accruing from the Southern Cameroons were included without distinction in the budgets of the Eastern Region of Nigeria, and expenditures were allotted to it not on the basis of its overall needs, but on those of the needs of the entire region.[96] Such a system made it extremely difficult to truly determine the capacity of the trust-territory to finance its own development. It was simply assumed that Nigeria was putting more into it than it was getting out. As a matter of fact, the Nigerian government claimed that during the period from 1943 to 1959, it subsidised Cameroon by more than one million pounds sterling.[97] When the CDC began largescale production in 1948, Southern Cameroons for the first time had a surplus of revenue over expenditure, leading to the creation of a special fund into which the sum of 1,163 000 pounds sterling was deposited over the next six years, used for the benefit of the trust territory as a whole.[98]

Despite the surpluses, a fiscal commission that studied Southern Cameroons' financial situation in 1954, reported fairly accurately that the territory could not be viable without external financial support. In fact, the budget of the new government for the first full year showed a deficit of about 285,000 pounds sterling. To guard against future deficits a special formula, known as the 'Chick Formula', was crafted by Sir Louis Chick, the Financial Secretary in the Nigerian Government, for stabilising the finances of the Southern Cameroons Government.[99] Under this formula, a federal constitutional grant was instituted to pay back to the Southern Cameroons government, every penny that the Federal government got from the territory and did not spend on federal services.[100]

In addition, a special advance of 300,000 pounds sterling was made available to the new government as working capital. The 'Chick Formula' assumed that the CDC would continue to be the major source

[95] Mokake, *Basic Facts on Cameroon History*, p.105.
[96] Fanso, *Cameroon History for Secondary Schools and Colleges vol. 2*, p.134.
[97] Ibid.
[98] Ibid., p.135.
[99] Mokake, *Basic Facts on Cameroon History*, p.105.
[100] Ibid.

of revenue for the trust territory.[101] But its poor performance in 1954 and subsequent years made it difficult for the Eastern Region to finance its own programmes.[102] In fact, during the early years of the Corporation's activities, most of its profits were re-invested or used to amortise loans.[103] Another plan to guarantee a fixed minimum revenue for the Southern Cameroons was designed in 1955 to replace the 'Chick formula'.

Under this system, the Federal government accepted the obligation to guarantee that the revenues Southern Cameroons would receive annually, over a period of three years from the Federation would not be less than 580,000 pounds sterling.[104] In other words, if the normal grant of 300,000 pounds sterling, plus the CDC's net profit fell short of the 580,000 pounds sterling, the Federal Government would make up the difference. This system was still nevertheless unsatisfactory as during the two fiscal years from 1956 to 1958, Federal grants to Southern Cameroons were 450,000 pounds sterling.[105] Another important development was that the Southern Cameroons Government drew up a five-year development plan covering the period 1955-1960, with capital grants from Britain amounting to 8.8 million pounds.[106]

The foregoing required a careful investigation into both the actual and estimated financial situation of Southern Cameroons before a formula similar to that applied in other regions, could be worked out for the territory. This study was entrusted to the Raisman Commission, during the fiscal years running from 1956 to 1959.[107] The commission's recommendations, were applied in the 1958-59's allocations to the Southern Cameroons, assigning to it, the proportion that was estimated to be due it from the import and excise duties, imposed by the Federal Government as well as receipt of the entire revenue from all personal income, mining royalties, and certain miscellaneous revenues, raised within the territory itself.[108]

---

[101] Ibid.

[102] Fanso, *Cameroon History for Secondary Schools and Colleges vol. 2,* p.135.

[103] C. E., Welch, Jr., *Dream of Unity: Pan-Africanism and Political Unification in West Africa*, Cornell University Press, Ithaca, New York, 1966, p. 164.

[104] Fanso, *Cameroon History for Secondary Schools and Colleges vol. 2*, p.135.

[105] Ibid.

[106] Ndongko, *Regional Development Planning.*

[107] Fanso, *Cameroon History for Secondary Schools and Colleges vol. 2*, p.135.

[108] Ibid.

In addition to the new allocation, debts totalling 700,000 pounds sterling and accrued interests made under the old system of revenue allocation were cancelled by the Nigerian Government. All the same, Southern Cameroons still suffered a deficit of some 200,000 pounds sterling in the first budget estimates that the new formula applied. It was only through the unexpectedly high revenues that the 1958-59 budget was finally balanced. There were also, as earlier indicated, capital grants to Southern Cameroons from both the United Kingdom and Nigeria. An annual grant of about 300,000 pounds sterling came from Nigeria for the period from 1955 to 1958, including an expenditure of 1.2 million pounds sterling on the Victoria-Bamenda Road in 1959.[109]

In 1956, the British Colonial Office made a grant of 1.3 million pounds sterling for various aid projects including roads, technical education, agriculture, communications and other development projects. An outright British grant of 450,000 pounds sterling was also made in early 1958 to help meet the territory's budgetary deficits.[110] All these did not stop Southern Cameroonians from feeling that their territory was not receiving the financial attention it deserved from the British Government, or its just share of Nigerian revenues.[111] Those who were dissatisfied with the income allocation to the territory, were convinced that it would do better if Southern Cameroons managed its own finances.[112] This credence received a boost in 1959 when a study showed that in certain circumstances, Southern Cameroons could be potentially viable, although not as an independent economy.[113]

It was within this context of economic backwardness that the impetus for the demand of a separate regional status emerged in British Cameroons. This was as it appeared as though the stagnation of the interwar period would not be broken, while Nigeria and French Cameroon progressed with aid from metropolitan governments. Enugu and Lagos apparently paid no attention to the plight of the territory, where economic development according to the Cameroon National Federation's (CNF) memo, did not make the slightest advance from where the Germans left it.[114] A British Administrator commented early

---

[109] Ibid.

[110] Fanso, *Cameroon History for Secondary Schools and Colleges vol. 2*, pp.292-293.

[111] Ibid.

[112] Ibid., pp. 298-299.

[113] Welch, Jr., *Dream of Unity: Pan-Africanism and Political Unification*, p. 186.

[114] Ibid.

in 1949 upon the rapidly widening gap in the degree of progress between the trust territory and the rest of Eastern Nigeria. [115]

It became natural to expect that only a regional government for the British Cameroons and much greater attention from the administering authority would alleviate these economic disparities. Only the plantations (placed under public ownership through the CDC in 1947) could be considered a major undertaking.[116] Thus, the major instrument of economic improvement seemed to only slightly change for the better. The plantation issue was further complicated by the Bakweri Land Committee demands, which petitioned the Trusteeship Council in support of its claims over plantation lands alienated to the Germans.[117] This Committee, requested the return of land to its indigenous owners. The CDC also had to struggle with uncertain budgetary subsidies from Great Britain, Nigeria, and the Commonwealth in its early period, to survive, reason why its lifeblood after Cameroon's independence, depended on heavy loans from various bilateral and international sources.

Aside widespread feelings of economic stagnation were grievances on social domination resulting from the immigration of alien groups into the Southern Cameroons. When the Kumba-Mamfe road was opened and plantations expanded after WWII, thousands of Nigerian workers got attracted by the relatively high wages and available land in the trust-territory.[118] These men, temporary rootless, ambitious to earn money, usually unmarried or separated from their wives, aroused the resentment of indigenous Cameroonians. [119] The British government did not place any obstacle on the way of Nigerian migrants, in keeping with the fact that the Cameroons formed an integral part of the Federation. As a result, a complex social problem, given the rapidity with which Nigerians, more particularly the Igbo monopolised many local enterprises.[120]

Apart from the foregoing structures and activities, there were other small-scale industries that provided jobs and cheap commodities in Southern Cameroons, like the Britind Industry in Moliwe, the Ombe

---

[115] Ibid., pp. 163-164.

[116] D. E. Gardinier, *Cameroon-United Nations Challenge to French Policy*, London Institute of Race Relations, Oxford University Press, 1963, p. 60.

[117] Ibid.

[118] Welch, Jr., *Dream of Unity: Pan-Africanism and Political Unification*, p. 164.

[119] Ibid.

[120] Ibid.

Textile Industries, which provided cheap umbrellas, shoes and wears to the people.[121] The issue of the economic viability of British Southern Cameroons to become an independent state became a great problem. A plebiscite was held in British Cameroon in 1961, because Southern Cameroons was deemed to not be economically viable to sustain itself as an independent state as reported by the Chick Commission. Consequently, to attain independence, the territory had to be linked either to the Federal Republic of Nigeria or the Republic of Cameroon.[122] It was with respect to the foregoing that at independence and reunification, the authorities of the Federal Republic of Cameroon decided to earmark the policy of planning as a channel for economic development in the country.

III- French Cameroon

This section is devoted to economic developments in Cameroon after the departure of the Germans from the territory. It lays emphasis on the mandates and trusteeship periods, wherein a series of development strategies were employed to satisfy French economic needs and so-called development of the territory.

A) Mandate Period

The economy of French Cameroon was largely dominated by agriculture during the mandate period, emanating from former German plantations. Much effort was not only vested on increasing peasant agricultural production and plantations, but also, on outspreading commercial activities and improving the territory's infrastructure.[123] By the time of the outbreak of the First World War and assumption of French control, the Germans had already made considerable economic advances in Cameroon, especially in the coastal and southern districts of the territory. There was a well-established monetary economy through European traders' presence and most especially the German administration, which established trade systems, plantations, built roads and railways and set-up public works.[124] These developments had made further inroads into the traditional economic activities and techniques

[121] Mokake, *Basic Facts on Cameroon History,* p. 141.
[122] Ibid.
[123] Fanso, *Cameroon History for Secondary Schools and Colleges vol. 2*, p.227.
[124] Takang, "The Cameroon Development Corporation, 1946-2020."

through appropriation of land, employment of labour and the introduction of taxation.[125]

Although the disorders of the First World War in the territory had forced German merchants and technicians to leave, temporarily destroying trading networks and markets, it left largely intact economic buildings, a number of all-season roads, plantations, railway lines and ports.[126] As soon as the French occupied part of Cameroon, their new administration pre-empted some former German plantations and sold others to non-Germans. Immense efforts were made in preventing German businessmen and farmers from returning to their trade in plantations respectively. [127] These efforts were also noticed through the substitution of German's ethics with French values, markets, products and techniques.

This was such that by 1925, the French administration had liquidated 166 German firms holding 366 different properties. Of these, 219 properties were sold at public auction, 107 were pre-empted, and 40 simply passed to the government because they originally belonged to the German State.[128] Disposal of German property to non-Germans almost completely precluded the return of its citizens to French Cameroon. A few Germans did however return after 1926 with various French and British trading companies.[129]

For an effective economic exploitation of the territory, the French colonial administration instituted two basic philosophies: *politique de protectorat* and the economic policy of *mise en valuer.*[130] The former was a shift from the integration of indigenous French Cameroonians into French political, economic and social life (Assimilation), to the slow development of the indigenous community towards eventual assimilation, with the separation of European communities from Africans' until assimilation was achieved (Association). The *mise en valeur* policy introduced a heavy tax burden and use of conscript labour

---

125 Fanso *Cameroon History for Secondary Schools and Colleges vol. 2*, p.226.
126 Ibid.
127 Oyono, "L'Allemagne et le statut international du Cameroun", p.124.
128 Fanso *Cameroon History for Secondary Schools and Colleges vol. 2*, p.226.
129 Ibid.
130 Le Vine, "The Cameroon Federal Republic", p. 270.

(*corvée*), reinforced by the *indégenat* [131] system.[132] Worthy of note is that it was within the framework of the *politique de protectorat* that the *mise en valeur* policy, was instituted in 1923, by the then French colonial minister, Albert Sarraut, who called for the extensive local economic development of colonies as the basis of fruitful relations between them and France.[133]

The forgoing policies were to be achieved through a labour tax, known as *prestation*,[134] under which all males of *Sujet* status, were obliged to furnish the administration with ten days of conscript and unpaid labour a year.[135] After ten days, if the worker desired to remain on the project, he was paid a minimal fixed rate for estimated portions of work done. Although accepted in exceptional cases, a Commutation of *prestation* at the rate of two French Francs per day of labour was made possible in 1925. Initially, the recruitment of workers for *prestation* was done through local chiefs, who were paid a lump sum for the work done. But when the chiefs began to abuse the system, the government gave the task to local administrative officials.[136]

The bottom-line of the *mise en valeur* policy was to first of all derive maximum economic returns for France from its colonies, before serving the interest of these colonies and the rest of the world.[137] Its application to French Cameroon, resulted in a fivefold upsurge of the territory's total trade between 1922 and 1938, fruitfully battering the worst years of the great depression that began in 1929.[138] France through this policy, was urged to provide loans to all her colonies so as to enable them develop and promote their economies. In this backdrop, the French government decided to set up the *Fonds d'Invertissement pour le Developpement Economique et Sociale (FIDES)* in 1928, to provide loans and grants to her colonies.[139] French Cameroon was not left out as a series of FIDES projects were realised in the territory, such as the

---

[131] This was a comprehensive set of violations and penalties that were used at will almost by all local French administrators against the indigenes, without control was aimed at deterring the political advancement of French Cameroon.
[132] Mokake, *Basic Facts on Cameroon History*, p.54.
[133] Le Vine, "The Cameroon Federal Republic", p. 270.
[134] Ten days of hard labour as compensation of Tax payment.
[135] Fanso, *Cameroon History for Secondary Schools and Colleges vol.* 2, p.228.
[136] Ibid.
[137] Mokake, *Basic Facts on Cameroon History*, p.54.
[138] Ibid.
[139] Kum, "Wum Area Development Authority (WADA), 1965-1994", p.79.

bridge over the Wouri River, the Electricity Dam at Edea and the modernisation of the Douala port.[140]

In the same light, a series of roads, railways, and ports were constructed, with priority given to those linking them to the hinterlands, where plantations were found, to ensure the easy transportation of raw materials to the coast for onward shipment to Europe.[141] The French colonial administration did everything possible to improve on the Douala, Kribi and Garoua ports. The Douala and Garoua ports were used to handle French Cameroon imports and exports.[142] The need for the transportation of perishable agricultural products greatly encouraged air traffic in the movements of mostly fresh meat from the Ngaoundere airport to the southern part of the territory. French Cameroon was also linked to the outside world at the time by international airports like Yaounde and Douala.[143]

Many more new roads were built and existing railway lines extended by some 128 kilometres to Yaoundé, with a branch of 37 kilometres from Gtele to Mbalmayo.[144] By 1929, basic road infrastructures had been constructed. For instance, the Douala-Yaounde Road had been constructed in 1927, while the construction of the Sangmalima-mbalmayo road was already in an advanced stage.[145] The Mbalmayo-Otele railway line was completed by the end of 1927.[146] By the time the Second World War came to an end, the Douala port had been enlarged and air services introduced. It is however realised that French interests in the territory concentrated around Douala, Yaoundé, Foumban, and Kribi. Out of this "fertile crescent", were large areas at least as underdeveloped as the Southern and Northern regions of Cameroon.

Various studies of the economy of French Cameroon during the mandate period show that the territory made only modest economic progress as compared with developments in education and health.[147] Nevertheless, the French took greater interest in developing their part of the territory than did the British, investing more capital, with many

---

[140] Mokake, *Basic Facts on Cameroon History,* p.54.

[141] NAB, File no. 1946/2- An Ordinance to Provide the Establishment of the Corporation known as the Cameroon Development Corporation (CDC).

[142] Mokake, *Basic Facts on Cameroon History*, p.55.

[143] Ibid., pp. 55-56.

[144] Fanso, *Cameroon History for Secondary Schools and Colleges vol. 2,* p.227.

[145] Ibid.

[146] Mokake, *Basic Facts on Cameroon History,*.56.

[147] Fanso, *Cameroon History for Secondary Schools and Colleges vol. 2,* p. 226.

French citizens coming to work in Cameroon.[148] This means that at independence French Cameroon had a much higher GNP per capita higher education levels, better health care, although still rudimentary and a better infrastructure than British Cameroons.[149]

Despite the excellent foundation laid by the Germans, French Cameroon's economy failed to sufficiently advance, for several reasons. First, the League of Nations mandate conferred something less than full French sovereignty over Cameroon whose eventual, though remote, goal was self-government.[150] As such, the possibility of Cameroon ever being assimilated to France's Equatorial African colonies was non-existent. Heavy investment in a territory with such an international status was considered by the French as too risky. Second, for a long time after 1918, France was more preoccupied with recovering from the First World War than with heavy investment in their African mandated territories and colonies. Third, France was also unwilling to make generous grants or loans to Cameroon because it was not certain that as a mandate the territory would remain French.[151] It was reported in a letter to the French Minister of colonies on October 28th 1936, that the country was more and more visited by German subjects with scientific and touristic voyages, being at the centre.[152]

It has further been estimated that the working conditions on railway lines in French Cameroon in 1944, forced well over 86 percent of the recruited labour in the Bafang region to escaped to British Cameroons.[153] Countless East Cameroonians fled from their regions usually recruited for forced labour, into British Cameroons, Gabon, Spanish Rio Muni and Fernando Po.[154] Able-bodied men were captured during the night in their villages by 'mysterious agents and led to work in camps in faraway regions unknown to their wives, children and relatives. [155] It was reported in the 1930s that forced labour had reached repellent proportions in the territory. By 1933, however, the use of forced labour had diminished and as a result of pressure on the permanent mandates commission of the League of Nations and hostile

148 DeLancey et al., *Historical Dictionary of the Republic of Cameroon*, p.6.
149 Ibid.
150 Fanso, *Cameroon History for Secondary Schools and Colleges vol.* 2, p.227.
151 Ibid.
152 Oyono, « L'Allemagne et le statut international du Cameroun », p.124.
153 Mokake, *Basic Facts on Cameroon History*, p.56.
154 Fanso, *Cameroon History for Secondary Schools and Colleges vol.* 2, p.228.
155 Ibid., p. 229.

publicity created by the situation, the French administration did drastically reduce its use by 1952.[156]

As far as the development of agriculture was concerned in French Cameroons, the administration enabled an increase in the production of cocoa, bananas, palm products and rubber among the indigenes and on the plantations through the introduction of new methods. Coffee became an important export commodity with the production of the *Arabica* variety largely in the hands of small holders and indigenous peasants, most of them in the Western grasslands. The *Robusta* variety was produced in the south. Coffee cultivation was also carried out in Ebolowa, Nkongsamba and Dschang, producing a very high output. In 1937 for instance, 4000 tons of coffee was harvested and by 1952 the quantity had increased to about 13000 tons.[157] On the other hand, cocoa was the most vital crop grown on these estates and exported to Europe in large amounts. But its cultivation was entirely in the hands of the indigenes; and by 1937, the territory was producing 27000 tons of Cocoa.[158] In order to improve on its value and quantity, a cocoa station was set up, to study and improve on the plant.

Aside the foregoing crops in French Cameroon were Banana plantations. This was basically cultivated in the volcanic regions of Mbanga, Penja and Njombe, where by 1938, about 28000 tons were exported, since there was a banana company responsible for the sale of French Cameroon Banana to France.[159] Timber began to be exploited on large scale, with more than 200,000 hectares of forests being used for commercial purposes before the outbreak of WWII.[160] Palm plantations were also found in the southern parts of the territory, and palm oil mills were opened in Bafia, Dschang, Edea and Kribi so as to improve on the quality of palm oil.[161] As a result of the foregoing developments, French Cameroon's foreign trade increased by nearly 500 percent during the interwar period, from 96,000,000 CFA francs in 1922 to 467,171,000 CFA francs in 1938.[162]

This very vibrant economy was nevertheless shattered by the great depression that broke out in 1929, affecting the whole world. The

---

[156] Ibid.

[157] Mokake, *Basic Facts on Cameroon History*, p.55.

[158] Ibid., p.54.

[159] Ibid., p.55.

[160] Fanso, *Cameroon History for Secondary Schools and Colleges vol.* 2, p.227.

[161] Mokake, *Basic Facts on Cameroon History*, p.55.

[162] Fanso, *Cameroon History for Secondary Schools and Colleges vol.* 2, p.227

effects of this depression hit the indigenes hardest, especially when the French Administration decided to increase the head tax by 7 percent in the midst of this fall in agricultural prices.[163] The great depression also affected the administration's financial standing as revenue got from the collection of taxes drastically reduced. Even the French government could no longer assist in the development of the territory as before. In spite of these effects on the indigenes and their inability to pay the head tax, the French colonial administration still decided to reduce civil servants' salaries as well as those of traditional authorities and made matters worse, when the cost of administration was increased by 13 percent. [164] With all these, the possibilities of indigenes revolting as a result of increasing hardship finally caught the attention of the French administration.

Visible effects of this great depression were noticed on the drop in the price of agricultural products, forcing the French administration to greatly reduce the cost of railway transport as well as prices in trade. A state-guaranteed loan of 10,000,000 francs CFA, authorised in 1930 to extend the railway line from Nkongsamba to Chad, was never granted, because of the territory's international status.[165] This also limited France's economic activities in East Cameroon. During the depression, prices of principal African products dropped by as low as 60-70 percent. Finally, the admission of Germany as a member of the League of Nations in 1926 and her strong campaign to regain Cameroon and her other former colonies thereafter made France unwilling to consider concessions. For all these reasons, French Cameroon made only modest economic progress during the mandate era.[166] Effective transportation for export crops, even when they could be produced, presented serious problems.[167]

B) The Trusteeship Period

The dominant feature of colonial rule in Cameroon was the selective nature of development, in which administrative structures and education played a subordinate role. The trusteeship period was marked by

---

[163] Mokake, *Basic Facts on Cameroon History,* p.55.
[164] Mokake, *Basic Facts on Cameroon History,* p.57.
[165] Fanso, *Cameroon History for Secondary Schools and Colleges vol.* 2, p.227.
[166] V.J. Ngoh, "The Political Evolution of Cameroon", 1884-1961, PhD thesis, Portland State University, 1979, pp. 33-37.
[167] Ibid.

the political and ideological scenes, rather than economic changes, to the extent that politico-ideological relationships began to dominate social relationships as a whole. In French Cameroon, educational expansion led to the emergence of an anti-colonial nationalism, the creation of independence parties and finally, the Basa revolt.[168] After the Second World War, relations between colonies and mother countries underwent a profound change as colonial powers came out of it considerably enfeebled, whereas in the colonies a desire for a different status began to take root. This was followed by a period of great political uproar amongst both Europeans and Africans, and the debate on the question of sharing power with the indigenes and the manner in which this should be achieved often took on a dramatic form.

In the case of Cameroon, there was not only the Brazzaville Conference (1944).[169] Since, economic objectives remained paramount for Europeans, it can be considered that it was through pressure from the local populations that the predominance of these objectives were challenged by the need to create a political structure, which would no longer be based only on a military force, but required to justify its own existence.[170] As such, education became both the end-product and the instrument for modifying relationships between the colonial masters and their subjects. It became the point at where, conflicts both crystallised and developed. The paradox is that it was from the moment when education was raised from its status as a supplier of recruits for minor posts to that of an agency for legitimising the colonial system, that this very legitimacy was called into question. [171]

In order to strengthen its legitimacy, the colonial power was forced to develop education, both horizontally and vertically, in areas where demand was making itself felt, such as, development zones, and the logic inherent. With the FIDES plans for French-speaking Cameroun.[172] The historical dimension and regional context of disparities in any system of education do not fail to operate, from a desire to possess all the European's knowledge the next step was a demand to possess all the European's power.

---

[168] Ibid.

[169] Jean-Yves Martin, *Social differentiation and regional disparities: educational development in Cameroon,* ORSTOM, Paris, 2008, p.37.

[170] Ngoh, "The Political Evolution of Cameroon, 1884-1961", p.38.

[171] Martin, *Social Differentiation and Regional Disparities*, p.38.

[172] Kum, "Wum Area Development Authority (WADA), 1965-1994", p.76.

At the end of World War II and creation of the UN, French Cameroon was transformed from the League of Nations Mandate to a United Nations Trust Territory and unified into the French Union. By accepting this system, France undertook to honour the political objectives stated in Article 76 of the United Nations Charter: "Progressive development towards self-government or independence".[173] It was in this regard that on 30th April 1946, the French National Assembly passed a law establishing FIDES, a long term programme for the development and modernisation of France's overseas territories.[174]

This was because only very limited progress had been made during the interwar period, in the economic and social domains of French Cameroon. The French did not want to invest on a territory, whose international status as a mandate of the League of Nations made its future relations with France indeterminate. Reconsidering to invest on it during the trusteeship period was because there were hopes for a continuation of relations with the territory at independence.[175] From 1947, the French took measures to promote the economic and social advancement of the territory on a much larger scale especially with the institution of FIDES. In Cameroun the funds were utilized to finance two economic plans: 1947–1953 and 1953–1957. These development plans over a period of 10 years amounted to 80 billion French francs.[176] The foregoing amount was far higher than all of French Equatorial Africa, partially due to Cameroon's special status as a trust territory of the United Nations.[177]

The funds for the programme were to be made up in large part of contributions from grants from the Central Fund for Overseas Territories (CCFOM) for participation in its economic and social plans. Other investments were to be provided by private concerns.[178] The first economic plan concentrated on developing the infrastructure of the territory.[179] A considerable part of the work undertaken involved major construction works, such as the extension and modernisation of the Douala seaport, the building of bridges, including the Bonaberi bridge

---

[173] LeVine, "The Cameroon Federal Republic." p. 271.

[174] Fanso, *Cameroon History for Secondary Schools and Colleges vol. 2*, p.121

[175] Ndongko, *Regional Development Policy in Cameroon*, p. 30.

[176] Ibid.

[177] DeLancey, et al. *Historical Dictionary of the Republic of Cameroon*, p.168.

[178] Fanso, *Cameroon History for Secondary Schools and Colleges vol. 2*, p.121.

[179] Ibid.

over the Wouri River complete with a railway linking the Douala-Nkongsamba lines, the development of telecommunications, renovation of railway equipment, building of airfields, and improvement of the road network, especially between Douala and its hinterland, which would permit the transportation of products to the internal and overseas markets.[180]

Investments were allocated to the various regions in relation to their estimated profitability, and the gap between the North and South was widened. Although a permanent highway was built in the Northern region in 1950, linking it with the South, and the planting of cotton and a programme of agricultural improvement that began in 1952 plus, an investment in schools, the relations between Moslems and pagans were to remain unchanged; and in the south-western zone the projects and improvements were on a much larger scale, particularly in the area of urban and educational development including the economic and social structures.[181]

Among some other major economic projects sponsored by the French government in Cameroon under the two four-year Economic Plans was the impressive technological, electrical and metallurgical complex, ALUCAM, established in Edea. This hydro-electric industrial complex was built to provide electricity for the city of Douala and for the Allumium industry.[182] The project involved building the Sanaga River and generators to provide electricity, and the construction of a plant for the processing of aluminium. This was a very important and long-term project implanted in the territory.

Work on the complex costed an estimated 26,000,000,000 CFA francs and employed between two to three thousand Cameroonians, although it was expected to employ only 600 of them and 100 French technical and managerial staff when completed.[183] It was hoped at the time that since electricity generated by the plant would be far more than ALUCAM and the surplus would serve as the basis of the industrialisation of the entire region. ALUCAM became fully operational in 1956, producing approximately 45, 000 tons of aluminium per

---

[180] Ibid.

[181] Ibid.

[182] LeVine, *The Cameroon Federal Republic*, p. 32.

[183] Fanso, *Cameroon History for Secondary Schools and Colleges vol. 2*, p.122.

annum.[184] However, limited industrial and infrastructural growth occurred during this period.[185]

The second plan was intended to deal more directly with the welfare of French Cameroonians. It devoted greater attention to such social aspects of development like schools, health facilities in the rural areas, agriculture and technology. In terms of agriculture, Cameroon made rapid progress in the production of export and commercial crops. From the beginning of the 1940s, French colonial authorities encouraged a policy of agricultural diversification based on mono culture crops, like coffee in the West, cotton in the North and cocoa in the south of the territory. The three most important export crops from which the territory drew much of its income were cocoa, coffee and bananas.[186] These crops accounted for a full 70 percent of the value of export crops. Of this, Cocoa alone accounted for 50 percent of the total export earnings of Cameroon, while coffee and bananas together accounted for 20 percent.[187] Palm products, timber, groundnuts, cotton and tobacco accounted for 30 percent of the value of exports.[188]

While cocoa cultivation was almost entirely in the hands of Cameroonians, coffee and banana were a monopoly of white farmers until after WWII. Cameroonians, mainly the Bamelike only forced their way into the production of both crops and to gain an equal share in the export markets with whites in the 1950s.[189] Cocoa production, which was vigorously promoted by the administration in all areas with requisite soil and climatic conditions, was most successful in the centre-south region from the Yaoundé area, South to Ebolowa and Ambam.[190] More than half a million inhabitants of the region depended on the crop for welfare. The banana crop was mainly grown in the Mungo region, while Arabica coffee was cultivated mainly in the western highlands among the Bamelikes and Bamouns.

Total investments in French Cameroon's public and private sectors at all levels of government from January 1946 to June 1959 stood at 95 424 200 000 francs CFA. [191] Of this, the French state provided

---

[184] Ibid.

[185] DeLancey, et al. *Historical Dictionary of the Republic of Cameroon*, p.6.

[186] LeVine, *The Cameroon Federal Republic*, p. 32.

[187] Ibid.

[188] Ibid.

[189] Fanso, *Cameroon History for Secondary Schools and Colleges vol. 2*, p.122.

[190] LeVine, *The Cameroon Federal Republic*, p. 36.

[191] Fanso, *Cameroon History for Secondary Schools and Colleges vol. 2*, p.121

39 698 000 000 francs CFA as grants and 9 214 500 000 francs CFA as loans.[192] Private investors put in approximately 21 000 000 000 francs CFA into privately-held enterprises, and some 15 658 700 000 francs CFA in semi-public enterprises in which the Governments of Cameroon and France also participated. Cameroon's contribution at the territorial and communal levels of investment stood at 9 873 000 000 francs CFA.[193]

It is worth mentioning that the economic and social advances made in French Cameroon from 1946-1959 had both positive and negative consequences.[194] On the positive note, the economic advances raised the standards of living of many Cameroonians. There also emerged in the Cameroon society, significant numbers of people belonging to such economic and social groups as small producers of export crops, salaried labour, a small middle class engaged in agriculture or commerce, and a civil service class.[195] Investments and rapid increase in the number of wage-earning Cameroonians led to the growth of labour unions accompanied by French social legislation and social security. [196]

On the negative side, French investments in the territory were concentrated in an area of just about one-tenth of the entire territory, the so-called "Fertile Crescent" or the region served by the rail road, with Douala as the centre.[197] All these developments were through force labour, which was only abolished thanks to pressure from the UN in 1952.[198] This was the region in which the major export crops were produced. Secondly, economic and social advances were more urban than rural in the territory. This situation stimulated a movement of the rural unemployed to towns and cities, principally Douala and Yaoundé, leading to a rapid growth of these towns and social problems as overcrowding, inadequate housing, electricity and water.[199] Looking critically into FIDES assistance, it did less for indigenous welfare, but instead boosted the fortunes of European-owned firms in the

[192] Ibid.
[193] Ibid.
[194] Fanso, *Cameroon History for Secondary Schools and Colleges vol. 2*, p.122
[195] Ibid., pp.122-123.
[196] Ibid, p.123.
[197] LeVine, *The Cameroon Federal Republic*, pp. 283-286.
[198] Gardinier, *Cameroon-United Nations Challenge to French Policy*, p. 57.
[199] Fanso, *Cameroon History for Secondary Schools and Colleges vol. 2*, p.123

territory.[200] Toward independence, FIDES was renamed *Fonds d'Aide et du Coopération (FAC)*.[201]

Lastly, except in the production of cocoa, much was not done to facilitate the entry of Cameroonians into commercial agriculture and the import-export trade and internal commerce[202]. In the commercial sector, large colonial trading firms, controlled the whole-sale and retail trade, while the colons, the Greeks and Lebanese controlled both the retail trade and trade in agricultural produce. Banks were unwilling to make loans accessible to Cameroonians to enable them enter into the competition with whites in these areas. Only the economically dynamic Bamileke; were able to render the discriminatory policies of credit agencies of little significance by using *Njangi* and other financial devices to force their way into the import-export trade and retail markets before independence.[203]

C) Independence and Reunification

We cannot understand the dynamics of Cameroon's post-independence development drive without presenting the circumstances that led to its independence and reunification. Self-government and reunification of Cameroon came because of pressure on the UN emanating from political events in French and British Cameroons, geared towards finding a solution to the question of the status of both trust territories.This shall enable us understand in detail why the Republic of Cameroon adopted certain development policies as soon it attained its independence from France and its consequent reunification with the British Southern Cameroons.

As far as French Cameroon was concerned, nationalist activities developed there in the 1940s, with the coming on stage of people who moved from individualistic to mass interests, geared towards exerting pressure on colonial powers and concerned bodies for their autonomy.[204] The principal ideas and connections between political actors within the territory and beyond especially in British Southern Cameroons, the United Nations and abroad, included self-government, independence and reunification. All these led to the legalisation of trade

200 DeLancey et al. *Historical Dictionary of the Republic of Cameroon*, p.168.

201 Ibid., p.169.

202 Gardinier, *Cameroon-United Nations Challenge to French Policy*, p. 37.

203 Fanso, *Cameroon History for Secondary Schools and Colleges vol. 2*, p.122.

204 Ibid., p. 312.

union activities in the territory in 1944.[205] Foremost of these was the Cameroon Trade Union Federation (CTUF), which embarked on the marked propaganda campaign against French colonial activities in the territory. The CTUF activities resulted in the creation of the *Assemblement Répresentative Camerounaise (ARCAM)*, a Representative Assembly in 1946, that became a worthy political avenue for the most able politicians to express their grievances.[206]

It was in the backdrop of the creation of ARCAM, that trade union leaders founded the *Union des Populations Camerounaise* (UPC*)* in April 1948, the first true nationalist party in French Cameroon.[207] Its political programme was: complete independence and reunification of the two Trust Territories (French and British Cameroons). Soon after its creation, it established and maintained contacts for many years with Southern Cameroons' political groups. The UPC even assisted in the formation of the French Cameroon Welfare Association, (later Union) with the dual purpose of mobilising French Cameroonians resident in British Cameroons and spreading the unification idea. This party at one time or the other, supported most Southern Cameroons political leaders.[208]

The UPC participated in several conferences of nationalist groups from both British and French Cameroons where ideas about reunification and independence were often discussed. This frequent UPC participation in Southern Cameroons' political meetings made the reunification issue a permanent factor in the politics of the territory.[209] In 1955, its leadership, fleeing from arrest after the party was banned in French Cameroon, established its control centre in Kumba and soon made a common course with the Kamerun National Democratic Party (KNDP) leadership. In 1957 it participated in the election into the Southern Cameroons House of Assembly, but failed to win a seat. Later in the year it was banned by the British administration from the territory, including its leaders, that had been under surveillance since 1955.[210]

But before the UPC was banned, it had made every Southern Cameroonian aware of reunification and even left behind an indigenous

---

[205] Ibid.

[206] Gardinier, *Cameroon-United Nations Challenge to French Policy*, pp. 39-40.

[207] Ibid., p. 44.

[208] Fanso, *Cameroon History for Secondary Schools and Colleges vol. 2*, p.314.

[209] Mokake, *Basic Facts on Cameroon History Since 1884*, p.107.

[210] Ibid.

Southern Cameroons' group, One Kamerun, to continue propagating the idea and that of independence in their own territory. That aside, the UPC moved faster in French Cameroon, structuring itself as a nation-based party, with branches all over the territory.[211] However, the major issue was the type and intensity of the relationship it was going to nurture with France after independence. [212] In this regard, the UPC leaders: Felix Moumié and Um Nyobe, demanded a thorough break with France and the construction of a socialist economy.[213] French officials opposed this demand and suppressed the party, leading to a bitter civil strife.

The French instead encouraged the creation of alternative political parties and leaders as they gradually granted increasing powers to elected assemblies, sailing from *ARCAM* to the *Assemblée Territorial Camerounaise* (ATCAM) and finally the *Assemblée Legislative du Cameroun (ALCAM)*, put in place under the sweeping reforms of the 1956 Loi Cadre.[214] It was within this framework that legislative elections were held, starting work on a proposed statute in New Year 1957. The Assembly then increased the powers of the future Cameroon government and replaced the title 'Territory' with 'State under the Trusteeship', adopted and made law by decree of the French Government on 16 April 1957.[215]

The new state thus acquired the constitution, a government headed by a prime minister and a citizenship, distinct from that of France. The High Commissioner remained responsible for the country's defence and for its relations with foreign countries and its own flag, a national anthem and a motto. On 9th May 1957, the assembly took the title of ALCAM. The following day, André Marie Mbida became Cameroon's first prime minister.[216] Cameroon had thus become a state under the Trusteeship outside the French Union, although it continued to be represented in the French Parliament. Mbida's policies were doomed as his methods were deemed by his political opponents as being too harsh. Opinion in both France and Cameroon emerged that a peaceful settlement be sought with the UPC, which did not however work as on the 26th January 1958, Mbida rather issued a ten-year programme for an

---

[211] Ibid.

[212] DeLancey et al. *Historical Dictionary of the Republic of Cameroon*, p.7.

[213] Ibid.

[214] Gardinier, *Cameroon-United Nations Challenge to French Policy*, pp. 80-81.

[215] Ibid.

[216] Eyongetah, Brain, Palmer, *A History of the Cameroon*, p.103.

undetermined political future without independence and reunification.[217] The *Union Camerounaise* (UC) rejected the programme and Ahidjo and his followers in the cabinet deserted the government.[218]

In the meantime, constitutional reforms which gave French Cameroon its first push towards independence were being worked out in France. They created the office of prime minister as head of a ministerial government. When Ahidjo succeeded Mbida as prime minister in 1958, he began immediately to hold talks with France to see how independence could be worked out.[219] In October 1958 the French government signified its assent to Cameroon's independence. As a result of the findings of the 1958 UN Visiting Mission to Cameroon, the UN General Assembly was convoked on February 20, 1959. The 1959 statute on Cameroun and the praiseworthy report presented by the 1958 UN Visiting Mission spoke favourably for the territory's independence.

However, the UPC lost the elections that were organised by the UN and the General Assembly resolved on the 13th March 1959 that from 1st January 1960, French speaking Cameroon would become the independent Republic of Cameroon.[220]On January 1st 1960, Cameroon gained her independence under Ahidjo as the first president and became the Federal Republic of Cameroon. In 1961[221] Ahidjo and his ruling party, the 1961*Union /%* pledged to build a capitalist economy. This was through a series of secret agreements for the Federal Republic of Cameroon to maintain very close political, economic, and cultural ties with France.[222]

For British Cameroons, despite the process that had been introduced by the United Nations, President Ahidjo immediately embarked on reuniting the independent Republic of Cameroon with the still-to-be independent British Southern Cameroons.[223] After the independence of French Cameroon in 1960, the impending independence of Nigeria meant that Southern Cameroons had to decide in a plebiscite, between the alternatives of either remaining in an independent Nigeria or joining

---

[217] Le Vine, "The Cameroon Federal Republic", p. 279.
[218] Ibid.
[219] Fanso *Cameroon History for Secondary Schools and Colleges*, p. 314.
[220] DeLancey et al. *Historical Dictionary of the Republic of Cameroon*, p.149.
[221] Fanso *Cameroon History for Secondary Schools and Colleges*, p. 314.
[222] DeLancey et al. *Historical Dictionary of the Republic of Cameroon*, p .7.
[223] Ngoh, "The Political Evolution of Cameroon, 1884-1961", p.76.

an independent French Cameroon.[224] Before then, Southern Cameroons was administered from Enugu, the capital of Eastern Nigeria. When in 1947, Nigeria became regionalised, the Southern Cameroons became a province of the Eastern region. After this political sentiment was growing for greater Southern Cameroons autonomy.

In 1953, Dr. Emanuel L.M. Endeley, then leader of the "Cameroon's faction" in the Eastern House, won a domestic election on the issue of separation from Eastern Nigeria. The Lyttleton constitution", promulgated in 1954, recognised the Southern Cameroons' wishes and made it a quassi-federal territory, in effect giving it a regional status, with its own House of Assembly and Executive Council.[225] The Southern Cameroons House of Assembly met for the first time in October 1954 and Dr. Endeley was named Leader of Government Business.[226] When his electoral alliance had won a close election in 1957, he was renamed Leader of Government Business, a title which he held up till 1958 when new constitutional arrangements came into place. Within this new system, Endeley was named Premier.

In January 30th 1959, general elections in Southern Cameroons resulted in the defeat of Endeley's coalition in favour of Dr. John Ngu Foncha, who had campaigned on a platform of the reunification of the two Cameroons. Foncha thus became Premier, replacing Endeley who had campaigned in favour of association with Nigeria.[227] In May 1959, the United General Assembly at the end of the special session on Cameroon, recommended that separate plebiscites be held in the Northern and Southern Cameroons to decide their political future. It was still in line with these developments that Foncha left Cameroon after the 1959 elections for New York in order to present his views on the future of the territory to the trusteeship council and the Fourth Committee of the UN, as follows:

> Secession from the Federation of Nigeria will place Southern Cameroons in a position to negotiate terms for reunification with the government of any free section of Cameroon which desires it ... the building up of a Cameroonian nation once again is a matter which is our concern. The question of reunification is now quite clear: it will be accomplished by individual sections rather than dependent British ones under France and Britain.[228]

---

[224] Gardinier, *Cameroon-United Nations Challenge to French Policy*, p.96.
[225] Fanso *Cameroon History for Secondary Schools and Colleges*, pp .316-317.
[226] Ibid.
[227] Eyongeta and Brain, *A History of the Cameroons*, p.146.
[228] Ibid.

Reunification was hence, the dominant ideology at the time. A majority of Cameroonian students studying in Nigeria, like James Sabum, supported the idea of re-unification. He declared in an article headlined, "The case for Secession" as follows: "... the division of Cameroon was an arbitrary and immoral act designed to suit the imperialists ... I say it was a mistake; a mistake is not corrected by simply accepting or arguing that it has gone on for a long time. Time does not make a mistake right."[229] The forgone views of Foncha and Sabum were an indication that Southern Cameroonians needed a free hand, in deciding their fate. The political grouping which most affected Southern Cameroons politics at the time as already mentioned was the UPC, whose motto was reunification and immediate independence. The opposition of the UPC took place mainly at the UN. During a debate in the Fourth Committee, Ahidjo received his most serious challenge from the UPC which demanded that new elections be held because the 1956 elections were held without the participation of the UPC.[230]

After this, the UN decided that plebiscites be held in British Northern and Southern Cameroons and that the choice for voters would be between joining an independent Nigeria or the independent Republic of Cameroon. A referendum had already been held in Northern Cameroons in 1959 in which the people were asked whether they wished Northern Cameroons to be part of Northern Nigeria when Nigeria becomes independent or whether they wanted to decide at a later date.[231] It may seem surprising that the question was asked in Northern Cameroons and not also in the Southern Cameroons. But the UN realised that the majority supported the union with Northern Nigeria. The result was that Northern Cameroon voted 70,456 to 42,788 to decide their future on a later date.[232]

As concerns the Southern Cameroons, the General Assembly resolved that their administration was going to be separated from Nigeria when the country attain independence on October 1st 1960 and that only persons born in Southern Cameroons will vote in the Plebiscite.[233] Talks between Ahidjo and Foncha became more frequent from 1959 as both personalities met twice that same year, in New York

---

[229] Ibid., p.147.

[230] Fanso *Cameroon History for Secondary Schools and Colleges*, p. .

[231] DeLancey et al. *Historical Dictionary of the Republic of Cameroon*, p .7.

[232] Kum, "Wum Area Development Authority (WADA), 1965-1994", p.72.

[233] Eyongeta and Brain, *A History of the Cameroons*, p.155.

in February-March and in Buea in July, to discuss the form of the union and system of government to be adopted.[234] They also held talks in Yaounde, in January, Nkongsamba in April and May, November and December in Yaounde.[235] In these talks, both leaders were able to agree that territories would neither join the French Union, nor the Commonwealth and that their own federal institutions would be responsible initially for foreign affairs, defence, public liberties, nationality, higher education, immigration, posts and telecommunication and the federal budget.[236]

When Southern Cameroons gained independence, she was to decide her future through a UN plebiscite on the 11th February 1961. Thus, both the Northern and Southern Cameroons had to choose one of the following options: "a) Do you wish to achieve independence by joining the independent Republic of Cameroon? b) Do you wish to achieve independence by joining the independent Federation of Nigeria?[237] A greater section of Northern Cameroon voted to join Northern Nigeria, while Southern Cameroon voted to join the Republic of Cameroon. The results of the plebiscite in Southern Cameroons were received with joy in the Republic and Foncha became hero of the time. The Republic was greatly disappointed at losing the Northern Cameroons. Without the North the Ahidjo government realised that Foncha's hand would be strengthened and that his demands for maximum local autonomy for his part of the federation would be difficult to deny.

Reunification talks between Ahidjo and Foncha resumed after the plesbiscite in Southern Cameroons. The Ahidjo actively pursued its complaint until April 1961, when the UN ratified the plebiscite, and did not get down to the business of a full-scale consultation with its new partners on the shape of the new federation. A constitutional conference was held at Foumban from the 17th to 21st July between representatives of the Republic of Cameroon and Southern Cameroons, to resolve the differences between Ahidjo and Foncha perceptions on the nature of the forthcoming federation.[238] Pressure for agreement only produced the text of a proposed federal constitution in July, 1961 after much foot dragging by the Republic. This conference was followed by another

---

234 Ibid.

235 Ibid.

236 Gardinier, *Cameroon-United Nations Challenge to French Policy*, pp.95-98.

237 Kum, "Wum Area Development Authority (WADA), 1965-1994", p.72.

238 Gardinier, *Cameroon-United Nations Challenge to French Policy*, p.118.

meeting in Yaounde in August. The outcome was a draft Federal Constitution, which was soon approved by the legislatures in both territories, and on October 1st 1961 the Republic of Cameroon and Southern Cameroons re-united as the Federal Republic of Cameroon, and the trusteeship over the Southern Cameroons officially came to an end.[239]

The former Southern Cameroons became the State of West Cameroon and the former Republic of Cameroon became the State of East Cameroon. Ahmadou Ahidjo became the president of the Federal Republic and John Ngu Foncha, while remaining the Prime Minister of West Cameroon, became Vice President of the Federal Republic. And Charles Assale, Prime minister of East Cameroon.[240] Worthy of note is the fact that the establishment of the federal state greatly increased the economic, demographic and political importance of the territory. There was an urgent need to meet the development requirements of the newly created Republic. It was in this backdrop that president Ahidjo, earmarked some development targets, aimed at attaining economic sovereignty which to him was the final phase of national independence.[241]

It is worthy of note that before the independence and Reunification of Southern Cameroons, with French Cameroon, Kenneth Berrill had concluded a report in 1960, in the territory, stipulating that whichever way the territory turned out, it would still need an estimated 1,000,000 pounds per annum to maintain its rate of economic growth.[242] The key fact for Southern Cameroons was that its economy was far from being viable and that if it had to move forward sizable injections of development, capital had to be made. It was the United Kingdom's, Colonial Welfare and Development Programme that had been chiefly responsible for providing such funds.[243] It is therefore argued that with independence, Southern Cameroons could still have relied on substantial economic aid from Britain, but on a much more limited scale and within limited time frames. But the United Kingdom rather gave Southern Cameroons some 2,000,000 pounds (approximately 1,

[239] Ibid.
[240] LeVine, "The Cameroon Federal Republic", p.281.
[241] Kum, "Wum Area Development Authority (WADA), 1965-1994", p.73.
[242] LeVine, "The Cameroon Federal Republic", p.288.
[243] Ibid.

800,000,000 Francs CFA) as a parting gift and extended commonwealth preference for west Cameroon exports to September 1963.[244]

Conclusion

Chapter one examined the contextual setting of Cameroon's economic development policies. It logically divided into the period of the German protectorate that ended with the outbreak of WWI, ensuing to the League of Nations mandates, ending with WWII, resulting in the UN trusteeship. The later periods were both animated by Britain and France. The chapter, laid deep emphasis on the organisation of colonial economies in the British and French Cameroons, paying much attention to the different economic development patterns that both colonial administrations employed for their economic gains. The chapter examined the general motives of European colonisation especially the Germans and their economic development patterns in Cameroon. It continued with both the mandates and trusteeship periods in both British and French Cameroons, emphasizing on their economic development strategies in the territory, during these periods. It further brought out both the strengths and weaknesses of France's economic development strides in its part of the territory during the trusteeship period and ended with the independence and reunification struggles in territories in 1960 and 1961.

[244] Ibid.

CHAPTER TWO
POST-INDEPENDENCE ECONOMIC DEVELOPMENT GROUNDWORKS

Introduction

Cameroon's early independence political economic values were based on values such as: economic sovereignty, Capitalist-socialism (a cosmetic blend of the colonial capitalist economy and indigenous African economy), planning and planned liberalism. From the foregoing chapter, it can be said that the founding History of Cameroon, as a nation-state was influenced by external factors, meaning that the founding political philosophy on which the country rests is traceable to foreign sources. This was especially due to the set of entangling agreements France reached with its former territories in Africa prior to the attainment of sovereignty. According to international law, such agreements between two unequal partners are questionable. Cameroon's post-independence development was thus not based on its indigenous philosophical basis of existence from which its worldview emerged to support its own reality. The chapter further examines Cameroon's economic sovereignty drive, its regional development planning mechanism, laying emphasis on distribution of investments among the six economic and administrative regions: Northern Region, South-Centre Region, Littoral Region, West Cameroon Region, Western and Eastern Regions. It wraps up with the country's concept of balanced development paradigm, crafted to enhance rural exodus issues in Cameroon at the time.

I- The Planning Mechanism

The policy of planning was earmarked due to the complex and challenging problems of independence, taking a new dimension within the framework of larger demands and aspirations for national economic growth. The prevailing political mood at the time was one of optimism that the federation would attain self-sustained growth.[1] According to Ahidjo, planning was not only necessary, but conformed to the evolution of the world at the time. His view could be perceived in the

[1] LeVine, *The Cameroon Federal Republic*, p.161.

following terms: “The national construction which is our supreme mission cannot be happily pursued in the present circumstances without plans; planning is necessary in all fields of national activity. This is not an exclusive Cameroon ambition or necessity; the twentieth century is a century of planning”.[2]

President Ahidjo defined it as follows: "We intend to submit, from now on, our international economic relations to our internal development objectives, that is to say that we intend to promote a truly integrated economy, characterized by the effective control of the principal factors of development. It is, basically, a human socialism that seeks its way in a pragmatic way.”[3] Planning was complemented by the initiation of the Civic Service in the development drive, added to efforts of some former structures created between 1966 and 1971 namely: the Intergovernmental Committee for the Plan and Economic Development, responsible for ensuring the co-ordination that was essential before decisions were taken in the economic field, the National Committee for Development, the National Committee for Economic Reconversion and General Orientation of Co-operation, the National Investment Corporation, the Rural Development Fund and others, which combined their efforts with those of the Economic and Social council, The National Credit Council, the Cameroon Development Bank and the Chamber of Commerce.[4]

The planning scheme was based on fulfilling some key requirements, such as the full mobilisation of human resources and major legislative and administrative innovations, notwithstanding the attainment of a number of economic objectives: the creation of the north-south communication axis, greater production and consumption of meat, refinement of distribution patterns and facilities, increase in the production of primary export products, a higher volume of savings, development of better credit facilities, and full development of the potentials for the creation and operation of various types of cooperatives.[5]

This 20 years plan was initiated by two medium term plans, covering the periods 1960-1965 and 1966-1971.[6] Ahidjo’s choice of Five-Year Development Plans was as a prelude to meeting the development needs

---

[2] Ahidjo, *Political Philosophy*, p.82.

[3] Chauleur, «Un « libéralisme planifié ».

[4] Ahidjo, *As Told by Ahmadou Ahidjo,* pp.54-55.

[5] Ibid.

[6] Ndongko, *Planning for Economic Development in a Federal State,* pp. 130-131.

of Cameroonians, emanating from independence and reunification. One of the earliest and prominent examples that did adopt such a model of development was Russia, which launched its first Five-Year Development Plan in 1928, aimed at finding the necessary food by forced collectivisation of agriculture.[7] India at independence in 1947 copied Russian methods and planned for certain improvements over a limited period with First Five Years Plan being implemented in 1950.[8] Gaining inspiration from these, Cameroon adopted the five-year development plans as catalysts for a rapid transformation of the territory.

Although centralized, development plans were profoundly democratic in Cameroon. First, they sort to orient, incite, influence and persuade rather than compel; second, they were worked out amidst a dialogue at all levels (village, communities, regional councils, divisional councils and national development councils), between authorities, producers, consumers, and in the final analysis the whole population.[9] It was in this view that a plan was elaborated in 1960 to run for a 20-year period. The initial efforts to achieve this were in two medium phases as already mentioned above: First and Second Five Years Development Plans.[10] Whatsoever, the initial plan substantially remained the framework for the two and future plans. The first plan did not have a regional breadth, since it was originally crafted for East Cameroon, before the federation and also because of the lack of feasibility studies of possible development projects in West Cameroon, making it difficult to be extended there.

The cost of the plan was equally of interest at the time. For the first five years, the plan estimated a total investment requirement of approximately 4,5 to 5 billion francs CFA.[11] Although the plan made no projections for the full 20 years, the utilization of its increment and investment percentages led to an estimate of its total cost by 1980 at over 1.1 billion US dollars.[12] It was nevertheless deemed exceedingly "utopian" in its financing aspects, as it specifically admitted that

---

[7] S.H. Wood, *World Affairs: 1900 to Present Day*, Longman Group Ltd, 1978, pp. 68-69.
[8] Ibid., p.281.
[9] Ahidjo, *Political Philosophy*, p.82.
[10] H.Philippe, *Analyse du sous-développement en Afrique noire: l'exemple de l'économie du Cameroun,* Paris presses universitaires de France, 1968, pp. 249-254.
[11] LeVine, "The Cameroon Federal Republic", p.348.
[12] Ibid.

between 40 and 45 percent, at least for the first five years, had to come from outside sources.[13]

Since most of Cameroon's development funding came on the basis of bi-lateral agreements, the possibility arose that these sources, especially France, either could not or were not going to maintain their then rate of aid. The alternative was thus, increased dependence on multilateral and or international aid and investment, but Henry warned in relation to the whole continent, that: "the net result of this reorganisation may well be a net decrease in the aggregate volume of aid received by Africa and not the expected increase".[14] The 1960 plan had three key aspects, in the following areas: agricultural reform and reorganisation, prospects for industrialisation and *le grand project* (the north-south rail way axis).[15]

A) Economic Sovereignty

One of the principal motives for which Cameroon's planning mechanism was adopted was to enhance the country's economic sovereignty that was yet to be attained. Although Cameroon's immediate and subsequent post-independence economic and social development drives were inbred from the British and French colonial capitalist economies, its economic sovereignty was primordial. The colonial administration had played a dominant role in upholding economic and social developments of the country's mandates and trusteeship periods. It was this same philosophy that newly independent Republic inherited for its socio-economic development quest. One of the major challenges at independence was that of attaining economic sovereignty.

It is worthy of note that France concluded secret agreements with Cameroon on 31st December 1958 in the following fields: military and financial cooperation, cultural affairs, administrative relations, civil aviation and aeronautics, military assistance, and a consular and legal convention.[16] This thus constrained Cameroon's post-independence development drive. This was in spite President Ahmadou Ahidjo, viewed development and economic development in particular as an

[13] Ibid.

[14] P.M. Henry, "The United Nations and the problem of African development", *International Organisation, XVI,* no. 2, spring 1962, p. 362.

[15] LeVine, "The Cameroon Federal Republic" p.348

[16] DeLancey et al., *Historical Dictionary of the Republic of Cameroon*, p.338.

integral part of the last conquest of national sovereignty.[17] For him, sovereignty was not complete, as long as economic dependence, characteristic of underdevelopment, remained, as long as economic independence did not come to complete political liberation.

Sovereignty is not an end itself, but a means of improving the nation's living conditions. Such improvement implies agricultural production in quantity and quality, its diversification not only depending on foreign markets but also on local needs and constant improvement of marketing channels.[18] It also implied industrialisation, because without it there could be no true development. The industry was out to promote all sectors of the economy. This perception was equally to allow agriculture modernise and make progress. Cameroon thus aimed at fitting its development policy into a context of vast diversified and general cooperation.[19] All this was to enable an effective economic take-off of the newly independent and reunified state. This situation is better expressed by Ahidjo in the following words:

> We have won our internal and external political sovereignty completely and totally. But political sovereignty which is not based on economic sovereignty is just like a house without a foundation ... the economic domain cannot be isolated from the social, scientific and more especially from the political domain, whether as regards internal or external policy. Economic problems are dominated by social and political considerations and social and political questions have always had important economic repercussions. That is why in elaborating our economic policy we have directed it towards political and social objectives.[20]

This fundamental preoccupation of Cameroon's leadership, as indeed of most Cameroonians was the problem of economic development of the country. To a large extent, the manifold problems of unification took on new meaning when seen within the context of the larger imperatives of national economic growth.[21] It was within the economic sovereignty perspective that a development planning mechanism was elaborated in 1960, anticipating a doubling of the average per capita income of the country in 20 years and the product of a national growth rate of approximately 4.6 percent.

---

[17] Ibid.

[18] Ibid.

[19] NAB, File No. 271/ S.2 (Qb/a 1969), "Five Year Development Plan, 1971-1976," 1969, p.147.

[20] Ahidjo, *The Political Philosophy of Ahmadou Ahidjo*, p.87.

[21] LeVine, "The Cameroon Federal Republic", p.347.

B) The Agricultural Reform

Concerning the agricultural reform, it envisaged a reorganisation of the rural economy, involving the creation of "a communal structure of rural life, oriented towards cooperative development at the human, social and economic levels".[22] Within each divisional set-up, there were : *des communautés villageoises* (village communities), embracing 20,000 to 30, 000 inhabitants, apparently on the models provided by similar projects on the Nile Delta, in Iran and Chad, and organised to provide cooperative marketing and production facilities for output and to permit maximum coordination of governmental social and development services within the area.[23] The operation of the various village communities absolutely fell under the jurisdictional supervision and control of the Ministry of Rural Development, operating in cooperation with national political agencies.[24]

Some of the bases for this projected reorganisation already existed. The extent and growth of production and marketing cooperatives had already been noted, especially those involved in major export crops like cocoa, coffee, and the like.[25] East Cameroon had some 1,500 cooperatives, of which, about 1,300 were financial in nature. In addition to the cooperatives, five Agricultural Modernisation Centres were created to coordinate development, research and technical aid relating to the principal crops grown in the five geographical zones, served by the centres.[26]

In conception, the rural reorganisation plan was grandiose, but certainly feasible. It must be pointed out that, the implementation of this portion of the 1960 plan involved solving some of the knottier social and political problems of which reference has already been made.[27] For example, unless "the Bamiléké problem" was resolved and unless the violence which had disrupted much of the economic life in the South West could be stopped, little progress was to be made toward agricultural reform in these very areas, that were most critical to Cameroonian agricultural production.[28]

---

[22] Ndongko, *Planning for Economic Development in a Federal State,* p. 132.
[23] LeVine, "The Cameroon Federal Republic", p.349.
[24] Ibid.
[25] Ibid.
[26] Ibid.
[27] Ibid.
[28] Gardinier, *Cameroon-United Nations Challenge to French Policy,* p.103.

C) Industrialisation

During the early years of independence and reunification, Cameroon earmarked the import substitution industrialization model. The goal was to reduce the country's dependence on imported goods, by promoting industrialization, expanding infrastructure, and improving social welfare, including the building of schools, hospitals, and other public facilities, under the planning scheme. As far as the industrialisation potential in the federation was concerned, two facts stood out: (1) that the greatest possibilities laid in the East Cameroon and (2) that major industrial projects designed to produce items for export were out of the question for the federation. The latter was one of the conclusions reached in a 1960 report prepared by a French firm assigned to study the possibilities for industrial development in Cameroun.[29] Given the high cost of capital and construction, the poverty in infrastructure, limited natural resources of the federation and difficulties involved in trying to compete in markets dominated by industrial nations, only limited industrial expansion in the country.[30] The consequences of this were obvious.

It was in the foregoing backdrop that the Cameroon's first and second five years development plans, stressed more on industrialization, trusting this was going to briskly attain its expected development goals, despite its financial constrictions. The dominant political sentiment at the time was one of optimism, that the country would attain self-sustained growth.[31] It is argued that some political leaders at the time did virtually equate development with industrialisation.[32] This was nevertheless so costly and slow in reducing poverty and stimulating Cameroon's socio-economic development.[33] Collint, Hansen and Wingender buttress these views in the following words:

> Early views of development assumed that most of the impetus for development and economic growth would necessarily come from the industrial sector, which was thought to offer the potential for rapid rates of productivity growth. In contrast, the

[29] Societe d'Etudes pour le Développement Économique et Social, *Rapport pour les possibilités de développement industriel du Cameroun*, Paris, La Société, 1960, p. 2.
[30] LeVine, "The Cameroon Federal Republic", p.350.
[31] LeVine, *The Cameroon Federal Republic,* Ithaca and London, Cornell University Press, 1971, p.161.
[32] C. Zuvekas, *Economic Development: An Introduction,* London, Macmillan, 1979, p.209.
[33] J. Seitz, *The Politics of Development,* New York, Basil Blackwell Inc, 1988, p.15.

agricultural sector in most developing countries was seen as backward and stagnant, with limited potential for growth.[34]

According to the report, East Cameroon's industrial development had to be directed toward the creation of industry, most of which was on a fairly small scale, designed to service just local markets.[35] Some dozen or so enterprises, including meat canning, flour milling, biscuit production and the manufacture of matches, tennis shoes, soap, plywood, cement and plastics would have had utility within the range of the Cameroon's limited economic potential.[36] Aside the foregoing, it called for the establishment of agro-industrial structures were innate in the process, through Five Years Development Plans, with an accent on industrial development. The plan also called for the establishment of regional development institutions combined with plantations and agro-industrial structures.

The Edea aluminium plant, the single exception to the "no large industry" rule, was constructed, it should be recalled, to take advantage of the extremely cheap hydroelectric power available at the mouth of the Sanaga River.[37] However, its expansion seemed to be economically unprofitable, principally because bauxite still had to be brought into Edea from outside sources and because the world market for aluminium was already quite inelastic. This did not discourage expansion of the already-existing facilities for the manufacturing of aluminium utensils made from the Edea ingots.[38] Such economic reality had to dictate that such production be directed to internal, rather than external markets.

Finally, a large area of uncertainty existed, regarding the exploit-tation of extensive bauxite deposits at Martap near Tibati.[39] This uncertainty was compounded by the fact that these ores were going to be available only when the Douala-Chad railway was extended more than 400 miles north from Yaoundé to reach the deposits and by the fact that this extension could not be completed for at least five to seven years.[40] Further, the unpredictable state of world aluminium market and

---

[34] D. Collint, C.W. Hansen and A.Wingender, "Two Blades of Grass: The Impact of the Green Revolution", Centre for the Study of African Economies (CSAE) Working Paper WPS/2016-30

[35] Fanso, *Cameroon History for Secondary Schools and Colleges*, p.171.

[36] LeVine, "The Cameroon Federal Republic", p.350.

[37] Ibid.

[38] Ibid.

[39] Ibid.

[40] Ibid.

the extremely high initial costs of transportation on the railway posed other problems. The major issue in the planning scheme was that the successes earmarked were limited, especially in the domain of agriculture. Apprehending that industrial development was more exorbitant and slower in reducing poverty and stimulating socio-economic change, greater attention was moved towards improving the country's agricultural economy in the early 1970s.[41]

D) The North-South Railway Axis

Apart from its industrialisation option, the government of the Federal Republic invested enormously on the North-South railway axis all in a bit to integrate the federation. Since the German protectorate, the extension of Cameroon's railway pattern northward to the Chad Basin had always been an object of great interest. In 1930, the French administration undertook a survey of the expansion of the Douala-Yaounde line north to Ngaoundere and onward to the Chad territory itself. The project laid dormant but not forgotten, until 1945, when interest was revived by the French and in 1948 a series of studies begun to determine the economic, political and financial feasibility of the Douala-Chad railway.[42]With independence, the Cameroon Republic pushed the project even further, to the extent of adopting the studies made by the governmental agency charged with examining the project and seeking international financing for it. In 1962, the Cameroon government obtained a commitment of about 31 615 000 dollars for the construction of the first 206 miles (Yaounde to Goyom) within the first plan's framework.[43] Involved in the project were: France, the European Economic Community and the USA, which pledged 11 033 000 dollars, 12 396 000 dollars and 8 119 000 dollars respectively. Work was expected to begin in 1963 and expected to be completed in 1965.[44]

In May 1962, it was propounded that the extension of the railway would be to Ngaoundere (438 kilometres from Yaounde), then Moundou in Chad (another 241 miles), making a total of about 780 miles.[45] In April 1962, Ahidjo met with Tombalbaye of Chad and

[41] Kum, "Wum Area Development Authority (WADA)", p.109.
[42] Commissariat Général à l'Information, *Le chemin de fer Trans camerounaise*, Paris, Société Presse Associée, 1969, pp.151-154.
[43] Ibid.
[44] Ibid.
[45] LeVine, *The Cameroon Federal Republic,* p.171

discussed the possibility of a further extension to Fort Archambault (about 230 miles from Moundou).[46] Fort Archambault, is the southern terminal of the navigable portion of the Chari River, which passes by Fort Lamy, in the capital of Chad.[47] The political and economic ramifications of the project as a whole were far-reaching for the Cameroon and Chad-Central African Republic area of Lake Chad.[48] (1) The Douala-Chad railway would provide a new and profitable means of access to the sea for an area of more than 193000 square miles with over 2,700 000 inhabitants.[49]

The foregoing area in question, had limited and difficult access to seaports. The North Cameroon-Fort Lamy areas were served by the Benue from Garoua and by the Nigerian railway system's extension to Northern Nigeria and alternatively (for Chad) by the difficult overland connections and by river south of Brazzaville.[50] The new railway line was intended to shorten the distance to the sea; cut the time required to move goods in and out of the area, and eventually lower the cost of transportation from the region by over two-thirds; constituting one of the vital requirements for the realisation of the Cameroon plan; without which the development of the Cameroon north would have become almost impossible and eventually, opening it to a closer integration with the Equatorial African group, which the Cameroun was definitely interested in joining.[51]

In all, the first development plan was produced and in some haste by a French research and planning group, without adequate preliminary study. It was equally put together before reunification and as such did not take into account the entering of West Cameroon into the total economy of the Federation.[52] More still, there was the lack of comprehensive feasibility studies of possible development projects in the former West Cameroon at the time and this made it difficult to extend the plan immediately to that state. The total planned investment in East Cameroon projects was earmarked at 53 million francs CFA. The plan was equally unrealistic in some of its provisions, in that the results

---

[46] Ibid.

[47] Ibid. p.351.

[48] Ibid.

[49] Fanso, *Cameroon History for Secondary Schools and Colleges vol. 2,* p. 350.

[50] LeVine, "The Cameroon Federal Republic", p.351.

[51] Ibid.

[52] Fanso, *Cameroon History for Secondary Schools and Colleges* p. 170.

achieved only partially corresponded to the stated aims in the domains of infrastructure (railways), public education, health and housing.

Most seriously, very little was met in the field of agriculture, which was one of the plan's key points of emphasis.[53] Nevertheless, the first plan permitted the creation of structures necessary for the success of the second plan. According to Hugon, the first plan served as "*Period of Adaptation*" for subsequent development plans.[54] But before we examine the other economic values and plans, it will be judicious to give a pride of place to the politico-economic development institutions that set in after reunification, for an effective implementation of Cameroon's initial and subsequent economic values and planning mechanism in particular.

E) Politico-Economic Development Institutions

For a better perception of the legal binding and functioning of its economic development values and planning process, the government of Cameroon, instituted some structures in that regard. One of the most essential, was the Federal Constitution that created two decision making institutions with extensive economic and political powers and responsibilities at the national level. These were the Presidency and the National Assembly, with the regulative capacity to control and influence the planning process.[55] To this extent, the authority relating to matters of development planning, economic policies, control and organization of credit, establishment of national budget and the determination of taxes and all levies required to meet national government expenditure, were jointly exercised by both institutions. As far as the Presidency was concerned, the Head of state was responsible under the terms of the Constitution for ensuring the management of the affairs of the Federation. In this capacity, he defined the main lines of the planning policy (in a Presidential Circular), and took all major decisions. The National Assembly on its part debated and voted on the law to approve these development plans.

The planning machinery at the national level, was under the Ministry of Planning and Territorial Development, headed by the Minister who was responsible for the general co-ordination of studies and procedures concerning their preparation and control of execution. A special point of

---

[53] Ndongko, *Planning for Economic Development in a Federal State,* p. 132.

[54] LeVine, *The Cameroon Federal Republic,* p. 163.

[55] Ahidjo, *Political Philosophy*, p.82.

view was the territorial development. One of the operations recommended to achieve the planning goal was the creation of what it called “an Obligatory National Civic Service for stable young unemployed people of 18 to 25 years, and their distribution among reclassification centres.”[56] If the experiences of states like Ghana, Guinea and the Ivory Coast were of any consequence, then the one-party state lend itself admirably to the creation of just such a mobilization of surplus labour.[57]

The Department of Planning, in cooperation with the other Departments of the Ministry, were responsible for the preparation of medium and long-term development plans, controlling the execution of the plans, the planning of human resources and the development of the national territory.[58] At the provincial level, there was a Provincial Economic Service, responsible for: collecting, centralizing and forwarding to the Provincial Governor and Minister of Planning and Territorial Development. Economic data on the province and principally ensuring that the control forms concerning the execution of these plans, were kept up to date, and organizing their regionalization by undertaking the secretarial duties of Provincial Planning Boards.[59]

Apart from Provincial Economic Services, there were also Provincial Development Councils which dealt with all problems related to the specification of development targets and implementation of projects earmarked for each province. In particular, the Provincial Development Councils proposed regional action programmes and determine the order of priority of the operation to be adopted. Again, they analysed the local means available and encouraged the co-ordination of technical services, public agencies and private enterprises.[60]

At the divisional level, was a Divisional Development Committee, chaired by a Prefect. The Committee comprised local technical services, deputies, mayors and private citizens. It examined the methods and means employed to ensure the satisfactory execution of the plans as well as the progress made by their programmes. Again, it ascertained the results of programmes in the field of rural action and submitted its views on requests for subsidies by Local Councils. The Divisional Prefect was assisted in his duties by a Regional Development Officer,

[56] LeVine," The Cameroon Federal Republic", p.348.
[57] Ibid.
[58]Ndongko, “Regional Economic Planning in Cameroon”, *Intereconics*, No. 5, 1974, p.154.
[59] Ibid.
[60] Ibid.

a technical representative of the Ministry of Planning and Territorial Development.[61]

In effect, then, Cameroon so far attempted to combine at each level, both the policy and technical planning functions.[62] Under the Cameroonian planning system, technicians, politicians and administrators were brought together with a view to ensuring continuous cooperation in the formulation and execution of development objectives at the national, provincial and divisional levels. As a result, it was possible to initiate programmes that were necessary to help each province attain its economic and social potential.[63] It was also possible to undertake an overall regional economic and social analysis so as to ensure that all levels of the planning machinery proceeded from a common base of information.

F) Development Planning within the Federal Set-up

Development planning within the Federal set-up emerged and operated under the stimulus of the planned liberalism strategy, taking into consideration the unification of the territory, to Federal (East and West Cameroons). This actually began within the Second Development Plan that was elaborated under the auspices of the Federal Government. It was the first plan to be regionalised, formulated for the six economic regions under the federal setting, instead of the two federated states.[64] For the first time, the planning process gave consideration to the spatial dimension of national development. The plan struggled to remedy the defects and failures of the first plan.

The second plan did envisage a total investment of 165 million francs CFA, amounting to more than three times that scheduled for the first plan.[65] Of this amount, 45.6 percent was devoted to increasing overall production in the country, 35.1 percent for infrastructural development, 15.8 percent for social equipment and 3.5 percent for

[61] Ibid.

[62] Ibid.

[63] Ndongko, "The Political Economy of Regional Economic Development in Cameroon", Kofele-Kale, *An African Experiment in Nation Building: The Bilingual Cameroon Republic since Reunification*, pp.227-228.

[64] Ndongko, "The Political Economy of Regional development Planning in Cameroon", p.227.

[65] LeVine, *The Cameroon Federal Republic*, p. 163.

administrative cost and studies.[66] Agriculture was given a pride of place. This explains why the plan was named the "peasant plan". The Plan further called for the acceleration of agricultural commercialization, reform and reorganization.

An important facet of the plan involved the radical improvement of peasant export production through the diversification of cash crops. Major cash crops like cotton, cocoa, coffee and others were increased significantly. Wood, meat and livestock were also exported in greater quantities.[67] Efforts were made to increase the production of tea, rubber and palm products. Most export crops were marketed by cooperatives in both parts of the country. In addition, the Federal Government created agricultural modernization centres in the five geographical areas of the country to coordinate development research and technical aid relating to the principal crops grown in the areas, served by the five centres.[68]

The plan also called for the establishment of regional development structures, much like the "Small landholders development authorities" in Rwanda and Malaysia, which were going to combine plantations and agro-industrial structures.[69] In addition, these organisations were to supervise the creation of rural development funds and distribute agricultural credit. In the plan, West Cameroon was considered as one economic region, while former East Cameroon was divided into five regions. This plan was a regionalized one, which aimed at effectively developing each region's economic and social potentials, especially in farming, crafts and industrial expansion.[70] It was in this backdrop that a series of agricultural development structures were put in place in Cameroon.

The Third Five Years Development Plan (1976-1981), constituted not only of extending large scale plantations and agro-industrial structures, but also at creating new ones. Apart from creating and extending large scale structures, projects of integrated development were equally established, to operate with the active participation of the populations concerned.[71] One of the main aims in the third plan was to increase production and productivity in all sectors of the economy with

---

[66] Ibid., p.164.
[67] Kum, "The Wum Area Development Authority (WADA)", p.77.
[68] Ibid., p.166.
[69] Ahidjo, *Fondements et perspectives,* p.33.
[70] Ndongko, *Regional Development Policy in Cameroon*, p.45.
[71] Kum, "The Wum Area Development Authority (WADA)", p.111.

significant investment expenditures directed towards the private sector. Most governments in developing countries in the 1960s gave a relatively low priority to agricultural development and concentrated on industrial development. As a result of the complex nature of certain constraints, the interaction between them, the ineffectiveness of existing strategies and accentuation of certain problems through time, the various plans pursued different approaches and adopted different strategies and solutions.

Zuvekas[72] holds that some political leaders did virtually equate development with industrialisation. Whatever, in the 1970s, greater attention was placed on agricultural development and on improving living conditions in rural areas. This awakening was urged by the fact that industrial development was costly and slow in reducing poverty and stimulating socio-economic development.[73] This fact is commensurate with why despite all early efforts by the state of Cameroon and Cameroonians in general to promote economic development, the economy still faced serious difficulties. These difficulties were caused by the fact that there was a production gap, due to unfavourable climatic conditions and simultaneously a fall in the prices of some basic products in the international market.

In the frameworks of the 2nd and 3rd development plans, government action was geared towards promoting high and equilibrium growth, principally in the domains of agricultural modernization, development of industries, and the acceleration of collective equipment. But due to preponderant effects on agriculture and volume of exports on the economic sector of the country, there was a slowdown in production; rhythm of economic activities; national demand; public finance and the balance of payment. Added to these were the effects of world inflation and the heights in prices of petroleum products, which contributed to disequilibrium in the economies of the different countries of the world including Cameroon.[74]

Five-year development plans were essentially out to reduce socio-economic disparities between regions in Cameroon. Ndongko argues that from 1966, planning was out to "assert, symbolise and strengthen

---

[72] Zuvekas, *Economic Development: An Introduction,* p.209.

[73] J. Seitz, *The Politics of Development,* New York, Basil Blackwell Inc, 1988, p.15.

[74] Ibid., p.32.

national unity."[75] But this was hardly achieved as regional inequality was rather enhanced as the plans instead established the basis of inequalities with some sectors and regions favoured against others.[76] Friedman and Alonso support this view as they argue that the question of social and economic justice in the distribution of economic progress are as important and as difficult in terms of regions as in terms of social class.[77]

In the third plan, 63 percent of the total investments were allocated directly to productive projects comparing with 46 percent in the second plan.[78] The private sector did not develop as was expected, due to no solid base for its development. Rather, the plans were just like mere presentations of lists of items to be done, which were never fully completed. Unlike the second plan which relied more on external sources the third did essentially on national resources.[79] Following this situation, the Gros Domestic Product (GDP) of Cameroon fell from 8 percent in 1970, to 4 percent in 1971 and 3 percent in 1972, urging the government to put some measures in place so as to elevate the living standards of the masses.[80] Taking into consideration the agricultural and pastoral vocation of Cameroon, rural development was given a pride of place. This explains why the third plan was baptized "production and productivity plan". [81]

The plan came to add more impetus to the regional approach adopted during the period of the second plan (July 1966 to June 1971) aimed at meeting up with issues resulting from the diverse cultural, ethnic and linguistic backgrounds of the various regions.[82] This was with a view to ensuring a balanced distribution of investment resources. LeVine[83] states that the problem of labour migration both seasonal and permanent long complicated West and East Cameroon relations. This is to add to the fact that with the coming of the central services of the Federal

---

[75] Ndongko, "Regional Economic Planning in Cameroon", Research Report No. 21, *The Scandinavian Institute of African Studies*, Uppsala, Sweden, 1974, p.6.
[76] A. A. Amin (ed), "Cameroon's Economy and Reforms in Developing a Sustainable Economy in Cameroon", *CODESRIA*, DAKAR, 2008, pp.81-82.
[77] J.Friedman and W. Alonso (eds), *Regional Development and Planning*, Cambridge, 1964, p.4.
[78] Ibid., p.81.
[79] Ibid.,p 82.
[80] Seitz, *The Politics of Development*, New York, Basil Blackwell Inc,1988, p.15.
[81] Kum, "The Wum Area Development Authority (WADA)", p.110.
[82] Ndongko, "Regional Economic Planning in Cameroon", p.5.
[83] LeVine, *The Cameroon Federal Republic*, 159.

Government, it decided to solve these problems in order to rationalize interstate labour exchanges. The plan was drawn around a certain number of strategic operations, principally directed towards the public sector aimed at breaking the principal impediments of economic and social development in the country. [84]

This effort could be seen beginning from the Second to the Fifth Five Year Development Plans. The 1966 to 1971 Development Plan allotted a stunning 26,758 billion francs CFA to rural development and actually invested 18,650 billion francs CFA on rural production.[85] The 1971 to 1976 Development Plan set aside 25,545 billion francs CFA for rural development, amounting to 9.2 percent of planned investments.[86] The 1976 to 1981 Development Plan witnessed a phenomenal increase in rural development budget, which got a whopping 108.9 billion francs CFA.[87] Development Plans were principally out to create and extend existing plantations and agro-industrial structures. Projects and programmes under these Plans ranged from sectorial through integrated to regional agro-industrial structures. The major issue with development planning was how to fund the various projects earmarked.

G) Development Funding and Debt Trap

Financing development in Cameroon during the post-independence period emanated from two main sources: domestic and foreign. The former constituted of drawing funds from domestic resources, while the later was characterised by direct private foreign capital investments, public foreign loans and grants from its bilateral and multilateral cooperation endeavours.[88] Early in the period after independence, underdeveloped countries engaged in seeking means to come out of underdevelopment. This fact could be likened to the economic goals of these newly independent African States. Their great desire for

---

[84] NAB, File No. DVA/J.2/2, (Qb/a 1960), "Five Years Development Plan", 1960, p.3.

[85] Ndongko, "The Tracing of Economic Development in Cameroon", *Africa Development*, Vol.11. No.3, p. 67.

[86] Ibid.

[87] Ibid., p.69.

[88] M. J., Abéna Etoundi, « La planification économique au Cameroun : aperçu historique (1960-2000) », Thèse de Doctorat Ph. D en Histoire, Université de Yaoundé I, octobre 2010, p. 411.

immediate development had one principal obstacle: financing growth and development.

According to Mboudou, financing the growth and development of a country is to mobilize the necessary financial resources with the aim of investing susceptibly to the development of that country.[89] For a better perception of how development was funded in post-independent Cameroon, it will be appropriate for us to have some knowledge of how it was financed in French and British Cameroons before independence and reunification. In French Cameroon, for instance, public development projects were financed mainly by the French oriented FIDES. Two development plans were put through this structure between 1947 and 1959, amounting to 96 million francs CFA.[90]

Southern Cameroons on her part drew up a five-year development plan covering the period 1955-1960, with capital grants from Britain amounting to 8.8 million pounds.[91] This explains why after reunification, unlike in East Cameroon, the bulk of West Cameroon trade remained for a long time with Britain.[92] It was with respect to the foregoing background that at independence and reunification, the authorities of the Federal Republic of Cameroon decided to earmark the policy of planning as a channel for economic development in the country. Generally, at the time African states gained sovereignty, internal resources were apparently insufficient and most African countries depended, more on external sources for financing development.[93] Thus, while developed countries relied principally on internal accumulation, underdeveloped ones contrarily relied on external sources. LeVine examining the second plan supposes that it was utopian in its financing respect, since up to 50 percent of its funding came from outside sources.[94]

The resources for financing the various development plans' projects could have, in principle, been provided by drawing on domestic

---

[89] A.M. Mboudou, "Le financement du développement au Cameroun", Thèse de Doctorat de 3éme Cycle, Sciences Economiques, Université de Yaoundé, 1981, p.2.
[90] Ndongko, *Regional Development Policy in Cameroon*, p. 30.
[91] Kum, "The Wum Area Development Authority (WADA)", p.79.
[92] NAB, File No. PMO 422 (Qb/a 1962/2), "General Economic Situation in West Cameroon Arising from Reunification", 1962, p.92.
[93] G.Ngango, *Les investissements D'origine extérieur en Afrique noire Francophone: Statut et incidence sur le développent*, Paris, Présence Africain, 1973, pp.319-320. Cited in Mboudou, « Le financement du développement au Cameroun, » p.2.
[94] LeVine, *The Cameroon Federal Republic*, p.164.

resources, thereby restricting consumption through higher tax rates or utilising idle resources of the country and or mobilising foreign public and private funds.[95] However, Cameroon just like any other less developed country with apparently limited domestic resources, chose to finance development through both means. The rational underlying the country's central government's policy to seek financial resources internally and externally stemmed from the total planned investments of both the 1960-1965 and 1966-1971 plans, that far exceeded available domestic savings, urging planners to rely on direct private foreign capital investments, public foreign loans and grants to fill the gap.[96] As a matter of fact most of Cameroon's development funding came through bilateral agreements and there was the possibility that these sources of aid, especially from France, either could not maintain or discontinue as time went by.

In the face of such speculations, the alternative was increased dependence on multi-national and/or international aid and investments. It was in this backdrop that speaking of Africa as a whole on the issue of over dependence on external aid, Henry warned that: "The net result of this reorganisation may well be a net decrease in the aggregate volume of aid received by Africa and not the expected increase."[97] Whatever, reposing on the essence of external funding for development plans by the FRC and Africa as a whole, did not mean the lack of internal sources to effectively finance development plans.

The problem with African states and Cameroon in particular was the lack of adequate economic policies, properly mobilised and orientated to the needed areas of the national economy. For instance, in most African states at the time, potential savings had not been totally transformed to effective savings. In some cases, savings made were poorly used, while some were transformed to sumptuous and ostentatious than productive expenses.[98] These circumstances preceding Cameroon's independence and reunification worked a great deal in influencing Cameroon's foreign policy orientations, based on international cooperation and non-alignment. Foreign public aid to

---

[95] Kum, "The Wum Area Development Authority (WADA)", p.79.

[96] Ndongko, *Planning for Economic Development in a Federal State*, p. 131.

[97] P. M. Henry, "The United Nations and the Problem of African Development", *International Organization,* XVI, No. 2, 1962, p.162.

[98] Mboudou, "Le financement du développement au Cameroun", p.2.

Cameroon was accepted no matter its source of origin, on condition that it was not linked to any political obligation.[99]

It was with regards to the foregoing that early in the period after independence, underdeveloped countries engaged in seeking means to come out of underdevelopment. This fact could be likened to the economic goals of newly independent African States. Their great desire for immediate development had one principal obstacle: financing growth and development. According to Mboudou, financing the growth and development of a country is to mobilize the necessary financial resources with the aim of investing susceptibly to the development of that country. [100]

The Debt Trap: Seeking means for rapid development, was as a result of limited means for financing growth in Cameroon. Mboudou argues that funding growth and development during that period depended much on mobilizing the necessary financial resources that was done mostly externally.[101] In fact, many freshly independent nations depended more on external sources for financing development because internal resources were apparently insufficient.[102] However, such a mechanism gained its roots from the colonial days. In French Cameroon for instance, public development projects were financed mainly by FIDES, whereby two development plans were put together with assistance from it between 1947 and 1959, amounting to 96 million francs CFA.[103] Southern Cameroons on its part drew up a five year development plan covering the period 1955-1960, with capital grants from Britain, amounting to 8.8 million pounds.[104] This is why after reunification, unlike in East Cameroon, the bulk of West Cameroon trade remained for a long time with Britain.[105]

LeVine in his analysis of development plans supposes they were utopian in nature given that Cameroonian authorities depended largely

---

[99] N AB, "Five Year Development Plan", p. 148.

[100] Mboudou, "Le financement du développement au Cameroun", p.2.

[101] Ibid.

[102] G.Ngango, *Les investissements D'origine extérieur en Afrique noire Francophone: Statut et incidence sur le développent*, Paris, Présence Africain, 1973, pp.319-320. Cited in Mboudou, « Le financement du développement au Cameroun, » p.2.

[103] Ndongko, *Regional Development Policy in Cameroon*, p. 30.

[104] Ibid.

[105] NAB, File No. PMO 422 (Qb/a 1962/2), "General Economic Situation in West Cameroon Arising from Reunification", 1962, p.92.

on external sources for their financing.[106] This was in spite resources for financing them could have in principle, been provided by relying on domestic resources, through restricting consumption via higher tax rates or utilising the idle resources of the country. The government of Cameroon however chose to do so through both internal and external resources since the total planned investments of the first two plans far exceeded available domestic savings.[107] According to Sikod, the first plan was made up of 72 percent external financing, 37 percent for the second, 25 percent for the third, with it remaining important in the fourth and fifth plans.[108] This grossly had the country indebted to foreign partners and institutions.

Much of the financing came through bilateral agreements and there was the possibility that these sources, especially from France, could either not be maintained or discontinued as time went by. In the face of such speculations, the alternative was increased dependence on diverse foreign sources. Foreign public aid to Cameroon was therefore acknowledged no matter its origin, on condition that it was not linked to any political obligation.[109] Reposing on the essence of external funding in Cameroon did not however mean a lack of internal sources to effectively finance development. This was such that in 1973 Cameroon's debt stood at 431.4 million US dollars (approximately 215, 700, 000 000 francs CFA). This remained so heavy on the economy despite the discovery of offshore oil deposits in the Gulf of Guinea in the mid-1970s, significantly affecting the country's once predominantly agrarian economy and society.[110]

It was hoped that this oil discovery and exploitation would enable a positive growth and help meet Cameroon's debt burden. It was however not the case as this rather negatively shaped the governing elite's behaviour, thereby raising the country's debt to eightfold, from that in 1973 to 3,367.4 million US dollars (approximately 1,837,000,000,000 francs) CFA in 1983.[111] During this period, there was very little public investment in infrastructure, mainly for political reasons. Thus, it was not until the arrival of President Paul Biya that the country's two main

[106] LeVine, *The Cameroon Federal Republic*, p.164.
[107] Ndongko, *Planning for Economic Development in a Federal State*, p. 131.
[108] Sikod, "The Completion point of the HIPC initiative; what it means for the Cameroon Economy."
[109] NAB, "Five Year Development Plan", p. 148.
[110] Bertelsmann Stiftung, "Cameroon Country Report", p.3.
[111] Ibid.

cities, Douala and Yaoundé got linked by a paved road, although earlier planned and promoted by President Ahidjo.

To repay these debts, Cameroon relied almost entirely on the production and sale of primary products (Cocoa, Coffee and Cotton) and petroleum to foreign markets. Most of the debt was dominated by the public sector meaning, these products were transferred to foreign creditors by way of debt service payments. As a matter of fact, the heavy accumulation of external debt triggered the increase in the internal debt, contracted by the state vis-a-vis its own citizens, in local currency. In the struggle between adjusting the economy and repaying its debts, poverty rose in the country because the economy's performance was not good, meaning a further accumulation of debts. This predicament was further made difficult with the collapse of world market prices of primary products in the mid-1980s. There was every need to rescue it and Cameroon embarked on several measures (internal and external) in handling the crisis. With the crisis, Cameroon's debt increased on a per capita basis, making it one of the worst in the world at the time.[112]

In 1996 the official country's national debt was estimated at 10 billion US dollars (approximately 500,000,000,000 francs CFA).[113] Working with the World Bank and the IMF in making serious reforms within the country, it was granted significant debt relief under the Heavily Indebted Poor Countries program. The government of Cameroon had been exclusively meticulous when it came to external debts accumulation. The economic crisis situation therefore came to highten the country's debts burdern as Abena Etoundi remarks : *L'arrivée de nouveaux fonds extérieurs et le montant élevé des intérêts à payer, n'ont fait que maintenir le lourd fardeau de la dette. En l'espace de quelques années 1992-1996, la dette du Cameroun a doublé pratiquement partant de 2,9 milliards de dollars à un peu plus de 4 milliards de dollars américains.*[114] It was in these efforts that individual countries cancelled Cameroon's debt as per agreements reached in the Paris Club (an informal group of creditors who seek to find solutions to the payment difficulties of debtor nations). Total debt relief from the Bank was about 2 billion US dollars (approximately 200,000,000,000

[112] DeLancey et al. *Historical Dictionary of the Republic of Cameroon*, pp. 124-125.
[113] Ibid.
[114] Abéna Etoundi, "La planification Economique au Cameroun : Aperçu Historique (1960-2000)", p. 411.

CFA francs). The savings in debt servicing payments equalled about 100 million US dollars (50,000,000,000 CFA francs) per year, and this was used for social service development projects. External debt (public and private) was estimated at 2.555 billion US dollars (1,277,500,000,000 CFA francs) by the end of 2006.[115]

II- Africa or Cameroon Socialism

Cameroon's earliest post-independence economic development pattern to meet its economic sovereignty goal, was embedded in President Ahidjo's African Socialism concept. This economic development philosophy was elaborated in Ebolowa in 1962 as part of the statement on general policy at the fourth Congress of the *Union Camerounaise*.[116] Its underlying notion was the denial of the existence of social classes in Africa and thus aimed at promoting the interests of less privileged groups in the country such as: farmers, labourers, women, and the unemployed.[117]

President Ahmadou Ahidjo distinguished classical socialism that emphasised nationalisation from African socialism that was based on village communities, collective labour, and manpower investment. Capitalist socialism, African or Cameroon Socialism was an expression of Cameroon's ideology in the consecrated vocabulary of the 1960s. The prime theme of this whole political, economic and social philosophy was to promote socialism among humanity, as reflected in the African lifestyle.[118] The ultimate intension of Cameroon Socialism was to achieve a continuous balanced development in the necessary stability; social justice through modern technical means by concerting national effort and foreign aid together in a coherent and realistic plan.[119] This step cut Cameroon clean from classical capitalism whose merits, even when undeniable, did not often succeed in masking its anarchy and social injustice.[120] This was about promoting equality in all spheres of national life.

---

115 Ibid.

116 DeLancey et al. *Historical Dictionary of the Republic of Cameroon*, p. 24.

117 Ibid.

118 Kum, "The Wum Area Development Authority (WADA)", p.74.

119 Ibid.

120 Ndongko, "The Political Economy of Regional Economic Development", pp.227-228.

Cameroon's stance was not without a proper examination of the other side of Leninist socialism as practised elsewhere, as this would have meant a denial of African personality and its role in the concert of nations, notwithstanding its physical and moral liberty.[121] African Socialism was thus, a blend; as it borrowed techniques from abroad and did graft on to Cameroonian realities. It was therefore characterised by African community spirit, respect for spiritual values, and the central place of man in the society.[122] During the years following the independence of African states, many people spoke of platforms like capitalism, socialism, neo-capitalism, neo-colonialism and so forth. To Ahidjo, it was Cameroon Socialism as he puts it:

> We Cameroonians rarely speak of capitalists, socialists and neo-colonialists because we believe that these are mere words. We have chosen to carry out our economic and social development within a liberally planned framework; that is to say within a system of liberty, within which private national and foreign enterprises work together; a system of development in which the state has not only an interest, but which it plans a system of development which presupposes that the state, with a view to creating new industries and enterprises ... You may be tempted to tell me "You are heading for socialism." Precisely, it is our system of socialism. You can call it Cameroon Socialism.[123]

Although not scientific, Cameroon socialism was believed would be profitable to the country. It was not synonymous to nationalisation because nationalisation was harmful. Nationalising food, for instance, was not going to last for long because Cameroonians were going to find themselves with empty shops, consequently marking an end of Cameroon Socialism. The African socialism philosophy was abandoned in 1965. [124] One could assume it was one step, in a series of moves, to offset the socialist orientation of the *Union des Populations du Cameroun (UPC)*. Following poor dividends African Socialism was replaced by the planned liberalism policy.[125]

III- Planned Liberalism

Planned Liberalism also termed, planned development was the key theory in Cameroon's economic development philosophy. The main

[121] Ahidjo, *As Told by Ahidjo*, pp. 53-54
[122] Kum, "The Wum Area Development Authority (WADA)", p.74.
[123] Ahidjo, *As Told by Ahidjo*, pp. 53-54.
[124] DeLancey et al. *Historical Dictionary of the Republic of Cameroon*, p. 24.
[125] Ibid.

poles of this concept were double: encouraging the private initiative[126] and relying on market forces, as well as government regulation of investment and judicious allocation of resources. It did also regulate, manage natural resources and orientate foreign investments towards the common interest.[127] Foreign investments were organised into specific economic sectors or geographic areas.[128] It was greatly interventionist and nationalistic.[129] Under planned liberalism, the state regulated and managed natural resources and oriented foreign investment towards the common interest. It also partnered with foreign entities to set up various parastatals and extending existing ones, providing jobs to Cameroonians. Planned liberalism, in addition, encouraged private enterprise and investment and rational exploitation of production factors and market forces.[130]

Major actors in the execution of this policy were private individuals and foreign companies, on the one hand, and para-public enterprises and the national government, on the other. The private investment initiative was encouraged in all sectors so as to enable economic development be endogenous. In other words, the implementation of an economic nationalism: "of the people, by the people and for the people”. Conceived in 1965 following the abandonment of African Socialism, Planned Liberalism was a deliberate attempt at ideological neutrality. It sought to integrate the best elements of capitalism and socialism in respect to private initiative and national sovereignty.[131] It encouraged private investment, local and foreign, but government was to play a strong and significant role in guiding development into sectors of the economy and geographical areas that were deemed as priorities.[132] As such, it became a partner to numerous economic enterprises in order to execute certain highly prized economic ventures in the country. [133]

The most dynamic factor of planned liberalism was its choice for liberalism in the economic sector. The prospects of this choice were that legitimate profit would not only stimulate enterprise and fertilize

[126]DeLancey et al. *Historical Dictionary of the Republic of Cameroon*, p.308.
[127] Dongmo, “Green Revolution and Food Self-Sufficiency”, p.2.
[128] Ibid.
[129] Ibid.
[130] Ibid.
[131] Ibid.
[132] Chauleur, “Un libéralisme planifié.”
[133] DeLancey et al. *Historical Dictionary of the Republic of Cameroon*, p. 11.

imagination, but also follow an orderly, selective, non-anarchic dynamism and full development.[134] Planned liberalism provided more favourable psychological effects of freedom and trust than in the results of action due to compulsion. This was particularly in matters of the economy, especially on investments. The policy was regarded in relation to the world's situation at the time as in great conformity to the interests of Cameroonians. As far as planned liberalism was concerned, Ahidjo intimated that:

> ... private investments, whether Cameroonian or foreign, will always be welcome in Cameroon and will find guarantee of their full profitability in the provisions of our Investment Code which precisely has been designed in the spirit of our liberal option. We wish however, to add that this option does not exclude the possibility ... the necessity, of a public or semi-public sector, an instrument, in Government's hands for stimulating, controlling or orienting the national economy as a whole and for safeguarding the fundamental interest of the state.[135]

The Planned Liberalism philosophy, encouraged investments in the private sector and the rational exploitation of production and market forces as it was understood that abandoning the population to itself would lead to disastrous economic and political consequences.[136] Thus, President Ahidjo, rejected all organisations of collectivist type, and preferred to organise and control the economy through the use of democratic procedures and active participation of the populations in the development drive of the country.[137] In line with this policy, the government of the Federal Republic of Cameroon saw the need for a development plan, to work toward integrating the economies of the territory.[138]

Planned development was therefore out to work towards the economic unity of the Federal Republic of Cameroon, favoured by the excellent communication facilities in the East, that provided advantageous routes of egress for products of West Cameroon, particularly those of the grassfields area. Ethnic ties between the two states provided the basis of expanded and advantageous commercial intercourse.[139] The problems of labour migration, both seasonal and permanent had long complicated relations between both territories, the central services of

[134] Ibid.
[135] Ahidjo, *As Told by Ahidjo*, p.54.
[136] Kum, "The Wum Area Development Authority (WADA)", pp.74-75.
[137] Ahidjo, *As Told by Ahmadou Ahidjo,* p.54.
[138] Fanso, *Cameroon History for Secondary Schools and Colleges vol.2,* p. 170.
[139] LeVine, "The Cameroon Federal Republic", p.345.

the federal government decided to solve the problems and rationalise interstate labour exchanges.[140]

IV- Foreign Policy Orientations

At independence, the development ordeal of much of the World and Africa in particular, attracted attention from the global community. In fact, the ostracized repercussions of colonialism introduced a worldwide division of nations into two classes, namely the "developed and underdeveloped."[141] This splitting up drew the contour line of international economic inequality and there was an urgent need to bridge the gap.[142] One of the most urgent problems confronting most developing countries at the time was sharing the benefits of socio-economic growth, science and technology, usually concentrated in the cities against the predominantly rural communities. [143] For him, this new prevalence explained the emphasis on rural development in many development literatures, national development plans and political platforms.

How Cameroon's development was funded can also be understood through its early post-independence foreign policy orientations, that spined around two fundamental and complementary principles, namely: national independence or non-alignment and international cooperation. The country's foreign policy was largely pro-Western and more especially pro-French. During Ahidjo's presidency, France enjoyed a very privileged position in Cameroon. This situation could be explained not only because Cameroon was a former French colony, but also because Ahidjo's rise to power depended most, on French manipulations.[144] France's monopoly over Cameroon, was nevertheless brief

---

[140] Ibid.

[141] W. Krause, *Economic Development the Under-Developed World and American Interest,* San Francisco, Wards Worth, 1961, p. 27.

[142] Ibid.

[143] F.C. Okafor, "Integrated Rural Development Planning in Nigeria: A Spatial Dimension", *Cahier d'Etudes Africaine*, Vol., No.2, 1986, p.83, Cited in C.A. Ngwa and C.M. Lambi, "An Evaluation of the Upper Nun Valley Authority's Agricultural Innovation in the Ndop Plain (Cameroon), Since 1970", *Epasa Moto, (Bilingual Journal of Arts, Letters and the Humanities)*, University of Buea, Vol. 4, No.1, March 2009, p.50.

[144] K. E. Mbuh, "Canadian Financial and Technical Assistance to Cameroon (1962-2006)," Masters Dissertation, Department of History, University of Dschang, 2010, p. 47.

because after some time the country extended relations to other willing nations of the world in order to meet up with its development drive.

According to some studies as established by Chiek Anta Diop on "Negro" civilizations from ancient Egypt to modern times, African civilizations failed because they were not sufficiently exposed to external influences.[145] This is to imply that civilizations can only survive by constantly assimilating new contributions. For Ahidjo therefore, independent Africa could only escape the fate of traditional Africa if she kept her doors wide open to the pregnant wind that blew from abroad at the time, especially from more advanced nations of the world.[146] This assertion could be better elucidated in the following address he made during the Fourth Congress of the *Union Camerounaise* (UC), held in Yaounde, from the 4th to the 8th July 1962:

> Let us make it precise and clear: the nations of the world with which we wish to enter into relationship should consider us as partners on an equal footing and respect our sovereignty. But the spirit of frank and loyal cooperation which we desire to see kept alive in international relations is if this spirit demands free confrontation, if it preserves our freedom of choice and decision … (non-alignment).[147]

Cameroon's foreign policy was equally influenced by its inherited particular ties with Europe. In this light, she could in no way fail to approve or give accord to certain priority issues in her relations with Europe and France in particular. Although the strategy of employing diplomacy at the service of development appeared to be budget consuming at the time, its economic effectiveness however remained multi-dimensional. To begin with, it supplied the temporarily shortage of cadres by directing bilateral and multi-lateral technical assistance towards depressed sectors.

Again, it helped to reduce the shortage of capital by acting as purveyor of grants-in-aid and organizing relations of cooperation, intended to promote investments in the country. Finally, it organized inter-state trade so as to facilitate the marketing of national products under the best conditions.[148] The effectiveness of diplomacy at the service of development was perceived when President Ahidjo spoke in the conference of Cameroonian Ambassadors on the 15th November, 1965 in Yaoundé that:

---

[145] Ahidjo, *Contribution to National Construction*, Paris, Présence Africaine, 1964, p. 46.

[146] Ahidjo, *As Told by Ahidjo*, p.66.

[147] Ibid.

[148] Ahidjo, *Political Philosophy of Ahidjo*, p.84.

> ...We must have no illusions about it. Political independence has certainly permitted us to become sole masters of our destinies, but this is a potentiality. Real independence, the veritable independence means economic victory, victory over underdevelopment, over all its manifestations, whether moral, intellectual, spiritual ... we must consider our diplomatic missions abroad as widows open on the outside world ... it is your duty, gentlemen, wherever you are and whatever the occasion, to seek out people of good will who will help us in the struggle against poverty, sickness and ignorance.[149]

The authorities of the FRC thought that it was a grave error to disregard East Asian countries, which were ceaselessly increasing in weight in world politics. Thus, Cameroon was opened to any country, which intended or was ready to establish relations with her on the basis of equality, reciprocity, mutual respect of sovereignty and of non-interference. In this light, an economic and commercial goodwill mission was established and sent to certain European countries in order to prepare the grounds and find ways and means of cooperation.[150]

The principle of non-alignment on its part for the Cameroon government at the time meant non-interference in the internal affairs of other countries. It equally signified tolerance and peaceful coexistence between states with different political, social, and economic back-grounds. It further called on the peoples of the world to work together in the promotion of a world with equal and liberal people, dominated by fear and mutual respect.[151] Cameroon's policy of non-alignment could be better perceived in an address presented by Ahidjo during the second session of the Cameroon National Union (CNU) party, on the 23rd July 1965 in Yaoundé as follows:

> Our non-alignment does not mean a refusal to cooperate with industrialized nations of whatever bloc. On the contrary, we welcome any policy of cooperation which implies participation in the fight against underdevelopment and accession of all nations to a dynamics of greater wellbeing and prosperity, aiming at the making of a world society based on a technical infrastructure, common to all regions of the globe. Contributing to the building of a universal civilization, where both the one who gives and the one who receives enriches his basic personality. Our policy means free choice in the face of all problems, the only determining factor being the national interest.[152]

Given the colonial ties between Cameroon and some European countries such as France, Great Britain and the Federal Republic of Germany (FRG), Cameroon never did hesitate to open cooperation ties

---

[149] Ibid.

[150] Ahidjo, *Contribution to National Construction*, p. 49.

[151] Ahidjo, *Fondement et perspective*, p. 121.

[152] Ahidjo, *As Told by Ahidjo*, p.96.

with them after independence and reunification. Although considerable priority was given to Franco-Cameroon cooperation at the time, with some attention placed on West Germany, which financed development projects in the country, making it second in importance to the former.

V- Regional Development Planning: Fundamental Basis

The regional development planning emerged within the framework of Cameroon's Planned Liberalism precept. It was nevertheless more ingrained in the differential impact of the British and French economic policies, that defined the economic disparities between the various regions of Cameroon and persisted with the Federal Constitution of 1961.[153] As mentioned earlier, the Federal government created two decisions, introducing structures with extensive economic and political powers in order to curb these problems: the Presidency and National Assembly, with regulative aptitude to control and influence the planning process.[154] They thus had authority over development planning, economic policies, credit control and organization, establishment of national budget and determination of taxes, notwithstanding all levies required to meet government expenditure. Specifically, the President of Cameroon was responsible under the terms of the Constitution for ensuring the management of affairs of the country. He defined the main lines of the planning policy (in a Presidential Circular), and took the major decisions, while the National Assembly on its part, debated and voted on the law to approve development plans.[155]

The idea of a regional development policy through Five Year Development Plans was to harmonize development in the country. The central aim was to eliminate economic and social disparities between the various regions of Cameroon, thereby integrating their economies.[156] This idea was crafted during the second five year development plan (1966-

---

[153] Ndongko, "The Political Economy of Regional Economic Development in Cameroon", N. Kofele-Kale, *An African Experiment in Nation Building: The Bilingual Cameroon Republic Since Reunification*, Westview Press, Boulder, Colorado, 1980, p.227.

[154] Ibid.

[155] E. Mbu, "An Imperial Presidency: A Study of Presidential Power in Cameroon", Kofele-Kale, *An African Experiment in Nation Building: The Bilingual Cameroon Republic Since Reunification* pp.138-150.

[156] Fanso, *Cameroon History for Secondary Schools and Colleges, Vol.2.The Colonial and Post Colonial Periods,* London, Macmillam Publishers, 1989, p.170.

1971) to complement the 20 year plan put in place between 1960, aimed at doubling the real per capita income of the country by 1980.[157] In the plans, the Cameroon Government elaborated strategies aimed at tackling rural development with emphasis on self-reliance and regional development. This was not only because 85 percent of the country's population lived in rural areas, but also because regional and national development could not progress without a wider examination, planning, management, and utilisation of the rural areas.[158] Rural exodus which was one of the principal motives of the establishment of this development paradigm in Cameroon, could be best understood in the following extract:

> It is a widespread tendency for the local population to discard the rural areas in favour of the urban areas. This rural exodus is largely the result of the absence of socioeconomic amenities in the rural areas, which tends to push the population away from villages, and the comparatively better amenities in the urban centres, which tends to pull the deprived folk into the major cities. The sum total of these push and pull factors creates the conditions for rural exodus. The desire for a larger income and the relative low earning capacity in rural areas is a significant factor in this equation. Government attempts to overcome this rapid urbanization by improving conditions in the rural areas and providing adequate facilities in the urban areas to cater for the influx of rural migrants. All villages in the country have been particularly hard-hit by the rural exodus, while the cities have grown tremendously as a result of this phenomenon.[159]

The Cameroon government set out to achieve the regional development planning by increasing the funding of rural development projects. This effort could be seen beginning from the Second to the Fifth Five Year Development Plans. The 1966 to 1971 Development Plan allotted a stunning sum of 26,758 billion francs CFA to rural development and actually invested 18,650 billion francs CFA on rural production.[160] The 1971 to 1976 Development Plan set aside 25,545 billion francs CFA for rural development, amounting to 9.2 percent of planned investments.[161] The 1976 to 1981 Development Plan witnessed a phenomenal increase in its rural development budget, which got a whopping 108.9 billion francs CFA.[162]

The actual regional planning idea began in 1966 during the period of the Second Five-year plan (July 1966 - June 1971) continuing with the

---

[157] Ndongko, *Planning for Economic Development in a Federal State: The Case of Cameroon, 1960-1971*, Munchen, Welt Form Verlage, 1975, pp. 130-131.

[158] Ahidjo, *As told by Ahmadou Ahidjo*, p.55.

[159] DeLancey et al., *Historical Dictionary of the Republic of Cameroon*, p.333.

[160] Ndongko, "The Tracing of Economic Development in Cameroon", p. 67.

[161] Ibid.

[162] Ibid., p.69.

Third Five Year Plan (July 1971 - June 1976). It was aimed at harmonising development in the country and work towards eradicating economic and social discrepancies, between the different regions of the country and integrating their economies.[163] Strategically speaking, it was aimed at merging the federated states of East and West Cameroons economically. Regional development planning did also aim at integrating the diverse cultural, linguistic and ethnic backgrounds of Cameroon, with a view of ensuring a balanced distribution of its investment resources and fruits of economic progress.[164] The essence of regional planning was equally to "assert, symbolise and strengthen national unity.[165] In line with the foregoing, Friedman and Alonso, argue that: "the questions of social and economic justice in the distribution of the fruits of economic progress are as important and as difficult in terms of regions as in terms of social classes." [166]

Although commencing in the mid-1960s, regional development planning gained grounds in Cameroon in the early 1970s following the establishment of the United Republic and subsequently regions: The Littoral, North, East, West, Center-South and West Cameroon.[167] Regarding the distribution of regional investments, West Cameroon that was initially a Federated state was considered as a region alongside the rest in East Cameroon. Of the projected budgets indicated, that of West Cameroon did not feature among the first three in terms of actual investments.[168] This spurred resentment, not just in the minds of West Cameroonians, but also among regions that felt cheated in the budget distribution process.

In a bid to realise its planning mechanism, Cameroon endeavoured to combine at each level, both the policy and technical planning functions. Technicians, politicians and administrators were brought together with a view to ensuring constant cooperation in the design and execution of development objectives at the national, provincial and

---

[163] M. P., Chia, "WADA and the Rural Development of Menchum Division: A Case study of Bum Area," Maitrise in Geography, the University of Yaoundé I, 1988, p.6.
[164] Ndongko, Regional Economic Planning in Cameroon, Research Report No. 21, the Scandinavian institute of African Studies, Uppsala, 1974, p. 6.
[165] Ibid.
[166] J. Friedman and W. Alonso (eds.), regional development and planning, Cambridge, p.4.
[167] Ibid.
[168] Ndongko, "Regional Economic Planning in Cameroon", p.157.

divisional levels.[169] It was thus probable to initiate programmes that were necessary to help each province to attain its economic and social potential. It has also been possible to undertake an overall regional economic and social analysis so as to ensure that all levels of planning machinery may proceed from a common base of information.

Economic planning was regionalised in Cameroon, due to specific regional problems in the country. Regionalisation of development did not however mean regionalism, but rather, integrated development with a view to achieving an optimal national economy growth.[170] It was in this light that aside creating and extending agro-industrial structures, Cameroon's planned development policy nursed a plethora of schemes: Agro-pastoral shows, 'operation green revolution', self-reliant development, regional development and a host of others. President Ahmadou Ahidjo encouraged the creation of regional development structures, much like the "Small landholders development authorities" in Rwanda and Malaysia that combined plantations and agro-industrial structures.[171] It should be noted that each region in the country had specific main agricultural products as can be seen on table 1:

[169] Ndongko, "The Political Economy of Regional Economic Development in Cameroon", p.234.

[170] Ibid., p. 227.

[171] Ahidjo, *Fondements et perspectives du Cameroun,* Paris, Saint Lambert, 1976, p.33.

Table 1: Regional Economic Products (in tons), 1970

No.	Main Product (in tons)	East	West	North	Litto-ral	Centre-South	Former West Cameroon
1	Coffee	6297	32600	260	27380	5406	11430
2	Cocoa	7500	/	/	3368	94200	8000
3	Cotton	/	/	68000	/	/	/
4	Bananas	/	/	/	28000	350	61036
5	Groundnuts	7200	16000	53000	/	19988	/
6	Maize	18000	112000	26000	/	28000	/
7	Plantain	153000	73000	/	200000	273000	/
8	Manioc	111700	/	119000	92000	180390	/
9	Yams	/	18000	/	26000	12000	/
10	Sweet potatoes	560	47000	35000	/	5000	20000
11	Palm oil	/	/	/	9700	10000	17215

Source: Ndongko, "The Political Economy of Regional Economic Development in Cameroon", p.130.

Table I, demonstrates the main product of each of the six regions in Cameroon, during the period of regional development in the country in 1970. All these were to ensure that each region's economic and social potentials are effectively developed. It was in the foregoing backdrop that two medium term plans were crafted between 1960 and 1971 to tackle rural development in the country, with emphasis on self-reliance and regional development.[172]Cameroon's idea to "assert, symbolise and strengthen national unity,"[173] through the planning mechanism and more precisely the agro-industry strategy was nevertheless hardly achieved as regional inequalities were rather enhanced as the first two plans instead established the basis of inequalities with some sectors and regions favoured against others.[174]

---

[172] Ndongko, *Regional Development Policy in Cameroon*, p.45.
[173] Ndongko, *Regional Economic Planning in Cameroon*, p.6.
[174] Amin, *Cameroon's Economy and Reforms*, pp. 81-82.

A) Regional Distribution of Investments

Considering the Cameroonian policy of sustaining a balance between regions, the planning process gave adequate attention to the spatial dimension of economic development of the nation. This important feature of planning in a unitary setting was reflected by the nature of decisions, taken in the process, with respect to allocations of public and private resources between the various regions. However, the lack of any comprehensive feasibility studies of possible development projects in former West Cameroon made it difficult to immediately extend the initial Plan (1960-1965), to that state. Consequently, the total planned investment of 53 billion francs CFA was earmarked for projects in East Cameroon. It should be pointed out that the 1966-1971 Plan was the first regionalized one, formulated for the six economic regions under the federal setting.[175] It was the first time, that the planning process took into consideration, the spatial dimension of national development.

As far as the distribution of planned investments between the regions, the bulk went to the littoral region which in 1965 accounted for 10 percent of the country's total population.[176] The South-Centre region, which had 20 percent of the total population, was allocated the second largest share, i.e., 12.2 percent. Projected investment in West Cameroon region, which contained 21 percent and of the total population in 1965, was approximately 11.8 percent of the total planned investment. [177] For the 1971-1976 plan, investment distributions were not made on a regional basis as was in the 1966-1971 plan. Rather allocations were made on sectoral and project bases. The information contained in the plan on the pattern of resource allocation, did not lend itself to regional analysis with a view to determining the volume of planned investments that was earmarked for each province.[178] It was, therefore, very difficult and frustrating to determine whether or not investment allocations under the 1971-76 plan was actually out to foster the government policy of maintaining balance amid the different economic and administrative regions of the country. Table 2 recapitulates industrial endowments invested upon by the federal government, within the different regions in Cameroon.

---

[175] Fanso, *Cameroon History for Secondary Schools and Colleges*, p. 350.
[176] Ndongko, "Regional Economic Planning in Cameroon", p. 157.
[177] Ibid.
[178] Ibid.

Table 2: Industries under the Investment code from 1961 to 1969

No.	Industry	Location/Region	Volume of investment in millions of francs CFA
1	Energy industries, Primary products	Littoral	10854
2	Processing industries	West and Littoral	10847
3	Aluminum production	Littoral	9827
4	Forestry industry	Center-South, West Cameroon, East	3200
5	Textile and shoe production	West, Littoral and North	2710
6	Chemical Industry	West and Littoral	489
	Total investments		37927

Source: "Investments and Economic Development: Cameroon", *Bulletin de l'Afrique*, paris, July 1970, p.12.

Table 2 examines the different regional industries that benefitted financial assistance from the federal state of Cameroon, between 1961 and 1969. The total amount being 37, 927 million francs CFA with the Littoral region, benefitting most being the economic capital with the highest number of industries.

B) Appraisal of the Cameroonian Experience

With regard to the general performance of regional planning in Cameroon, it became difficult to judge the separate effects of various area development programmes in the different plans. This policy was generally focused on specific problem areas and on those with specific resource potential for development. This is why under the authority of the Head of State and other moral forces of the nation the structures most likely to promote development got into the process of being built, during the Second Five Year Plan (which was a regionalized one).[179] This made Cameroon's GDP to increase from 194.5 billion francs CFA in 1966/67 to 296.8 billion francs CFA in 1970/71, making an annual growth rate of 9.6 percent.[180] If account is taken of the annual population growth of 2.1 percent and an annual average increase in the

[179] Fanso, *Cameroon History for Secondary Schools and Colleges vol.2*, p. 170

[180] Kum, "Refitting Economic Sustainability in Cameroon (1986-2006): Retorts of a Miscarried State", *Annals of the Faculty of Arts, Letters and Social Sciences,* the University of Yaoundé I, No.20, New Series, 2018, p. 180.

general price level of 3 percent, then the real growth rate of GDP per capita was 4.5 percent per year between 1966/67 and 1970/71.[181] This rate was double the per capita income between 1960 and 1980 a fundamental objective of Cameroonian perspective planning.

With respect to the three major sectors of the Cameroon economy (primary, secondary and tertiary) the share in percentage of the primary sector in GDP decreased from 36.7 percent to 32.0 percent between 1966/67 and 1970/71, while that of secondary and tertiary sectors fluctuated between 19.9 percent and 20.9 percent and respectively 44.2 percent and 47.10 percent, during the same period.[182] The fluctuations in the shares of the secondary and tertiary sectors were explained by the uneven sectoral shifts which took place within the various regions and the major industries that comprised them. The steady decrease in the share of the primary sector in GDP was a clear indication of the planning effort to reduce this sector's dominance in the Cameroonian economy.

Concerning the actual sharing of the regional investments, the projected investments, for the six economic and administrative regions in the Second Five Year Development Plan, indicated that the Littoral Region was to have the largest proportion of total planned investments followed by the Centre-South region.[183] However, for the year 1966/67's actual investments in the latter region, were indeed higher than in the former region. Furthermore, although the 1966-71 Plan indicated that the West Cameroon region was to receive the third largest share of planned investments among the six regions, this projection was not fulfilled in 1966/67[184]. Rather, the Northern region became third in terms of the actual investments that were undertaken whilst West Cameroon was fourth. Concerning the Western and Eastern regions, their respective positions were maintained.

In regards to undistributed investments, planned and actual capital expenditures in 1966-1967 were close to the estimates made in the 2nd plan, that is 38.1 percent as compared to 38.2 percent. For the remaining four years of the 1966-1971 plan, information on its execution did indicate the actual volume of investments that were finally undertaken in each region. It was thus difficult to say whether or not the various

[181] Ndongko, "Regional Economic Planning in Cameroon", p.157,

[182] Ibid.

[183] Ndongko, *Regional Economic Planning in Cameroon*, pp. 20-21.

[184] Ndongko, "Regional Economic Planning in Cameroon", p.157.

regions maintained their respective positions as they did in 1966-1967. In the case of the Third Development Plan, the report on its first year (1971-1972) execution again did not indicate the volume of actual investments undertaken in each region, probably because it was not regionalized like the 1966-1971 Plan.[185] It was hard to determine available data whether or not economic development under the policy of "planned liberalism" at the regional level in Cameroon was successful, particularly in view of government policy in maintaining a balance between all regions of the country. The results of this policy were nevertheless encouraging at the national level.[186]

Although a lot was done to improve the economy of West Cameroon, considered to be lagging in several respects, almost all of its projects such as: Powercam, Cameroon Bank, National Lottery as well as the National Produce Marketing Board (NPMB) eventually got ruined, due to poor management.[187] The Victoria deep sea port as well as Tiko wharf, which served the Federated State, declined in importance to the advantage of the Douala Sea Port. The Public Works Department (PWD) carried out good road maintenance as public transport was well organised.[188] West Cameroon system of driving changed from left to right. Vehicle inspectors made sure that only cars that were in good mechanical conditions that could guarantee lives and property were allowed to ply the road. [189] A. N. Jua kept the Tiko, Bota and Victoria seaports or Wharves, busy as the CDC, West Cameroon Marketing Board and Cameroon Development Agency helped to stimulate development and kept the economy buoyant.[190] Many unfulfilled promises were made to revive the ports, only for government to suddenly divert its attention toward the construction of the Kribi port.[191]

C) Balanced Development

The balanced development philosophy was innate in the regional paradigm, based on distributing progress throughout Cameroon, by redressing existing inequalities among the various regions of the

---

185 Ibid.
186 Ibid.
187 Mokake, *Basic Facts on Cameroon History Since 1884*, p.154.
188 Ibid.
189 Ibid.
190 Takang, "The Cameroon Development Corporation, 1946-2020", pp. 80-81.
191 Ibid. p. 155.

country. These imbalances were immensely embedded within the federated states of Cameroon, especially as the former West Cameroon was very much underdeveloped than East Cameroon as well as the different regions/provinces of the federation.[192] West Cameroon for instance lacked such vital economic structures and basic social amenities as industries, rural infrastructure, schools, hospitals and recreational facilities.[193]

Whatever, there was general spatial imbalance in development and infrastructural distribution in the whole territory, leading to an undesirable socio-economic relationship between rural and urban settings. This situation urged most of the youths in rural areas to drift to towns for greener pastures.[194] The government of the Federal Republic of Cameroon took upon itself the challenge of providing solutions to this trend, in order to enable a compatible development of all its regions.[195] The emphasis on balanced development throughout the country's various regions was basic to the Cameroon's planning process.

This involved regional, sectoral, and personnel aspects. The regional aspect consisted of a judiciously balanced allocation of programs and resources across the geographical areas of the country.[196] The sectoral, concerned restructuring the country's economic potential across the agricultural, industrial, extractive, and tertiary sectors. In terms of personnel, the balanced development paradigm aimed at equalizing opportunities for posts allocation among various regional and ethnic interests, requiring enormous state intervention, distorted the economic rational in the location of industries, and sometimes led to administrative mediocrity.[197] Government of Cameroon defended the balanced development option as an aspect of planning, for a young developing country. The origin, of these imbalances that existed were in part, the colonial legacy, whereby economic activities as well as missionary and Western education developments were concentrated

---

[192] Ndongko, "A Comparative Analysis of French and British Investment Policies in Cameroon", *Pan African Journal,* Vol. VII, No.2, Summer, 1974.

[193] Ibid.

[194] Kum "The Socio-Economic Impact of the Liquidation of the Wum Area Development Authority (WADA) on Wum Central Sub-Division 1989- 2004" Maîtrise Dissertation, Department of History, University of Yaoundé I, 2004, p.20.

[195] Ibid.

[196] DeLancey et al., *Historical Dictionary of the Republic of Cameroon*, p.56.

[197] Ibid.

near the coast and especially in the "fertile crescent" bound by Douala, Edéa, and Yaoundé. [198]

However, the implementation of balanced development during the Ahmadou Ahidjo era led to much dissatisfaction in the southern parts of the country as he placed weighty emphasis on projects in the northern areas. Before the 1990s, little was heard of this philosophy in government circles.[199] There was need to reverse the country's investment incentives so as to enable that private and foreign capital moved to the more neglected provinces and regions of Cameroon. [200] The idea of maintaining a balance between the regions was a political necessity and its implementation was compulsory.[201] In fact, the hidden idea of regional planning and balanced development was fostering national unity in the country, rather than the immediate maximisation of aggregate economic growth rate. This made economic growth within the policy a precondition of political stability in Cameroon.[202] It is worthy of note that the country's sound record of development progress predated its good fortune in the development of its limited petroleum resources in the late 1970s.

In 1972, the Cameroonian government decided that its economic priority would be agriculture oriented and launched the "green revolution".[203] The aim was to achieve food self-sufficiency and government invested massively in cash crops, such as cocoa and coffee, thanks to oil revenues and debt.[204] A price stabilisation fund was created for many commodities, such as the *Office National de Commercialisation des Produits de Base (ONCPB)*.[205] This is how companies like *Société Camerounaise de Palmerais* (SOCAPALM), for palm oil production and *Hévéa Cameroun* (HEVECAM) (rubber) benefited from massive public investments which led to very modest results, notably very low productivity and only owing their survival to the

---

[198] Ndongko, "The Political Economy of Regional Economic Development in Cameroon", p. 248.

[199] DeLancey et al., *Historical Dictionary of the Republic of Cameroon*, p.56.

[200] Ndongko, "The Political Economy of Regional Economic Development in Cameroon", p.248.

[201] Ibid.

[202] Ibid.

[203] Kum, "The Operation Green Revolution 1973-1986: Sustaining Cameroon's Planned Development Precept, *World Journal of Education and Humanities*, Vol. 3, No. 2, 2021, p.67.

[204] Ibid.

[205] Ibid.

financial assistance of international donors.[206] A plan to develop rice cultivation was implemented in the North Province. Although the beginnings were promising, the *Société d'Expansion et de Modernisation de la Riziculture de Yagoua* (SEMRY plan quickly failed due to the prohibitive cost of rice (50 percent above world prices) and the stagnation of production despite massive public investment.[207] The production of sugar, wheat, fertilisers or skins did not fare any better and despite massive state aid, the projects, often poorly dimensioned, went bankrupt more or less quickly.

Conclusion

Chapter two has examined early post-independence economic development groundworks. It laid emphasis on Cameroon's utmost desire to attain its economic sovereignty, through a series of mechanisms, ranging from development planning, African socialism, planned liberalisms, the institution of development management institutions and others. The chapter equally gave a pride of place to how development was funded in Cameroon during early independence period, based on both internal and external sources, notwithstanding its foreign policy orientations. The country's debt trap entanglements were equally examined in the chapter notwithstanding some of the efforts that were employed to save it from the predicament. The chapter has further laid emphasis on the regional planning mechanism that Cameroon instituted during the second five years development plan period and within its planned liberalism precept. The fundamental basis of this development model was traced, notwithstanding the distribution of investments among the six economic and administrative regions: Northern Region, South-Centre region, Littoral Region, West Cameroon Region, Western and Eastern Regions. After its succinct appraisal, the chapter concluded with the concept of balanced development with the context of the country's economic trends.

---

[206] The Ministry of Planning and Territorial Development, *What you Should Know about the IIIRD Plan*, Temporary Edition, Yaoundé, No Date, p.79.

[207] Ibid.

CHAPTER THREE
AGRICULTURAL DEVELOPMENT STRATAGEMS

Introduction

Chapter three dwells on Cameroon's agricultural development strategies during the period preceding the economic crisis that broke out in the mid-1980s. Cameroon's planned development policy initially laid emphasis on industrial development, later realised to be costly and slow to spur socio-economic developments in the country. In the early 1970s, the government endorsed agriculture as the primary basis to boast real development in the country, perceived to be the centre piece of its economy. The chapter opens with the early post-independence efforts meant to enhance the country's agricultural economy. Aside that it examines Cameroon's self-reliance development model that was fashioned to subordinate Cameroon's international economic relations to domestic development objectives, depending principally on local efforts and labour. This gave rise to the country's Food self-sufficiency drive, in order to ensure a sustainable production of food for local consumption and sale to its neighbours. It was in order to meet the foregoing principles that the Agro-industry strategy, Operation Green Revolution and Agro-pastoral shows were instituted in Cameroon.

I- Early Measures

Except for some areas, the economies of the two Cameroons were separate for over 40 years before independence and reunification. As of July 1962, only the most rudimentary common economic measures had been undertaken by the new federation. These included the introduction of the franc CFA as the common currency in both states, the promulgation of the first federal budget and taking of various steps to ease the flow of goods and trade between both states.[1] The economy of the federation was nevertheless based almost entirely on agriculture. The predominant pattern was subsistence farming, though no considerable portion of the agricultural sector was devoted to the production of exportable crops. Millet, cassava and various tuberous vegetables were the principal crops produced almost exclusively for

[1] LeVine, "The Cameroon Federal Republic", p.284.

local consumption.[2] Whereas palm oil produced in East Cameroon was mainly consumed locally and that which was produced in West Cameroon constituted its fifth most valuable export crop.[3]

Cameroon's laudable shift towards promoting its agricultural economy stemmed from the fact that during the period of the first and second five years development plans, its planning mechanism had stressed more on industrialization, trusting this was going to briskly attain the expected development goals. Despite the sector's financial constrictions, the dominant political sentiment at the time was one of optimism, that the country would attain self-sustained growth.[4] It is argued that some political leaders at the time did virtually equate development with industrialisation.[5] This was nevertheless so costly and slow in reducing poverty and stimulating Cameroon's socio-economic development.[6] Collint, Hansen and Wingender buttress the foregoing in the following words:

> Early views on development assumed that most of the impetus for development and economic growth would necessarily come from the industrial sector, which was thought to offer the potential for rapid rates of productivity growth. In contrast, the agricultural sector in most developing countries was seen as backward and stagnant, with limited potential for growth. [7]

The period from 1973 to 1978, made agriculture the mainstay of Cameroon's economy and allowed the country to record real growth, thanks to the development of the oil sector. [8] In fact, in agrarian societies, such as those that predominated Africa, agricultural development was an essential prerequisite to overall national economic development.[9] The forgoing views on industrialisation for rapid change did not work and in crafting a third plan early in the 1970s, agriculture was reconsidered as the crucial and most important stage to real

---

[2] Ibid.

[3] Ibid., p.285.

[4] LeVine, *The Cameroon Federal Republic,* p.161.

[5] C. Zuvekas, *Economic Development: An Introduction,* London, Macmillan, 1979, p.209.

[6] J. Seitz, *The Politics of Development,* New York, Basil Blackwell Inc, 1988, p.15.

[7] D. Collint, C.W. Hansen and A.Wingender, "Two Blades of Grass: The Impact of the Green Revolution", Centre for the Study of African Economies (CSAE) Working Paper WPS/2016-30.

[8] J. M., Moudio, "The dynamics of food security policy in Cameroon (2008-2019)", *American Journal of Public Policy and Administration,* Vol.6, Issue 1, 2021, pp 12-43.

[9] G. Toenniessen, A. Adesina, and J. Devries, "Building an Alliance for a Green Revolution in Africa", Annals of the New York Academy of Sciences, 2008, p. 233.

development, especially as food insecurity increasingly became a major concern, just as Toenniessen, Adesina, and Devries examine below:

> Most of Africa's people live in rural areas and depend on agriculture for their livelihoods. These predominantly small-scale farmers face many challenges, including food insecurity, rising poverty, and natural resource degradation. To increase the productivity, portability, and sustainability of their farms, they need greater access to affordable yield-enhancing inputs, including well-adapted seeds and new methods for integrated soil fertility management, as well as to output markets where they can convert surplus production into cash.[10]

It should be noted that it was the foregoing lag that made Cameroon's GDP to fall from 8 percent in 1970, to 4 percent in 1971 and 3 percent in 1972, urging government to adopt alternative measures to those adopted earlier during the independence era. This was to elevate the living standards of its masses. [11] Hence, rather than depend solely on industrialisation, initially perceived as the most practical way out for her development needs, agriculture was merged to the former, with the later taking precedence. Cameroon thus, decided to not totally side-line industrialisation, but created and extended structures that were going to blend both activities with emphases on agro-industrialisation and plantation agriculture. Ndongko acknowledges this when he opines that one of the most remarkable events in the country's political economy in the 1970s was the promotion of the agro-industrial enterprises and its agricultural economy, based on plantation production.[12]

It was in this backdrop that the third plan extended existing large-scale plantations and agro-industrial structures: *Société de Développement du Cacao (SODECAO)*, Cameroon Development Corporation CDC and others) and created new ones: *Société de Développement du Coton (SODECOTON)*, Upper Nun Valley Development Authority (UNVDA), *Société D'expansion et de Modernisation de la Riziculture de Yagoua (SEMRY)* and others. These included projects of integrated development nature: The Rural Migration projects of North-East Benue, Doulo-Ngane and Guider, all situated in the North Region; *Zones d'Actions Prioritaires Intégrées (ZAPI)* in the Centre South and East; the Wum Area

---

[10] Ibid.

[11] Seitz, *The Politics of Development*, p.15.

[12] Ndongko, *Labour Resistance in Cameroon: Strategies and Labour Resistance in the Agro-Industrial Plantations of the Cameroon Development Corporation*, African Studies Centre, Leiden, 1993, p.16.

Development Authority (WADA) and others. [13] All these trends were to boost production and productivity in all sectors of the economy and reduce rural exodus. This plan was baptized "production and productivity plan". [14]

Unlike the second plan which relied more on external sources, the third one did fundamentally on national resources.[15] There was therefore cause to take advantage of the country's most precious means: unused labour of the thousands of youths in rural settings. [16] This labour force was going to measure Cameroonians' efforts and find a solution for the problem of "disguised unemployment", which was common in the countryside. A series of financial and commercial institutions were equally instituted to assist in this direction: the Cameroon Development Bank, *Fond Nationale pour le Dévélopment Rurale* (FONADER) and others, which combined their efforts with those of the National Credit Council (NCC), NPMB, and Chamber of Commerce to provide loans and material assistance to the youths and foregone structures for the purpose of improving on their activities. [17] This allowed the government to retain a fraction of nominal world market prices on export crops to finance public consumption and investment needs. [18]

It was absolutely indispensable therefore for special efforts to be made at all levels to develop the agricultural sector in Cameroon, so as to raise the standard of living of all those that engaged in it, which at the time constituted 85 percent of the population.[19] Government's determination to throw off underdevelopment was a big step towards human and social progress as president Ahidjo attributed Cameroon's failures to ignorance as seen subsequently: "in Cameroon, people do not die of hunger or cold as they do in other countries; Cameroonians die rather of the ignorance of their possibilities, of the ignorance of the potential forces that lie within their reach". Giving priority to

---

[13] The Ministry of Planning and Territorial Development, *What you Should Know about the IIIRD Plan*, p.79.

[14] Ibid.

[15] Amin, "Cameroon's Economy and Reforms in Developing a Sustainable Economy in Cameroon", pp.81-82.

[16] Ahidjo, *As Told by Ahmadou Ahidjo,* p.58.

[17] Ibid. pp.54-55.

[18] E. Douya, "Cotton Supply Response in Cameroon", in *CODESRIA*, Dakar, 2008, p.66.

[19] Kum,"Wum Area Development Authority (WADA)", p.113.

agricultural growth as it was at the time is reminiscent of Anderson and Lorch's views, which hold that:

> ... very few countries, particularly in the developing world have experienced rapid economic growth without agricultural growth either preceding or accompanying it. This is because agricultural growth is a catalyst to broad-based development. At the micro level, for instance, it provides eventual savings for entrepreneurial development in the informal sector. At the macro level, it provides raw materials which are a strong base for industrial development.[20]

The state's intervention in the agricultural sector was direct and indirect. Indirect intervention could be seen as a continuation of the French and British colonial policies through marketing boards which had a monopoly over the agricultural export trade. Through structures like the National Produce Marketing Board, which was a strategy that allowed the government to retain a fraction of the nominal world market prices of export crops to finance public consumption and investment needs.[21] This policy was coupled with guidance of farmers by providing subsidized inputs through parastatals. Direct intervention involved state corporations, controlling activities formerly carried out by the private sector. The government sought to increase agricultural productivity through the establishment of the modern sector involving the expansion of plantation farming organisations like the CDC and the Cameroon Sugar Company (CAMSUCO).

The slogan: "grow more food", had been launched in West Cameroon early in the 1960s. This functioned so well that in the early 1970s, policy makers in the United Republic of Cameroon decided to style it a nationwide mantra.[22] Agric-Shows had always been crafted in this part of the country, to accompany it.[23] Its first two shows were launched in 1966, in the Wum and Nkambe Divisions.[24] These exhibitions helped change the minds of populations in the areas and youths in particular, who began to look at agriculture as a dignified career and highest in importance for an agricultural economy like theirs.[25] The preceding structures and ideas were production targets for agricultural activities during the period of the third plan. It was in line with these

---

[20] P. Anderson and R.P. Lorch, *Agricultural Growth is the Key to Poverty Alleviation in Low Income Developing Countries*, In the Unfinished Agenda: Perspectives on overcoming Poverty and Environmental Degradation, Washington D.C, 2001, p.87.

[21] Douya, "Cotton Supply Response in Cameroon", p.66.

[22] Kum, "Understanding Agro-pastoral Shows in a Planned Economy."

[23] NAB, File No. 748 QC/a/1966/2, "Agricultural Shows", 1966, p.6.

[24] DeLancey et al. *Historical Dictionary of the Republic of Cameroon*, p. 11.

[25] NAB, File No. 748 QC/a/1966/2, "Agricultural Shows", 1966, p.6.

that the government of Cameroon launched the Self-reliance and food sufficiency strategies that inspired the Operation Green Revolution, Agro-pastoral shows, farm credit bodies and related structures to permit the rural masses to get the maximum of them.

Although just 13 percent of Cameroon's land was arable, some 70 percent of its population engaged in agriculture, which produced about 44 percent of its GDP. Agricultural products were often categorized as "food" crops (cassava, cocoyam, banana and plantain, sorghum, millet, and maize) and "cash" or "export crops" (banana, cocoa, coffee, palm produce, rubber, and cotton). Cameroon became self-sufficient for food and even exported large quantities to neighbouring countries like Gabon, Equatorial Guinee, the Central African Republic and others.[26] Cash crops provided an important contribution to export income, and many Cameroonians were employed in the raising and processing of these crops.

For many years the government of Cameroon tended to place more emphasis on these crops, but as farmers became unable to satisfy domestic food demands, more research and funding were made available to assist them meet these exigencies.[27] Most food crops were produced by women and cash crops by men. Lack of credit, migration of young people to urban areas, failure of government to provide adequate support for agricultural inputs (pesticides, fertilizer, etc.), lack of proper infrastructure (for example, roads), and lack of research and adequate education were among several problems affecting agriculture.[28] In addition, population growth outpaced food crop expansion.

II- Self-Reliance Development

The self-reliance development pattern was launched in Cameroon in 1975, as a follow up of its planned liberalism concept. It was an integrated national development stride through effective control of the main factors of production by the government and people.[29] Interestingly, self-reliant development, subordinated Cameroon's international economic relations to the objectives of domestic development, depending principally on local efforts and labour.[30] In its fundamental sense,

[26] Ibid.

[27] DeLancey et al. *Historical Dictionary of the Republic of Cameroon*, p. 25.

[28] Kum,"Wum Area Development Authority (WADA)", pp.118-119.

[29] Dongmo, "The Green Revolution and Food Self-sufficiency."

[30] DeLancey et al., *Historical Dictionary of the Republic of Cameroon*, p.338

self-reliance is therefore a state of mind that esteems one's own mental and material resources as the primary stock to draw on in the pursuit of one's objectives, and finds emotional fulfilment not only in achieving the objectives but of having achieved them primarily by using one's own resources.

By self-reliance, the production policy in Cameroon was more sensitive to the local consumption market, a greater mobilization of financial and monetary policy towards savings and investment, and an enhanced labour and income policy in the labour market.[31] This was to enable that village communities contribute to developing their infrastructure and social services, by applying their knowledge and skills to the resources at their disposal. This ties with Anyanwu's observation that the development of related skills and attitudes of a people can enable them to satisfy their basic needs, to grow self-reliant, and to minimise precarious dependence on agencies external to their communities.[32]

Self-reliance in the Cameroonian context did not differ significantly from the principles of self-help, closely related to the later as perceived by Ghari,[33] that it is being promoted through cooperation throughout the developing world, as no egalitarian society should be persistently unable to meet their self-defined, local needs. It was thus successfully implemented and enforced by various state organs through the Five years development Plans to ensure that the country achieved its objectives of a self-sustained growth. The effect was Cameroon's movement towards a plantation economy, a process by which people were encouraged to be rural agricultural workers, a model of popular development geared towards the masses and the deserving rural working classes.[34]

Self-reliance enabled Cameroonians to exploit to their advantage, resources, by making use of the under-utilised labour; thereby enabling them handle their affairs.[35] This was because it improved the importance of people increasing their sense of responsibility, and

---

[31] Dongmo, "The Green Revolution and Food Self-sufficiency."

[32] C. Anyanwu, *Community development. The Nigerian perspective*. Ibadan: Gabesther
Educational Publishers, 1992.

[33] D. Ghari, et al., *The Basic Needs Approach to Development: Some Issues Regarding Concepts and Methodology*. Geneva: ILO Publication 1980.

[34] Dongmo, "The Green Revolution and Food Self-sufficiency."

[35] Anyanwu, *Community development. The Nigerian perspective.*

looking assistance as just supplementary, but never replacing popular initiatives or local efforts.[36] The emphasis was on democratising with reliance on what people could do for themselves. The principle of self-help means of offering ordinary citizens the opportunity to share in making important decisions about their living conditions.[37] This entails community participation at all levels of the project, a tendency that is noticeable in the communities under study. Worthy of note in the case of Cameroon just like most African countries was that it had initially relied on the export of cash crops: cocoa, coffee, bananas, rubber, timber, palm products and cotton, in order to provide the foreign capital needed for development expenditures.[38]

Much emphasis was thus placed on the expansion of the production of these crops, ignoring food crops.[39] In addition to export crops, some emphasis was laid on import substitution crops such as sugar, wheat, and rice, which had become popular in Cameroon but were not grown in sufficient quantity locally to provide for the country's needs.[40] Self-reliance was in fact, one of the bases of effective community development in Cameroon as was in most of Sub-Saharan Africa. This model was located centrally within the discourse of community development and connected to related concepts like self-help, mutual-help, indigenous participation and rural development as already mentioned earlier. According to it, community development depended significantly on voluntary cooperative efforts.[41]

Self-reliance explains the emerging trend in rural development in Cameroon during the period of planning for development, as an important point of take-off for better living. This emphasis was to involve young Cameroonians in planned programmes from which they were to gain skills that would enable them cope more efficaciously with the problems of their everyday life. It was thus "development on the basis of each region of the country's own resources, involving its populations based on the potentials of its cultural values and

[36] Fonchingong and Fonjong, "The Concept of Self-Reliance in Community Development", 199.
[37] Anyanwu, *Community development. The Nigerian perspective.*
[38] DeLancey et al., *Historical Dictionary of the Republic of Cameroon*, p. 11.
[39] Ibid.
[40] Ibid.
[41] Anyanwu, *Community development. The Nigerian perspective.*

traditions."[42] This is because they were going to delineate development according to their needs, values and aspirations.[43]

III- Food Self-Sufficiency

The needs for local alternatives and self-reliance have been voiced in more explicit terms by other scholars, such as Brett[44] who calls for cooperative and voluntary alternatives, while Sandbrook[45] emphasises the need for "small-scale community solutions". In the Cameroon's strategic plan, the agricultural sector was an important lever for economic and social development, as part of its strategies to combat food insecurity. Food self-sufficiency was launched in Cameroon in the 1970s alongside the self-reliance development policy. The central goal of increased food production, nevertheless, implies a long-term perspective and no dramatic achievements other than steady progress toward it should be expected.[46] The goal was to grow internal adequate food for the population and create a balance between food imports and food exports. Cameroon's enviable record was the combination of natural, economic, and political factors. Policies like the Green Revolution and the various institutions set up by government improved the level of food self-sufficiency. During the economic crisis of the 1980s, Cameroon's situation deteriorated.

In Cameroon, it emanated from economic, geographic, environmental, political and human capital factors. Given the dominant role of agriculture in socio-economic development, this was understandably the perception that sources of Cameroon's access to ample food were to be found in its agricultural potential and adequate policy planning. The country's food self-sufficiency goal, evolved within a development-oriented framework of what president Ahidjo officially labelled "Sahel

---

[42]J. Galtung et al. (eds.), *Self-Reliance: a Strategy for Development*. London: Bogle L'Ouverture publications, 1980.

[43] R. Preiswerk, Sources of Resisting to Local Self-Reliance. In: J. Galtung et al. (eds.), *Self-Reliance: a Strategy for Development*. London: Bogle L'Ouverture publications, 1980.

[44] E. Bret, *Adjustment and the State: Problem of Administrative Reform*, *IDS Bulletin*, 19(4): 4, 1988.

[45] R. Sandbrook, The Politics of Africa's Economic Stagnation. United Kingdom: Cambridge University Press, 1985.

[46] USAID, Annual Review of Agency's Four Priority Areas of Concentration Cameroon, 1983.

Vert" and the "Revolution Vert."[47] Among other problems, government subsidies for agricultural inputs decreased, leading to productivity drops. Food self-sufficiency was a long-awaited dream, for many developing countries, that made easy access to food, a reality in the daily life of the population. Launched in the mid-1970s, the Sahel vert project aimed at fighting gradual desertification in northern Cameroon by planting trees.

Upon its inception at the Agro-pastoral show in march 1973, the green revolution embarked on promoting the mass production of high consumption commodities such as rice, wheat, bananas, tomatoes, vegetables and corn, just to name a few. Though rice production was dismal prior to 1971, the state had identified various sites for its extensive cultivation in Yagoua, Mbo plains (Mungo), Nanga Eboko, and Doumé (East).[48] Major corporations that became involved in rice farming included the *Societé D'éxpansion et de Modernisation de la Riziculture de Yagoua (SEMRY)* and the 2000 hectares of lot of the *Société de Développement de la de la Riziculture dans la plaine Mbo (SODERIM)*.[49] Their primary goals were to increase the market share of Cameroonian rice, enhance agricultural revenues in these regions, provide jobs, supply the local consumption market with adequate food and bring large scale imports under control.[50]

Although food self-sufficiency was indeed a goal hard to accomplish by many African countries, Cameroon attained it for several years.[51] Exporting food to neighbouring African countries became a significant aspect of the country's food policy, making it a granary in the Central African Sub-Region. This desire to increase export production however conflicted with its food self-sufficiency goal.[52] According to the United States Agency for International Development (USAID), Cameroon had one of the brightest prospects among Sub-Saharan African countries with regards to her significant progress in self-sustained economic and social development as its broad economic philosophy and policies were those which the Agency's philosophy espoused. [53] The country came

---

[47] Dongmo, "The Green Revolution and Food Self-sufficiency."
[48] Kum, "The Wum Area Development Authority (WADA)", p.119.
[49] Ibid.
[50] Ibid.
[51] DeLancey et al., *Historical Dictionary of the Republic of Cameroon*, pp.170-171.
[52] Ibid., p.171.
[53] USAID, Annual Review of Agency's Four Priority Areas of Concentration Cameroon, 1983.

closest to being the model, which the USAID desired developing countries to emulate, except for some political issues.[54]

Despite these efforts made by Cameroon, food security remained a problem for the northern regions of the country, where drought was recurrent. It is indicated that due to this, 39 percent of women in the area suffered from malnutrition, and acute malnutrition affected 30 percent of children between six months and five years of age.[55] Countrywide, 26 percent of the population was undernourished, and 32 percent of children under five suffered from severe to moderate stunting.[56] The assessment of the national food situation carried out in 1985 indicated a deficit of 36 percent in cereals, 53 percent in pulses, 51 percent in vegetable oils and 74 percent in meat. [57] The Food and Agriculture Organization (FAO) and African Development Bank (ADB) announced in 2003 that Cameroon was one of 86 countries to be supported by a Special Food Security Program established to assist countries with food deficits.[58]

Although national agricultural production did not keep pace with demographic changes, it must be acknowledged that the volume of food imports increased tenfold between 1961 and 1998, from 32,000 tons to 348,148 tons. [59] Wheat and rice were the most important import items to Cameroon, representing 32 percent and 19.4 percent of total imports respectively. [60] These same products represented 80.2 billion francs CFA of the country's household consumption expenditure in 1996. Imports increased significantly from 72.101 billion in 1999/2000 to 80.2 billion in 2000/2001.[61] The rise in the household consumer price index and strong retrieval of food imports since 1996 seem to confirm the low growth of certain products (cereals, fish, animal products, etc.) relative to demand. [62] This situation prevented sustainable poverty reduction among host communities and those beyond. Food Self-

---

[54] Ibid.

[55] DeLancey et al., *Historical Dictionary of the Republic of Cameroon*, p.171.

[56] Ibid.

[57] J. M., Moudio, "The Dynamics of Food Security Policy in Cameroon (2008-2019)", *American Journal of Public Policy and Administration,* Vol.6, Issue 1, 2021, pp 12-43.

[58] DeLancey et al., *Historical Dictionary of the Republic of Cameroon,* p.171.

[59] Moudio, "The Dynamics of Food Security Policy in Cameroon (2008-2019)."

[60] Ibid.

[61] Ibid.

[62] Ibid.

sufficiency even though an ideological discourse, made feasible landmark contributions to the agricultural development process in Cameroon. Aside the Food Self-Sufficiency ideology emerged the agro-industry strategy in a bid to enhance the country's agricultural economy.

IV- Agro-Industry Strategy

The Agro-industry strategy was one of Cameroon's main development pillars. It was in line with its development that the country's policy makers, allocated not less than 60 percent of public funds reserved for agricultural development to the sector within the framework of its third and fourth Five Years Development Plans (1971-1981).[63] The Agro-industry strategy, was a development approach adopted by the government of Cameroon in 1968, whereby, agriculturally related industries were conceived, to speed the country's growth and self-reliant development.[64] It was purposely designed to set up industries that could process the Cameroon's principal agricultural products in a bid to change the country's status from a raw material exporter.[65]

This was achieved by converting her traditional agriculture through industrialisation to enhance rural development and quality of her exports and major domestic crops. The agro-industry was also intended to construct a national identity and counter regional acrimonies that could pose as set-backs to the Cameroon's most cherished to consolidate its independence and reunification at the time. This approach grew out of the country's planned and regional development strategies. State support for it actually began with the creation of the Palm Grove Company (SOCAPALM) in 1968.[66] Many more of them followed in subsequent years, actually making their marks in the country's agricultural development drive in particular and development in general.

These agro-industry endeavours were sought to transform Cameroon's traditional agriculture through industrialization, to enhance rural development, escape from the sturdy dependency on export crops and amend the quality of the country's export and major domestic crops. As time

---

[63] Ndongko, *Labour Resistance in Cameroon*, p.16.
[64] DeLancey et al., *Historical Dictionary of the Republic of Cameroon*, p.26.
[65] Ibid.
[66] Ibid.

went by, it was emphasised on, as an alternate of petroleum, the main source of export income in the country. This concept received new emphasis with the privatization program, disassembling many of the relevant parastatals originally established in the program.[67] Despite the backing of foreign consultants, constructors and financiers, the agro-industry strategy failed to meet Cameroon's expectations, without a substantial impact.

The agro-industry strategy was also one of such incentives, introduced for this same drive. The green revolution through this strategy, provided the impetus for the production of raw materials (food and cash crops) that could be transformed in the country to ensure that domestic consumption and exports of some finished goods were earned.[68] Government's decision to outlaw the export of raw timber in 1999 was an example of this strategy and the prospect was that finished lumber and wood products will be exported and as such, new industrial jobs will appear with the growth of timber processing factories.[69] These did not work as there was a considerable delay in the full implementation of decisions in that regard. Another philosophy still in line with improving the agricultural economy of Cameroon was the operation Green Revolution as shall be seen subsequently.

V. Operation Green Revolution

The Operation Green Revolution was the term used to describe a large increase in crop yields based on cultivation of high-response varieties of grain and intensive use of fertilizers, pesticides, improved seeds, irrigation, and machinery, with genetically modified (GM) crops sometimes included.[70] Cameroon's Operation Green Revolution emerged within the framework of its principle of planned development, which had as central aim, the advancement of economic and social developments in the country.[71] This in part reflected the deep concern that Cameroon's decision makers espoused Thomas Jefferson's "agrarian state" ideology that formed the standard of the American Republic at the end of the 18th century.[72] The philosophy could also be

---

[67] Ibid., p. 83.

[68] Ibid., p. 25

[69] Ibid.

[70] Ibid., p.196.

[71] Ahidjo, *As Told by Ahmadou Ahidjo*, p.54.

[72] Dongmo, "The Green Revolution and Food Self-sufficiency", p.2.

seen from the perspective of a nationhood-felt patriotic and naturalist ideology that developed to accommodate the demands of large, medium and small size farmers in search for self-sufficiency and right to sustainable development in Cameroon.

Agro-industrial structures were innate in the process, through Five Years Development Plans, with an accent on industrial development. But apprehending that industrial development was more exorbitant and slower in reducing poverty and stimulating socio-economic change, greater attention was moved towards improving the country's agricultural economy in the early 1970s.[73] It was in this regard that the government of Cameroon adopted a series of incentives, including the "Operation Green Revolution", for the purpose of meeting this goal. This philosophy was essentially embraced in an effort to meet the country's food self-sufficiency vision aimed at curbing poverty.[74] It was launched by President Ahmadou Ahidjo in Buea during the country's first agricultural show in 1973, it had to act as a prodigious stimulant to agricultural output.[75] Dawson, et al., document that green revolutions did record huge successes in southern Asia and beyond in the 1960s, benefitting smallholders.[76] The subsequent section shall lay emphasis on the origins of the economic policy in Cameroon.

A) Construing its Basis and Evolution

Most African economies embraced planning mechanism during the early years of independence, as the basis for their rapid transfiguration. According to Ahidjo, regarding Cameroon, planning was not only necessary, but matched the world's evolution at the time.[77] He appended that the country's supreme mission of national construction could not be happily pursued without plans as planning was necessary in all fields of national activity.[78] This was not therefore an exclusive Cameroon ambition or necessity, but a 20th century ambition with Russia being one of the earliest and most prominent examples to adopt.

---

[73] Kum and Kum, "Understanding Agro-pastoral Shows", p.1.

[74] Ibid.

[75] Ahidjo, Recueil *des discours Présidentielle de 1973-1978,* Centre de propagande Economique, Paris, 1978, p.11.

[76] N. Dawson, et al., "Green Revolution in Sub-Saharan Africa: Implications of Imposed Innovation for the Well-being of Smallholders", *World Development*, Vol. 78, 2016, p.1.

[77] Ahidjo, *As Told by Ahmadou Ahidjo*, p.82.

[78] Ibid.

Russia launched its first Five-Year Development Plan in 1928, aimed at finding the necessary food, by forced collectivisation of agriculture.[79] India at independence in 1947 copied Russian techniques, with its First Five Year Plan being implemented in 1950.[80]

Gaining inspiration from the USA, Russia and India, Cameroon adopted five-year development plans as catalysts for the rapid transformation of the country. This vision emerged from the complex and challenging demands of national economic growth in a freshly sovereign nation.[81] It was in view of the preceding developments that the 20-year plan was elaborated in 1960. This plan as already mentioned in the previous chapter was to develop three major spheres of the economy: industry, transport and agriculture. Initial efforts to this end were in two medium phases called: First and Second Five Year Development Plans.[82] The first plan (1960-1965) was launched before reunification and did not therefore take into account the entrance of former Southern Cameroons into the total economic configuration of the country. It was idealistic in some of its provisions, as the results achieved partially paralleled stated aims, with very little met in the field of agriculture, which was to be one of its key points of emphasis.[83]

The Second Five-Year Development Plan was elaborated under the patronage of the Federation. This plan remedied the defects of the first one, investing a total of 165 million francs CFA, with agriculture given a pride of place, triggering it to be named, "peasant plan", with emphasis on agricultural commercialization, reform and reorganization. It compelled a radical improvement on peasant export production through the diversification of cash crops such as cotton, cocoa and coffee, which increased significantly in volume. Agricultural modernization centres were created in the five geographical areas of the country to coordinate development research and technical aid related to the principal crops grown there, served by these centres.[84]

---

[79] S.H. Wood, *World Affairs: 1900 to Present Day*, Longman Group Ltd, 1978, pp.68-69.

[80] Ibid., p.281.

[81] Ahidjo, *As Told by Ahmadou Ahidjo.*

[82] H. Philippe, *Analyse du sous-développement en Afrique noire : l'exemple de l'économie du Cameroun,* Paris Presses Universitaires de France, 1968, pp.249-254.

[83] Ndongko, *Planning for Economic Development in a Federal State: The Case of Cameroon, 1960-1971,* Munchen, Welt Form Verlage, 1975, p.132.

[84] LeVine, *The Cameroon Federal Republic*, Cornell University Press, Ithaca and London, 1965, p.163.

Regional development structures, much like the "Small landholders development authorities" in Rwanda and Malaysia, were encouraged, to combine plantations and agro-industrial structures.[85] This was in order to effectively develop each region's economic and social potentials.[86] Ndongko, argues that from 1966, Cameroon's planning was oriented towards asserting, symbolising and strengthening national unity.[87] This was hardly achieved as regional inequalities were rather enhanced as the plans instead established the basis of discrepancies within almost all sectors, with some regions favoured against others.[88] Friedman and Alonso support this view and argue that the question of social and economic justice in the distribution of economic progress is important, but difficult to handle in terms of regions as well as social class.[89] The major issue with the first and second plans was the difficulty in financing the various projects earmarked.

The Operation Green Revolution was a term that described an increase in the rate of agricultural growth and productivity, based on the application of modern crop breeding techniques to the agricultural challenges of the developing world.[90] This notion is said to have developed in Asia and Latin America, to address rural poverty challenges and agrarian unrest in the late 1950s and early 1960s, involving a concerted effort, to apply scientific understanding of genetics to the development of improved crop varieties that were suited to the growing conditions of the developing world.[91] The Green Revolution delivered a massive and nearly immediate impact in some locations in the world, particularly in the irrigated rice-growing areas of Asia and wheat-growing hubs of Asia and Latin America.[92]

In Cameroon, the Green Revolution was embraced to ensure that the country's agricultural production dramatically increased, within the framework of its planned development scheme. By this, food

---

[85] Ahidjo, *Fondement et Perspectives*, 1976, p. 33.

[86] Ndongko,., *Planning for Economic Development in a Federal State: The Case of Cameroon*, p.46.

[87] Ndongko. "Regional Economic Planning in Cameroon", p.6.

[88] Amin (ed). *Cameroon's Economy and Reforms in Developing a Sustainable Economy in Cameroon*, pp.81-82

[89] J. Friedman, and W. Alonso, (eds), *Regional Development and Planning*, Cambridge, 1964, p.4.

[90] Collint, et al., "Two Blades of Grass: The Impact of the Green Revolution".

[91] Ibid.

[92] Dawson, et al., "Green Revolution in Sub-Saharan Africa.

production was expected to increase by 2.3 percent per year on average against the 5.4 percent for agricultural products destined for export. [93] Cameroon was a predominantly agricultural country given that most of its population lived on the soil. It was therefore absolutely indispensable that special efforts be invested, to develop this essential activity and raise the standards of living of all Cameroonians. Anderson and Lorch hold this view in the following terms:

> .... very few countries, particularly in the developing world have experienced rapid economic growth without agricultural growth either preceding or accompanying it. This is because agricultural growth is a catalyst to broad-based development. At the micro level, for instance, it provides eventual savings for entrepreneurial development in the informal sector. At the macro level, it provides raw materials which are a strong base for industrial development. [94]

It is in line with the preceding rational that the "Operation Green Revolution", was launched in Cameroon to ensure food self-sufficiency, an aspiration that many developing countries nursed at the time. This wish evolved and culminated in the country's development-oriented framework (planned development) in what President Ahidjo officially labelled the "*Sahel Vert*" and *"Revolution Vert* in 1973". [95] The *Sahel vert* project was crafted to counter desertification in the northern part of the country, through trees planting, while the green revolution on its part concentrated on promoting the production of high consumption crops like: rice, wheat, bananas, tomatoes, vegetables and corn.[96] It was institutionalized alongside Cameroon's socio-economic and political agenda: agro-pastoral shows.

The maiden agro-pastoral show that sanctioned the revolution was jointly organized by the ministries of agriculture (under Jean Keutcha) and that of livestock and animal industries (under Sadjo Agokay) in March 1973. [97] This accommodated the burdens of large, medium and small size farmers in search for self-determination and the right to sustainable development. On launching the shows, it was hoped they would promote food self-sufficiency and act as stimulants for Cameroon's agricultural economy.[98] It was also to assure the rational

---

[93] NAB, File No. 748 QC/a/1966/2, Agricultural Shows.

[94] Anderson and Lorch, *Agricultural Growth is the Key to Poverty Alleviation in Low Income Developing Countries*, p.87.

[95] Dongmo, "The Green Revolution and Food Self-sufficiency".

[96] Ibid

[97] Kum and Kum "Understanding Agro-pastoral Shows in a Planned Economy (1973-1987), pp. 773-774.

[98] Ahidjo, *Recueil des discours*, p.11.

use of natural resources, by appealing to all Cameroonians to make the maximum use of the soil as an irreplaceable focal point.

The Green Revolution regarded agriculture as a national base for feeding Cameroon's population and also as strength to its industry and most essentially, crucial factor for economic growth. [99] It was a complemented effort to the country's initial reliance on industrialisation for its rapid development. This thus implied steady and forward-looking change in attitudes, goals, means, methods, traditions and vital structures for an effective food sufficiency drive in the country. To boost food abundance, the mass production of high consumption commodities such as rice, wheat, bananas, tomatoes vegetables, and corn, became very imperative.[100] President Ahidjo, in order to add flesh to the foregoing, argued as follows: "in an independent and free country as ours, which desires prosperity, for its children, we must not content to produce just enough to eat, to pay our tax, to wear. We must do more".[101]

The Green revolution's philosophy further called on farmers to form groups to enable them better qualified for government assistance. This was because a bulk of Cameroonian farmers depended on subsistence agriculture and there was need for them to produce not just for family sustenance, but also for commercial purposes, with financial backing from the state. The government of Cameroon took appropriate measures to solve this issue by creating FONADER: the "farmers' bank", through Presidential Decree No. 73/24 of 29th May 1973.[102] This institution provided loans to Cameroonians in order to meet the operation Green Revolution's objectives.

With the proclamation of the Green Revolution policy during the Buea Agro-Pastoral Show in 1973, it was acknowledged that attention must be given to indigenous food crops.[103] Not only was the country to be self-sufficient in food, it also had to serve as a source of food for many of its neighbours. Although the country's agriculture continued to be plagued by low productivity and outdated technology, it nevertheless succeeded in fostering growth and development of both food and cash crops. This was in spite some major failures took place

[99] Collint, Hansen and Wingender, "Two Blades of Grass: The Impact of the Green Revolution", p.2.

[100] Ahidjo, *Recueil des discours*, p.11.

[101] Ahidjo, *As Told by Ahmadou Ahidjo*, p.59.

[102] Ibid.

[103] DeLancey et al., *Historical Dictionary of the Republic of Cameroon*, p. 11.

in an attempt to develop import substitution crops.[104] Generally, the green revolution's mandate included inter-alia the financial management of specific funds, disbursed by the state, domestic and or foreign bodies, to grant if need be guarantees to loans accorded by commercial banks to certain intervention bodies in rural areas; the provision with the Cameroon Development Banks and commercial banks of joint financing for rural development and above all the distribution of agricultural credits. [105]

Many agro-industrial projects that were created during this period, were significantly influenced by the Green Revolution's philosophy. For example, WADA, that was to play an important role in promoting and accelerating economic and social development in the rural communities of Menchum Division, assisted in coordinating FONADER loans, to farmers or groups of farmers, graziers and craftsmen who undertook agricultural activities considered profitable in the context of the objectives of the economic and social development plans of the country. [106] It further guaranteed loans granted by created bodies to cooperative societies, as well as farmers and stock breeders; granting advances for purchase of agricultural tools, materials and constructing storage facilities especially for the settlement of young farmers in rural areas.

By the green revolution, Cameroonian youths had to demonstrate immense taste for work, accountability and ability to ameliorate the quality of life in the villages, all in a bid to render the work of the soil its dignity and nobleness.[107] A series of structures were instituted to accompany the operation green revolution: National Fund for Rural Development in 1969; NPMB in Sep 1972; Cameroon Chamber of Commerce, Industry and mine in March 1986; *Société de Développement du Nkam* (SODENKAM); *Hévea Cameroon* (HEVECAM), in Dizangue in 1975 to counter growing rubber prices on the international market and others.[108]

---

[104] Ibid.

[105] N. Jua, Economic Management in Neo-Colonial States: A Case Study of Cameroon, Research Report No. 38, *African Studies Centre*, Leiden, Netherlands, 1990, p.25.

[106] Kum and Kum, "Understanding Agro-pastoral Shows in a Planned Economy", p.776.

[107] Ahidjo, *As Told by Ahmadou Ahidjo*, p.45.

[108] Ibid.

The training of rural consultants, agricultural technicians and engineers was carried out through various academic and professional institutions that emerged nationwide under state support such as: the regional colleges of Agriculture (Bamenda and Ebolowa), National School of Waters and forests (Mbalmayo), Agricultural Technical Colleges (ETA), *Institute de Recherche Agricole pour le Développement* (IRAD), Nature conservation School Garoua. Especially the education of senior Agricultural managers successively took place at the Agricultural science Institute (ITA), *Ecole Nationale Superieure d'Agronomie et des Sciences Agronomique* (ENSA) and the *Institute Nationale pour le Développement Rurale* (INADER), that formed the bulk of the then Dschang University Center. Another Important aspect of the Green Revolution was the institutionalization of agro-pastoral shows in the country's socio-economic and political agenda, with Buea hosting the inaugural show in March 1973.[109]

B) Inroads

Green revolutions transformed many rural economies in Asia and Latin America between 1960 and the 1980s, but their transfers to Sub-Sahara Africa had limited successes, due in part to locally inapt seed varieties and lack of human and institutional capacities.[110] This did nevertheless generally impart in Cameroonians, the spirit of broad-mindedness, innovation and responsibility, spurring agricultural growth thereby meeting government's socio-economic development goals.[111] Cameroon's food self-sufficiency dream initiated within its planned development framework also became a reality especially in the rice production sector, which had been very dismal before 1971. Rice production increased subsequently when the state identified various sites for its extensive cultivation within the ambits of the green revolution: Yagoua, the Mbo Plains, Nanga Eboko Upper Noun and Doume.[112]

Through this, food insecurity was momentously alleviated in the country as the cultivation of irrigated rice was encouraged, resulting in a steady decrease in imports. The Yagoua, Mbo, Nanga Eboko, Upper

[109] Kum and Kum, "Understanding Agro-pastoral Shows in a Planned Economy", p.1.
[110] Dawson, et al., "Green Revolution in Sub-Saharan Africa, p.204.
[111] L. N. Fonjong, "Changing Fortunes of Government Policies and its Implications", *Nordic Journal of African Studies*, 2004, p. 20.
[112] Ibid.

Noun and Doume sites were developed and financed through the following agro-industrial companies: *SEMRY*, UNVDA and the *Société de Développement de la Riziculture dans la plaine de Mbo SODERIM.*[113] A host of others were created, although not based solely on rice production like the forgoing. Solely rice producing structures benefitted from substantial funding from within and outside (Food and Agriculture Organisation (FAO) Cameroon as can be seen on Table 3.

Table 3: Financial Assistance to Rice Producing Companies between 1976 and 1987

No.	Name of Parastatal	Period	Amount Benefitted in Billions of francs CFA
1.	SEMRY	1979-1987	40 billion francs CFA
2.	SODERIM	1976-1987	7.1 billion francs CFA
3.	UNVDA	1981-1987	7 billion francs CFA
	Total	**1976-1987**	**54.1 billion francs CFA**

Source: Author's conception from information gathered in MINADER, "National Strategy for Rice Growing in Cameroon", p.5.

It is documented that this assistance enabled the rice market to grow from 15,000 to 60,000 tons between 1975 and 1980m especially after establishing the foregoing agro-industrial projects and accompanying funding on table 3.[114] They therefore increased the market share of Cameroon's agricultural produce, enhanced revenues in isolated regions, provided jobs (poverty alleviation), supplied local consumption markets with adequate food and brought large scale imports under control. Cameroon's Green Revolution was therefore crafted as a means to mobilize all the country's human and material resources towards agricultural boost, which greatly enhanced production and productivity, clipping down poverty and improving on its socio-economic developments.

In other words, agricultural production possibilities were enhanced, ensuring that there was a steady increase in quality and quantity of the agricultural produce that was so direly needed, to feed the country's

---

[113] MINADER, National Strategy for Rice Growing in Cameroon: (Milling) III, 2009, p.5, https://www.jica.go.jp/english/our_work/thematic_issues/agricultural/pdf/cameroon_en.pdf, consulted on the 07-03-2021.

[114] Ibid.

growing population.[115] The green revolution was therefore the way to go for Cameroon's agricultural economy. As a result of this funding, incomes grew at a howling rate of more than 7 percent per year, also due to the improved agricultural economy through the operation green revolution from 1973 to 1986.[116] This improvement could be justified by the factors behind the very foundation of the revolution as the then Vice Minister of Agriculture, Joseph Awunti (1976) puts:

> The green revolution calls on all Cameroonians to engage in agriculture in a realistic manner; modify ancient traditional farming methods so as to replace them gradually with more modern and scientific methods; replace low yielding cocoa, coffee, and food crops, planting materials with high yielding disease resistant varieties; readapt agricultural policy to the needs of the nation so as to be able to maintain a proper and careful balance between cash crops and food crops. [117]

Agricultural research on the other hand, which is often cited as the single-best investment in terms of increasing productivity and reducing poverty complemented these efforts. [118] With scientific research, genetically modified crops became the order of the day within the framework of the country's Green Revolution strategy. This greatly enhanced the development and spread of high yielding food crop varieties such as: rice, maize, sorghum, millet, root crops and legumes. [119] These efforts were realised in a large degree through the creation of research centres and programs in the country, prominent among were those that worked towards meeting the operation green revolution policy, within Cameroon's planned development framework: IRAD, concerned essentially with research on a wide range of crops: cereals, root and tuber crops, legumes and fruit trees.[120]

---

[115] P.C. Yuh, "Wum Area Development Authority (WADA): Catalysis for Rural Development", B.A. Dissertation, International School of Journalism, University of Yaoundé, 1977, p.76.

[116] Ernest Bamou and William A. Masters, Distortions to Agricultural Incentives in Cameroon,
Paper 42, December 2007, p.9, https://www.researchgate.net/publication/228618483, consulted on the 07th Maech 2021.

[117] Yuh, "Wum Area Development Authority (WADA): Catalysis for Rural Development", p.76-77.

[118] P. Pingali, D. Spielman, and F. Zaidi, "Changing Donor Trends in Assistance to Agricultural Research and Development in Africa South of the Sahara, in J. Lynam, N. Beintema, J. Roseboom and O. Badiane (eds.) *Agricultural Research in Africa: Investing in Future Harvests*, The International Food Policy Research Institute (IFPRI), Washington, DC, 2016, p. 140.

[119] Ibid.

[120] Bamou and Masters, "Distortions to Agricultural Incentives in Cameroon."

Related centres were the Ekona Biotechnology laboratory, the Faculty of Agronomy and Agricultural Sciences (FASA) of the University of Dschang and a host of others.[121] Other crops were introduced by the Wum Area Development Authority, such as soya beans, dwarf beans, potatoes, sorghum, yams, guavas, mangoes and others, through the Cameroon-West German technical assistance.[122] These research centres, programmes and incentives made Cameroon to be frequently cited among the few countries in Sub-Saharan Africa to have achieved satisfactory agricultural development during the period of study.[123] The agricultural modernization of Cameroon's food crop economy, both as a means of feeding the nation and developing its exports was significantly enhanced through the Green Revolution approach. [124]

Agricultural production greatly improved as Farmers were regularly paid and promptly for their labour. Many market roads were constructed which helped to ease the transportation of agricultural products. Some major roads were equally constructed like the Yaounde-Douala, Tiko-Douala, Yaounde-Ebolowa, and Ngaoundere-Garoua ones, which helped to reduce transport costs on agricultural products between these towns and cities.[125] There were equally the existence of three international airports at Douala, Garoua and Yaounde. In 1973, Cameroon withdrew from Air Afrique, which was largely dominated by the French and decided to establish her own airline called, Cameroon Airlines.[126]

Cameroon's Food self-sufficiency target was attained through the Green Revolution, especially as its prime objective was to grow internal adequate food for the population or have a balance between food imports and exports. This was a goal hardly achieved in many African countries at the time. This enviable record was thanks to the combination of natural, economic, and political factors in the country at the time.[127] This Food self-sufficiency goal, reached by Cameroon in the late 1970s can be said to have been because of its ability to grow adequate food for consumers or stabilize its trade balance, thanks to its agricultural potential and adequate planning. This excessive domestic

---

[121] Ibid.

[122] Interview with Gabuin Ndarikwi Johsnson, 84 years, Former Director of WADA, Bamenda, 2016.

[123] Ibid.

[124] DeLancey et al., *Historical Dictionary of the Republic of Cameroon*, p.197.

[125] Ibid.

[126] Ibid.

[127] DeLancey et al., *Historical Dictionary of the Republic of Cameroon*, pp. 170-171.

food production led to colossal import substitution and conservation of foreign exchanges; release of labour into the industrial sector; provision of raw materials for industrial growth; lowering of food prices, raising real wages and generation of employment in the country.

As already seen earlier, the Green Revolution was equally the basis for launching Cameroon's self-reliant development strategy in 1975, due to the successes it recorded in the sphere of food self-sufficiency.[128] This strategy remarkably subordinated the country's international economic relations to domestic development, depending principally on local efforts and labour.[129] It eliminated archaic methods and various constraints on small farmer production. Though directly targeted at the farmer, the rhetoric envisioned raising the awareness of the entire population toward respect for agriculture and optimum development of the soil.[130] The shared effect was Cameroonians' movement towards the plantation economy, a process by which they were encouraged to remain rural agricultural workers. This model of popular development was the country's idea geared towards the masses and deserving rural working classes to see into a more sustained agricultural economy.

Most Green Revolutions in Sub-Sahara Africa failed to achieve expected goals, because rural development initiatives were predominantly crafted and harnessed by states, which laid much emphasis on cash crop production. [131] In Cameroon, despite espousing the foregoing, its green revolution did also stress on indigenous food crops production and this did not only enabled it become self-sufficient in food, but also, the bread basket for many of its neighbours: Gabon, Equatorial Guinea, Chad and the Central Africa Republic.[132] However, government's insistence on the cultivation of export crops (Cocoa, coffee, Rubber and others), did not augur well for its planned development philosophy, especially due to the short-lived petroleum boom that interposed in the country in the late 1970s and outbreak of the economic crisis in the mid-1980s. Both incidents severely worked down on government's development efforts during the period of study as already discussed in previous sections.

---

[128] Dongmo, "The Green Revolution and Food Self-sufficiency."

[129] Ibid.

[130] DeLancey et al., *Historical Dictionary of the Republic of Cameroon,* p.196.

[131] Dawson et al., "Green Revolution in Sub-Sahara Africa", p.204

[132] DeLancey et al., *Historical Dictionary of the Republic of Cameroon,* p.11.

VI. Agro-pastoral Shows

Among other strategies at independence, Cameroon gave priority to agro-pastoral shows during the period of planning for development. Agro-pastoral shows were first introduced in West Cameroon before being integrated nation-wide. Cameroon's development efforts were initially managed through a series of five years development plans. These plans laid conditions for public investment and facilitated the flow of development assistance from foreign partners.[133] The Government intervened massively in rural development and this was directly through the establishment of state-owned agro-industries, rural corporations and settlements, and indirectly through various support programs. About 85 percent of the population of the country lived in rural areas and relied principally on agriculture for their livelihoods.

Peasant agriculture did not augur well during the period of the first and second five years development plans, as its growth and performance in output came rather from increases in the areas under cultivation than yield gains. With an agriculture essentially dominated by food products, whose growth rate represented 4.9 percent of the agricultural GDP in 2005/2006, Cameroon cannot isolate itself from the problem of hunger and, consequently, from the food insecurity that affects a large part of the population.[134] These plans did however envisage experimentation with other forms of intervention structures in agriculture and production.

Cameroon's unification in 1972 and the creation of a new Ministry of Agriculture led to a substantial modification in the colonial institutional structure of the agricultural domain. Considering the agricultural and pastoral vocation of the country at the time, rural development was given a pride of place in its third development plan, baptized: "production and productivity plan".[135] The third Five Years Development Plan, constituted not only of extending large scale plantations and agro-industrial structures, but also on creating new ones. Apart from these, some projects of integrated development were created, to operate with the active participation of the populations concerned thereby improving on agricultural output.

---

133 Kum and Kum, "Understanding Agro-pastoral Shows in a Planned Economy."

134 Moudio, "The dynamics of food security policy in Cameroon (2008-2019)",

135 Kum and Kum, "Understanding Agro-pastoral Shows in a Planned Economy.".

These projects were to insert the youths into rural development activities. Their possibilities complemented the initiation of the Civic Service in the development drive. All these were aimed at reducing rural exodus and luxury in urban centres among the youths in particular.[136] The forgone structures were production targets of agricultural activities during the period of the Third Five Years Development Plan. It was held that by these, food production will increase by 2.3 percent per year on average against 5.4 percent for agricultural products destined for export. It was in this light that the idea of food self-sufficiency evolved within a development-oriented framework of what was officially labelled "Sahel Vert" and the "Green Revolution."[137] Agro-pastoral shows were an important aspect of the Green Revolution in the country's socio-economic and political agenda. For a better perception of how agro-pastoral shows emerged and evolved, it would be essential to give a pride of place to West Cameroons.

Before Agro-pastoral shows became part of West Cameroon the Federal agricultural policy, with some general institutional structures and policies were put in place by the government to promote agricultural development in the country. One of the most prominent was the Department of Agriculture and Rural Animation, created in 1964 under the Federal Ministry of Planning.[138] Coordination in the department's efforts was seen more in areas of research, extension, availability of inputs and others, all in a bit to obtain changes in peasant behavior in view of their autonomy in decision-making. This was such that when future measures came, it would be easier for them to concur.

Agro-pastoral shows as already mentioned, were first instituted in West Cameroon, before being espoused nationwide. West Cameroon adopted Agro-pastoral shows as a means to contributing and promoting food self-sufficiency in the country in pursuance of the national development policy.[139] The slogan "grow more food" was thus launched by R.E.G. Burnley and his agricultural colleagues of West Cameroon in this regard. This worked so well that in the early 1970s, President Ahmadou Ahidjo, decided to make it a nation-wide event. When Cameroon got unified in 1972, those who were appointed to this

---

[136] Ibid., p.45.

[137] Fonjong, "Changing Fortunes of Government Policies", p. 20.

[138] Kum and Kum, "Understanding Agro-pastoral Shows in a Planned Economy."

[139] The Farmers Voice, "Agro-Pastoral Show 2010: Ebolowa says, "Yes we can", *The Farmers Voice*, Bafoussam, 16th March 2010, p. 2.

part of the country saw how this slogan worked. The main objective behind why Agro-pastoral shows were promoted in West Cameroon was not only because there was need for food self-sufficiency, but also because the idea of the green revolution was spreading worldwide and West Cameroonians too embraced it.[140]

Farmers were encouraged to grow not only cash crops like coffee, cocoa and banana, but also food crops. For instance, most of the Yams in West Cameroon before the advent of agro-pastoral shows, came from Nigeria, so farmers were encouraged to increase their yams cultivation capacities. What existed more in West Cameroon were plantains, cocoyam and Colocasia. Farmers were equally encouraged to remain attached to livestock of their respective areas: pigs, goats and sheep in the South West; in the North West the farmers reared cattle and other small ruminants like those of the former. These were the various crops and animals that farmers brought and exhibited during Agro-pastoral shows in the territory.

Agro-pastoral shows in West Cameroon were done both at provincial and divisional levels. For instance, the Wum and Nkambe Divisions' shows took place in 1966.[141] These were to help change the people's minds, so that they could look to agriculture as a dignified career and highest in importance to an agricultural country like Cameroon.[142] The first Agro-pastoral show that took place in Buea West Cameroon was on the 7th November 1967. This was organised and financed by the Bakweri council with the assistance of the technical officer of the Ministry of Agriculture, West Cameroon.[143] In effect, agricultural shows were not new to Cameroonians before 1973.

After the referendum of 1972, with East and West Cameroons uniting as the United Republic, President, Amadou Ahidjo decided that the latter's experience of agro-pastoral shows be adopted and practiced at the national level. Buea was chosen to host the first show in March 1973 and this was jointly organized by the ministries of Agriculture and Livestock and Animal Industries.[144] Eager to promote rapid development through Five Years development plans the government of Cameroon decided to refocus on Agriculture as the primary catalyst for

---

[140] Kum and Kum, "Understanding Agro-pastoral Shows in a Planned Economy."

[141] NAB, File No. 748 QC/a/1966/2, "Agricultural Shows", p.6.

[142] Ibid., p.33.

[143] Ibid.

[144] Kum and Kum, "Understanding Agro-pastoral Shows in a Planned Economy."

economic growth. Agro-pastoral shows were founded on the country's desire to grow adequate food for consumers.

Cameroon had vast expanses of exploitable land or sea, generally favourable climate, fertile soils, many plant varieties, industrious and hardworking labour that augured well for a rapid development of the country. Considering that Agriculture was the primary job provider that could employ about 80 percent of the population that depended on it, Agro-pastoral shows were deemed necessary to boost production.[145] Again, given its dominant role in socio-economic development, it was understood that Cameroon's access to food would be found in its agricultural potential and adequate policy planning. This was in spite many youths still found it difficult to get employed. The launching of Agricultural shows came along with the institutionalisation of periodic festivals held regularly in major cities and towns of the country. [146] This was to see into it that the problem of rapid economic development in the country was resolved.

In its Magazine entitled: "the Grand agricultural show Buea South West Province", the then Minister of agriculture Jean Keutcha said: ".... Such a manifestation brings together farmers, extension and research services, manufacturers; traders etc and thus play an important role of training and information of rural populations."[147] They were therefore to act as impetus to stimulate, incite, inform and also as a forums where farmers and youths in particular could learn and emulate from one another.[148] They were further created to speed up national agricultural production while encouraging all actors of the sector to work harder in order to ensure food self-sufficiency. In order to materialize government's encouragement, competitors (planters or growers, fishermen and stock breeders) of the country who presented the best products and farmers were awarded prizes. Government organized and encouraged shows at periodic and rotating intervals, at provincial and even very restricted territorial units. Giving priority to promoting Agricultural growth is reminiscent in the following views expressed by Anderson and Lorch:

> Very few countries, particularly in the developing world have experienced rapid economic growth without agricultural growth either preceding or accompanying

[145] Ibid.

[146] Fonjong, "Changing Fortunes of Government Policies", p.20.

[147] The Farmers Voice, "Agro-Pastoral Show 2010, p. 1.

[148] Ahidjo, *Recueil des discours Présidentielle de 1973-1978,* Centre de Propagande Economique, Paris 1978, p. 5.

> it. This is because agricultural growth is a catalyst to broad-based development. At the micro level, for instance, it provides eventual savings for entrepreneurial development in the informal sector. At the macro level, it provides raw materials which are a strong base for industrial development.[149]

It was in such basis that Agro-pastoral shows were adopted during the period of the Third and Fourth Five Years Development Plans (1971-1981). Both plans are often considered main pillars of Cameroon's agricultural development. Not less than 60 percent of the total planned budget for the plans was reserved for agricultural development.[150] During agro-pastoral ceremonies, competitions were organized, with appropriate compensations given to participants for efforts put at agricultural production both in quality and quantity. The spirit of emulation was also encouraged, given that this was perceived as the most favourable factor of technical progress that played a great role in promoting economic and social progress in the country. According to Simon Tamanjung, the then provincial delegate of agriculture for the South West Province:

> Agro-pastoral shows were normal events in former West Cameroon and occasional events in East Cameroon. The objectives of Agricultural shows were to "accelerate agricultural development so as to find an early solution of providing the population and the industrial expansion of the country," this meant a radical change from the subsistence farming techniques and improved marketing circuits resulting in higher incomes from agricultural pursuits.[151]

Agricultural shows were to urge Cameroonians and the youths in particular, to be conscientious of the problems plaguing the rural world.[152] They were also to orchestrate serene confrontations between agriculturalists, graziers, foresters, artisans, business people and industrialists, thereby, constituting an irreversible meeting point of diffusion and information where each of them could enrich their knowledge, compare experiences and appreciate the technical progress so far realised in their various domains of activity.[153]

Agro-pastoral shows transformed villages from places where the inhabitants would not remain essentially agricultural, living on one and the same activity, to places where apart from farmers, were going to be added an important tertiary population of trades, services, a secondary population of small local industries and even a resident population

---

[149] Anderson and Lorch, *Agricultural Growth is the Key to Poverty Alleviation in Low Income Developing Countries*, p.87.

[150] Ndongko, *Labour Resistance in Cameroon*, p.16.

[151] NAB, Agricultural Shows, p.33.

[152] Ahidjo, *Recueil des discours*, p.5.

[153] Ibid.

which consumed on the spot.[154] All of these motivations were to discourage the youths from migrating out of the villages, because in return to the training and other facilities which the state did provide for them, they had to, on the other hand provide their dynamic generosity to the drive for national development. It was in this direction that structures like WADA, SODENKAM, ZAPI, *Mission de Développe-meny d'Ombessa* (MIDO) and others were earmarked, so as to coordinate its intentions.[155]

Through such structures the youths were to show in an efficient manner their taste for work, accountability and quality to ameliorate the quality of life in rural settings. These structures were also founded from the nationhood-felt patriotic and naturalist ideology that emerged at the time, to accommodate the demands of large, medium and small size farmers in search for self-determination and the right to sustainable development. Apart from individual farmers that were indirectly connected to these structures, they were also encouraged to have their products exhibited during agro-pastoral shows.

Some major corporations that got involved in rice cultivation were the *Societé d'Expansion et de modernisation de la Riziculture de Yagoua (SEMRY)* and the *Societé de Developpement de la Riziculture dans la plaine Mbo* (SODERIM). [156] Agro-pastoral shows were therefore to encourage them and individual farmers increase production in quality and quantity. In fact, the importance of rice cultivation was noticed even before the Buea show especially with the identification of its cultivation in various extensive sites like Yagoua, Mbo plains (Mungo), Nanga Eboko, and Doumé (East Region).[157] Their primary goals were to increase the market share of Cameroonian rice, enhance agricultural revenues in the isolated regions, provide jobs, supply the local consumption market with adequate food and bring large scale imports under control. This was in effect to render the work of the soil its poise and dignity.

The first achievement of the Buea show was that agriculturalists present and consecrated best provincial producers, considered it a

---

[154] Ibid.

[155] Kum and Kum, "Understanding Agro-pastoral shows in a Planned Economy", p.774.

[156] NAB, File No. DVA/J.2/2, (Qb/a 1960), "Five Years Development Plan", 1960, p.3.

[157] Kum and Kum, "Understanding Agro-pastoral shows in a Planned Economy", p. 775.

practical assignment to conserve and improve on their performances. Again, those who were not well classified at this occasion were urged to work harder and did not only take the lead during the next show that took place in Ngaoundere, but emerged among the group of best producers.[158] In this way, structures put up during the third plan were to compete and either or not compensated as best or weaker structures during the shows. Prior to agro-pastoral shows, best farm competitions were organised at all levels as a means of motivating farmers.[159]

The foregoing is to say these were to be held from village to provincial levels. Such competitions and prizes won acted as incentives to farmers and as catalysts for rural development. After the Buea agro-pastoral show of 1973, was Ngaoundere in 1974, Bafoussam in 1977, Bertoua in 1981, Bamenda in 1984 and Maroua I 1987.[160] That of Ebolowa was announced in 1988, but never held, because of the outbreak of the economic crisis. The next section shall outline farm credit bodies and related structures in their role as incentives to Cameroon's agricultural economy.

VII- Agricultural Incentives

Other great strides in this light were the establishment of agricultural banks and other input institutions. Taking into account the fact that a larger number of the country's population depended on agriculture for livelihood, the state embarked on assuring that it did move from subsistent to commercial Agriculture. This was to be done with sufficient financial backings and measures to solve the problems of rural savings and agricultural credit. The Rural Fund for National Development (FONADER), the "farmer's bank" was therefore created by presidential decree No. 73/24 of 29th May 1973 to play this important role by promoting and accelerating economic and social development in rural areas.[161]

Generally, FONADER's mandate included inter-alia the financial management of specific funds placed at its disposal by the state, domestic, and or foreign bodies; granting if need be guarantees to loans accorded by commercial banks to certain intervention bodies in rural

[158]Ahidjo, *Recueil des discours*, p.12.
[159] Fonjong, "Changing Fortunes of Government Policies and its Implications", p.20.
[160] Kum and Kum, "Understanding Agro-pastoral shows in a Planned Economy", p.775.
[161] Fonjong, "Changing Fortunes of Government Policies and its Implications", p.59.

areas; provision with the CBC and commercial banks of joint financing for rural development and above all, distribution of agricultural credits. [162] This role was to be fulfilled in the following ways: providing aid and credit to farmers or groups of farmers who undertook agricultural activities considered profitable in the context of the objectives of the economic and social plans of the United Republic of Cameroon (URC); guaranteeing loans granted by created bodies to pre-cooperative groups, cooperative societies and Unions as well as to farmers and stock breeders; granting advances for purchase of agricultural tools, materials and constructing storage facilities especially for the settlement of young farmers in rural areas. [163]

This was to permit farmers work improve on the quality and quantity of agricultural production. Considering that small farmers constituted the bulk of the rural population in Cameroon, the importance of the credit to them could not be over emphasized. Even civil servants who owned economically viable farms were encouraged to benefit from the scheme. [164] The apparently simple procedures of applying for credit scared off rural dwellers, and FONADER became the tool of the wealthy urban Cameroonian who was well versed in the corrupt practices of the system.[165] The foregoing greatly defeated the broad objective of the bank. For these reasons, and in the wake of a crushing economic crisis, FONADER was reorganized in 1987.[166] Since then, several attempts at establishing a workable rural credit system had been attempted.

Considering that small farmers constituted the bulk of the rural population in Cameroon, the importance of loans to them could not be over emphasized. Although it was important to provide civil servants who owned economically viable farms with loans, it was however not to be to the detriment of subsistent farmers. On account of the fact that moving from subsistent agriculture to a market oriented one required necessary important financial means to the farmers, the government took such steps in order to solve the problems of rural savings and agricultural credits.[167] This helped broaden the scope of production by increasing the number of people involved in agriculture.

[162] Jua, "Economic Management in Neo-Colonial States", p.25.
[163] Ahidjo, *Recueil des discours,* p.45.
[164] Fonjong, "Changing Fortunes of Government Policies and its Implications", p.19.
[165] DeLancey et al., *Historical Dictionary of the Republic of Cameroon,* p. 267.
[166] Jua, "Economic Management in Neo-Colonial States", p.25.
[167] Ahidjo, *Fondement et Perspective*, pp.45-46.

Other related bodies included farm equipment bodies like the *Centre National d'Etudes et D'Expérimentation du Machinisme Agricole* (CENEEMA) involved with the production of agricultural tools and equipment to facilitate input needs.[168] Bodies to promote cooperatives like the *Centre National de Développement des Enterprises Cooperatives* (CENADEC) were equally put in place, to run cooperative activities within the framework of improved agricultural production.[169] Agricultural research units like the *Institute de Recherche Zoologique* (IRZ), agricultural training schools as well as bodies for the commercialisation of agricultural produce like the NPMB, were also established.[170] These bodies were expected to work in a coherent and coordinated manner in order to develop zones that were so far abandoned thereby improving on the national agricultural output.[171] The preceding incentives, made agro-pastoral shows flourish as farmers were able to improve on the quality and quantity of their produce.

Conclusion

Chapter three highlighted Cameroon's agricultural development strategies during the period before the outbreak of economic crisis. It has expounded why and how Cameroon's planned development scheme, initially laid emphasis on industrial development, but indorsed agricultural development in the early 1970s. The chapter unfastened with the early post-independence efforts, employed, to enhance the country's agricultural economy. Aside that were the country's self-reliance development model, fashioned to subordinate its international economic relations to domestic development objectives, depending principally on local efforts and labour. It has demonstrated that this gave rise to the country's Food self-sufficiency drive: to ensure a sustainable production of food for local consumption and sale to its neighbours, notwithstanding the Agro-industry strategy, Operation Green Revolution and Agro-pastoral shows were instituted in Cameroon. All the foregoing, in a bit to meet the agricultural

[168]Chia, "Wum Area Development Authority (WADA)", p.8.
[169] Ibid.
[170] Ahidjo, *Fondements et perspectives du Cameroun nouveau,* pp.46-48.
[171] E. Bilsorrow and F. Delargy, *The Impact of Rural Development Projects in Demographic Behaviour*, New York, UNFPA, 1985, p.87.

development needs of the country, before the outbreak of the economic crisis in 1986. The chapter argues that although Cameroon's policy makers made tremendous inroads in its agricultural policies, they met with immense drawbacks. Chapter four shall focus on the country's Economic development drawbacks, before 1986.

CHAPTER FOUR
ECONOMIC DEVELOPMENT DRAWBACKS

Introduction

Cameroon's early development drive was based initially on attaining its economic sovereignty, perceived as the final stage for her independence. A series of schemes and policies were instituted in the country ranging from planned development, executed through Five Years Economic and Social development plans; planned liberalism; Regional planning, balanced development, self-reliance development, food self-sufficiency, the Agro-industry strategy; operation green revolution and Agro-pastoral shows. After examining the foregoing, chapter four dwells on some of the challenges that hit the country's early economic development strides. It begins with agricultural constraints, revolving from poor cultivation technics, inadequate inputs, to poor or no financing of projects; the petroleum debacle that greatly worked down on production and state corporations' drain, where a lot of money was borrowed and invested on these structures, that turned out to be unproductive. All these culminated in the economic crisis that broke out in the mid-1980s.

I- Agricultural Constraints

In the aftermath of independence, the economic context of Cameroon imposed agriculture as a pillar to improve the country's economic situation. From 1960 to 1986, five-year plans were implemented entirely in Cameroon.[1] During the first five-year plan executed between 1960 and 1965, there was talk of doubling GDP per capita in record time. The second plan was devoted to improving the living standard of people in rural areas. The last three plans were reserved respectively for increasing production and agricultural productivity, increasing GDP per capita by at least 5 percent and increasing real income per capita to improve Cameroon's image. To this end, during these five-year plans, more than half of the investments had been intended for directly productive agricultural projects, and a large part of the investments was devoted to rural infrastructure and the rural

[1] Daka et al., "Public Agrarian Policies and Food Security in Cameroon", p.24.

economy and energy as well. A special place has been given to the agricultural sector.[2]

Much of the poverty and hunger in Cameroon's rural communities in the 1960s was caused by the lack of sufficient food production and income generation means from small-scale farming. Cameroon's agricultural policies came to work toward modernizing of food crop production both as a means of feeding the nation and developing exports. This was however not very utterly successful as farm productivity in some parts of the country remained subsistent due to the incessant use of traditional crop varieties and outdated farming methods.[3] In addition to this problem were increasingly depleted soils, shrinking plots of land due to the lack of interest in agriculture by some Cameroonians; scarce and defective water supply; crop losses from pests and diseases, inequitable land-distribution patterns, in efficient and unfair markets and poor agricultural and transportation infrastructures.

In Menchum Division for instance, some of the farmers operating under WADA Agricultural development programmes: Bloc Extension Farming (BEF); Group Framing Programme (GFP) and the Oxen Training and Farming Programme (OTFP) rejected some of the high yielding crops species it introduced such as the upland rice, corn and groundnuts on grounds that they had bad tastes and demanded too much attention and care.[4] Again, many farmers perceived these programmes as coming to embolden seclusion among them, unlike had been their normal communal lifestyle that was reflected at all levels of their daily lives.[5]All these tremendously worked down on the philosophy's successes in the area. Cameroon's oil boom of the late 1970s also slowed down the country's operation green revolution goals in that it introduced a series of resource misallocations.

The most fundamental were the classic Dutch Disease emanating due to unsustainable price incentives, which limited investment in smallholder agriculture, making it unattractive and increasing the

---

[2] A. Z. Tamekamta and J. K. Menkene, Eds., *L'urgence d'une révolution agricole au Cameroun*, Paris, L'Harmattan, 2013.

[3] EDIAFRIC, République du Cameroun : Mémento de L'économie Africain », *numéro spécial du bulletin de L'Afrique noire* No. 456, Paris, 1967 p. 23.

[4] Kum, "The Wum Area Development Authority (WADA) 1965-1994: Implantation, Economic and Social Conversions in Menchum Division, PhD Thesis, Department of History, University of Yaounde I, 2014, p. 215.

[5] Christopher Agem, 75 years, and Akwo Martin, 61 Years, (20th September 2015). Former Extension Farmers WADA, Wum.

number of unskilled workers seeking non-farm work. [6] Again, most parastatals, created to accompany the revolution at the time became unsustainable due to poor management and lack of specialists, capable of handling, redefining goals and drawing up suitable programmes for their activities. [7] This resulted in poor policy implementation and limited financial assistance to smallholder agriculture actors during the boom. There was also under-investment in new technology in the country. Although Cameroon had a significant public agricultural research capacity and development programmes, during the boom there were nevertheless very few incentives for technology adoption, so yields for most crops stagnated or declined. [8]

These problems were entrenched, because development efforts were designed and essentially championed by the state rather than private agencies, even in fields where it had neither the requisite expertise nor comparative advantage. [9] For instance, the Cameroon Development Bank that was initially supposed to finance development activities in the country, made agriculture the poor cousin of industry by reserving most of its funding for the later. [10] The state in wanting to reinforce the credits put FONADER at the disposal of farmers, which also rather granted more loans to civil servants or wage earners, than full time farmers.[11] Considering that small farmers constituted the bulk of the rural poor in Cameroon, the importance of loans to them could not be over emphasized.

Even though the Cameroon government took great steps to solve the country's economic development problems, its predominant role in this sphere, remained a severe cause for concern. [12] It played a significant role in guiding development into sectors of the economy and geographical areas, deemed as priorities. This made its agricultural policies to remain more confined to the production of export crops. This

---

[6] Bamou and Masters, "Distortions to Agricultural Incentives in Cameroon".

[7] SCET Cameroun, *Projet de Développement Rural intègre du département de la Menchum,* Vol. 3, Direction des études et projets, MINAGRI, Yaoundé, 1982. p. 206.

[8] Bamou and Masters, Distortions to Agricultural Incentives in Cameroon, p.6.

[9] Ngwa and Lambi., "An Evaluation of the Upper Nun Valley Development Authority's Agricultural Innovation in Ndop Plain (Cameroon) since 1970", 'epassa Moto' (A Bilingual Journal of Arts, Letters and Humanities), Vol.4 No.1, University of Buea, March 2009, pp.50-71.

[10] Jua, Economic Management in Neo-Colonial States", p.25.

[11] Fonjong, "Changing Fortunes of Government Policies and its Implications", p.19.

[12] Ahidjo, *Fondement et Perspective*, pp.45-46.

explains why in 1986, as the price of crops like cocoa and coffee fell drastically in the international market, poverty and food insecurity struck Cameroon, compelling the government to change its policy.[13] These political constraints on state support for agriculture were arguably compounded by challenges such as high population densities in areas best suited for agriculture, poor infrastructure and vulnerability to climate change. [14] The once largely self-sufficient economy in food production instead turned to import large amounts of basic foodstuffs.

Despite its tremendous inroads, Cameroon's agricultural policies were strained by a series of stakeholders. Its operation green revolution, was variously attacked for its use of genetically modified crops, widespread use of fertilizers and pesticides, and other technologies relevant to it as these were regarded as not tying with the people's realities.[15] Given the low cost of its expansion (agriculture requires relatively more minor resources than the industrial sector, for example) and the easy accessibility to the equipment that peasants need to be trained in using and maintaining, agricultural activity possessed for the Cameroonian government an obvious advantage over other sectors in the implementation of an economic development policy.[16] Because it remained practiced by a large part of the population, improving this activity would have more marked effects on the population. Thus, upon his accession to the supreme magistracy, President Amadou Ahidjo launched the five-year plans to make agriculture the country's economic base.[17]

These efforts have contributed in a few ways to improving the food and economic situation of the country, in particular by improving the quality and volume of production, advancing considerably towards food self-sufficiency, and developing cash crops. However, it should

---

[13] Global Forum for Rural advisory Services, https://www.g-fras.org/en/world-wide-extension-study/africa/central-africa/cameroon.html, consulted on the 12th March 2021

[14] J. Blanke, *How to make the Green Revolution a Reality in Africa*, The African Development Bank Group, 31-Aug-2017, https://www.afdb.org/en/news-and-events/how-to-make-the-green-revolution-a-reality-in-africa-17294, consulted on the 12th March 2021

[15] DeLancey et al., *Historical Dictionary of the Republic of Cameroon*, pp.196-197.

[16] A. Daka et al., "Public Agrarian Policies and Food Security in Cameroon: Problems and Challenges towards Agricultural Development", *European Journal of Humanities and Social Sciences, Vol* 1, Issue 4, July 2021, p.24.

[17] H. Mbouri Mbak, "La production alimentaire au Cameroun," in Traité sur la sécurité alimentaire au Cameroun, Areion Publishing., Paris, 2002.

also be noted that numerous difficulties have marred the smooth running of these plans. These difficulties led to an intense stagnation in the 1980s. Indeed, from 1969 to 1980, agriculture grew harmoniously and accounted for 30 percent of GDP. [18] From 1982 until 1985, overall growth declined.

This deceleration was mainly due to the decline in Cameroon's food sector. This sector had experienced a marked break from the previous period. The food crop on which Cameroon's agricultural growth was based collapsed by approaching zero growth, a decline of more than 3 percent in production per capita, without the export sector taking over. The latter continued its growth based on 2 percent per year.[19] The second half of the 1980s thus characterized the end of an accelerated growth cycle resulting in a decline throughout agricultural production, leading to a decrease in per capita production over the period, reducing the coefficient of food self-sufficiency.[20]

Moreover, the dynamics of the effort rested only on the state apparatus, favoured the emergence of an authoritarian state, rigid, inflexible, and hostile to private initiatives. These agricultural policies have favoured cash crops to the detriment of food crops. This marginalization of food crops has inevitably led to failure in achieving food self-sufficiency because food security is to have a diversified diet in sufficient quantity. Moreover, "the failure of all these strategies can be explained by a planning process which in practice only concerns technocrats and politicians, excluding producers".[21]

Talking about constraints in the agro-industrial sector, complexes like the CDC, noted for their good output in West Cameroon, declined in importance because of strong Francophone domination over it, leading to poor management and corruption with eventual privatisation.[22] This complex, covers about 38,000 hectares of land and employs more than 9,000 persons. [23] It grows, processes, and markets rubber and bananas for export and palm products mainly for domestic use. Minor crops such as coconuts are also grown. There are nine rubber estates (18,000 ha.), six rubber factories, seven oil palm estates (16,000

[18] Daka et al., "Public Agrarian Policies and Food Security in Cameroon", p. 24.
[19] Ibid.
[20] Ibid.
[21] Ibid.
[22] Mokake, *Basic Facts on Cameroon History Since* 1884, p. 154.
[23] DeLancey, et al., *Historical Dictionary of the Republic of Cameroon* p. 83.

ha.) and two mills.[24] The two banana estates (3,000 ha.) are managed in a partnership with the international Del Monte Company.[25] This was as the Corporation's lifeblood could only be secured with heavy loans from various bilateral and international sources that were eternally misappropriated.[26] During the early period after independence, the firm was run by British and Nigerian staff, which was so well done; and later by Cameroonians, through a board of directors under the government.

Whatsoever, despite all efforts, the gap between urban and rural settings remained, as the beautiful development concepts and platforms put in place seemed largely politically inclined. While most development experts and researchers agreed on the existence and extent of such disparities, they differed remarkably on matters relating to the causes and most suitable approaches to solving them. Ngwa and Lambi intimate that this conflict, among other issues, led to failure of the copious experimented development procedures, meant to meet broad social, economic and political issues in developing countries.[27]

II- The Petroleum Debacle

Cameroon's economic strategies of planned liberalism and self-reliance created milestone developments which evidently showed that the economy of the country was on an irreversible path to growth.[28] The indicators in many respects were symptomatic, especially in the second half of the 1970s, which marked the discovery and transformation of oil in the country's National Refinery Company in Limbe, incorporated as a major national income earner in the early 1980s, envisaged to produce 4 billion tons of crude oil by 1985.[29] This discovery of exploitable petroleum reserves was initially a great boost to the Cameroon's economy.[30] Once into production, petroleum soon became the country's

---

[24] Ibid.

[25] S.H. Bederman and M. W. DeLancey, "The Cameroon Development Corporation, 1947-1977", Kofele-Kale, *An African Experiment in Nation Building*, p.270.

[26] DeLancy, et al., *Historical Dictionary of the Republic of Cameroon* p. 83.

[27] Ngwa and Lambi, "An Evaluation of the Upper Nun Valley Authority's Agricultural Innovation, p.50.

[28] N. K. Takor and G. F Kum, "Incubation of the Economic Crisis in Post-Colonial Cameroon 1960-1987: An Experience in State Capitalism", *International Journal of Humanities Social Sciences and Education (IJHSSE)*, Volume 5, Issue 8, August 2018 p.56.

[29] Ibid.

[30] DeLancey et al., *Historical Dictionary of the Republic of Cameroon*, p. 11.

most valuable export.[31] It suffices here to mention that given the vision of the First Republic, the period (1960-1970) could be described as the decade of strategic economic planning while that from 1970 to 1980 was more or less gauged as an era of economic growth. This was more indicative because, the country enjoyed an economic growth rate that peaked to 7 percent per annum in most part of the 1970s.[32] From this growth rate the economy went into an all-time low economic performance, indicating a reversal of the growth trend.

Thoughts on the performance of Cameroon's economy have most often projected the period running from the late 1970s when oil was discovered to the mid-1980s as the glorious height of the economy. In far more measure, this conclusion leaves much to be desired in substance because the addition of oil to the country's Gross Domestic Product (GDP) opened an inveterate debate between oil pessimists and optimists. Better still, it divided public opinion into two as some perceived oil as a national blessing and others as a curse. The prospection of oil reserves by the French exploration company, Elf-Aquitaine (SNEA) and later its local subsidiary Elf-SEREPC in the Rio del Rey belt of Cameroon which started as far back as 1947[33] and stretched up to the mid-1970s was insignificant to the national economy. This is because, exploitation was very paltry. Oil production effectually started in 1978, with a total output of roughly 625,000 tons of crude oil.[34] Due to its political entombment, there was no consistent records on the scale of oil production in Cameroon from the genesis of commercial production to the outbreak of the crisis in the mid-1980s, as can be seen on Table 4.

[31] Ibid., pp. 11-12.

[32] Anderson, and Lorch, *Agricultural Growth is the key to Poverty Alleviation.*

[33] B. Gauthier B. and A. Zeufack, *Governance and Oil Revenues in Cameroon*, London, OxCarre Research Paper 38, October 2009, p.7.

[34] Jua, "State, Oil and Accumulation," in P. Geschiere and P.Konings, Pathways to Accumulation in Cameroon, Leiden, ASC, KARTHALA, 1993, p. 131.

Table 4: Cameroon Oil Production from 1978 to 1987 (million tons)

Year	Nicod Estimates	International Oil Estimates (IOI)	Other Estimates
1978	-	0,12	0,63
1979	14,8	1,00	1,71
1980	2,8	1,90	1,71
1981	4,0	3,40	2,80
1982	5,2	4,70	5,50
1983	6,3	5,80	6,00
1984	7,6	7,00	8,00
1985	7,6	8,40	8,24
1986	7,3	8,20	8,85
1987	7,0	8,10	8,28

Source: Bikas C. Sanyal, Wilfred A. Ndongko et al., *Development of the oil industry in Cameroon and its implications for education and training*, Paris, IIEP & MESIRES, 1990, p.33.

Table 4, recapitulates Cameroon's oil production trends from 1978 to 1907 in million tons, demonstrating its evolutive growth, during the period. Besides the lack of consensus of official statistics on oil production, there was no specific legislation regulating the sector. Instead, activities in the sector were governed by the 1964 mining law (Loi 64-LF-3) supplemented by the 1978 Law (Loi 78-14).[35] Under this regime, oil taxation in Cameroon was based on a complex system in many respects unique in the world. At the start of oil production in 1977, the then President of Cameroon decided to create an extra-budgetary account: *"Compte Hors-Budget" (CHB)* a board, to manage oil revenues.[36] This decision according to Jua was enigmatic because export revenues from the sale of cash crops were always budgeted.[37] "Cameroon's" decision to "save" its oil reserves abroad is argued, was sound for at least two reasons: first, to help in avoiding oil dependence and the Dutch Disease and secondly, because its boom was allegedly temporary as the rate of depletion of oil was believed to be very high.[38]

From a political economy perspective, the cautious approach by the post-colonial state to the "oil debate" was attributed to its determination to adhere to the course of "conservatism" on such issues. Symptomatic

[35] Takor and Kum, "Incubation of the Economic Crisis", p. 56.
[36] Jua, "State, Oil and Accumulation," p.131.
[37] Ibid., p.137.
[38]Gautrai and Zeufack, Governance and Oil Revenues in Cameroon, p.23.

of this policy was the throttling of structural economic transformation if it could engender political tensions, disrupt the apparent equilibrium that existed between the regions or socioe-conomic groups and ultimately threaten the power of the state.[39] In this spirit of totalitarianism, the state made the oil economy sacrosanct and secret. Gutrai and Zeufack carefully observe that: Instead of depositing 65 percent of its reserves in the *"Compted' Opérations"* in the French treasury, as per the CFA zone rules, President Ahidjo decided to keep a portion of oil revenues in US Dollars, in "escrow accounts" in foreign banks. The motivation announced then was to "avoid oil dependence" but also to have a "War Chest" (*trésor de guerre*), a fund for special projects...[40] This balance was supposed to be placed in the extra-budgetary account.

While there is evidence that the country's investment budget was funded mostly by resources from the "extra budgetary account" between 1980 and 1986, serious mismanagement occurred.[41] Building on the opacity and secrecy around the account and oil production in Cameroon and in spite of the fact that oil production in Cameroon peaked at about 65 million barrels per year around 1985-1986; the manifestation of the economic crisis was inevitable.[42] This was due to the fact that huge funds of the CHB were invested in unproductive parastatals. Illustrative of this financial drain was the increase in the funding of SODECAO from 200 million FCFA in 1982/1983 to an astronomical figure of 11.82 billion FCFA in 1984/1985.[43]

It is worth mentioning that in 1983, a few months after the investiture of Paul Biya as the second President of the country, an attempt was made through his "New Deal Policy" to reverse the status quo on national oil management.[44] This was initially done through a public policy discourse where he intimated that: "...if the accounts of oil revenue were not immediately included in the national budget, this was for technical reasons...But we will continue to discuss the best ways of

---

[39] Jua, "State, oil and Accumulation", p. 138.

[40] Gautrai and Zeufack, Governance and Oil Revenues in Cameroon, p.23.

[41] Takor and Kum, "Incubation of the Economic Crisis in Post-Colonial Cameroon", p.62.

[42] Ibid.

[43] Jua, "State, oil and Accumulation", p.150.

[44] Takor and Kum, "Incubation of the Economic Crisis in Post-Colonial Cameroon", p.62.

presenting these receipts which are public receipts and belong to the entire Cameroonian nation".[45]

This was the first time in the history of the oil debacle that such a subtle proclamation was made by a top state functionary. It marked a great departure from President Ahidjo's conservatism. However, the hope that President Biya's intended reversal of rule raised was ephemeral. From 1983 to 1987 when the crisis was officially announced, transparency remained an intractable problem as oil revenues were still not incorporated into the state budget in spite of the persistent advice from the IMF to do so for a more rational planning and programming process. The decision to manage the oil revenue on blind and expediency considerations only gave space for conspicuous consumption, endemic corruption, embezzlement and capital flights.[46]

The petroleum boost also made it such that its revenues be used to give higher prices to farmers, thus encouraging increased agricultural output.[47] Oil money was used to pay the costs for the imports of materials and technical skills needed for many development projects. And petroleum earnings were used to build financial reserves for difficult times that might arise in the future. Sadly, petroleum income was also used to pay the costs of many large, badly planned projects.[48] Much of the income was poorly used. Industrial development for many years emphasized large-scale projects such as the *Cellulose du Cameroun* (CELLUCAM) paper pulp facility that faltered due to the economic difficulties the country faced.

It was the discovery of petroleum in West Cameroon influenced Ahidjo to abolish the unitary system of government in favour of the Republic of Cameroon, so as to ensure strict government controls over the resources.[49] After the discovery of oil in 1978, the GDP growth rate increased sharply, remaining at an average annual rate of 8.2% until the end of the oil boom in 1986.[50] In that year farmers were offered a large increase in real producer prices for cocoa, coffee, and cotton. Those gains were quickly eroded by subsequent inflation, however, and on

---

[45] Jua, "State, oil and Accumulation", pp. 138-139.

[46] Takor and Kum, "Incubation of the Economic Crisis in Post-Colonial Cameroon", p.63.

[47] DeLancey et al., *Historical Dictionary of the Republic of Cameroon*, p. 12.

[48] Ibid.

[49] Ibid., p. 151.

[50] Moudio, "The dynamics of food security policy in Cameroon (2008-2019)", pp 12-43.

balance agricultural production was heavily burdened during the boom years.[51] During the boom, three distinct kinds of resource misallocation became increasingly severe. The most fundamental were classic Dutch Disease misallocations due to unsustainable price incentives, which limited investment in smallholder agriculture.

Prior to the oil boom, the sectoral balance had already leaned heavily against agriculture as a whole, and within agriculture resources were concentrated in the relatively small estate sector which produced no more that 10 percent of total agricultural output. These biases worsened during the boom, which made smallholder farming even less attractive and increased the number of unskilled workers seeking non-farm work. A second kind of misallocation occurred within government institutions, due to unsustainable management structures. Prior to the oil boom, an extreme centralization of decision-making had resulted in heavy red tape and fragmentation of responsibilities in the bureaucracy and the extension service. This resulted in poor policy implementation, and misallocation of what little expenditure was targeted to smallholder agriculture during the boom. A third kind of misallocation was under-investment in new technology.

Although Cameroon did have a significant public agricultural research and development program, during the boom there were few incentives for technology adoption, so yields for most crops stagnated or declined.[52] During this time, oil prices remained very low. Inflation was under control as the value of the Francs CFA remained strong and stable. All the foregoing problems were well known in Cameroon during the oil boom, but no real policy enhancement was instituted until the boom ended and only the liability crisis of the mid-1980s made reform unavoidable through the liberalization precept from the late 1980s. From 1973 to 1986, incomes grew at more than 7 percent per year.[53]

The lack of transparency in the management of oil rents has led to corruption. State investments generally proved to be irrelevant, and many state-owned enterprises soon turned out to be white elephants and went bankrupt. However, a minority took advantage of the state's control of certain economic sectors to 'place' themselves. It also appears that planning was inefficient. The cost of creating jobs was sometimes

---

[51] Bamou and Masters, "Distortions to Agricultural Incentives in Cameroon".

[52] Ibid.

[53] DeLancey et al., *Historical Dictionary of the Republic of Cameroon*, p.9.

disproportionate in some sectors. While the economic demands may in the long run benefit the country, the short-term effect is hardship for the majority of the population. Cutbacks in spending on education and health care, reduction of salaries and number of employees, and closure and privatization of many of the parastatals were accompanied by a reduction in the quality of life for all but the wealthiest and most politically connected of Cameroonians.[54] In all even though much of the country's early economic growth came from petroleum exports during its boom, it has been established that it was also sustained by the unsustainable expansion of agricultural areas and government borrowing.[55]

III- State Corporations' Drain

Cameroon earmarked parastatals as catalysts of rapid development at independence. In this backdrop, the state played a central role in promoting economic and social development due to the absence and or limited appropriate institutions capable of taking on the task of doing so.[56] For this reason, development efforts were championed by public rather than private firms, even in fields where the state had neither requisite expertise nor comparative advantage over the private sector.[57] The outcome was that the state became more of a liability than an asset in Africa, with parastatals becoming incapable of discharging their duties. State corporations scored incompatible results in many sectors of the economy with regards to the means that were put at their disposal. It is acknowledged that one of the most remarkable developments in Cameroon's political economy was the promotion of agro-industrial enterprises, based on plantation production.[58] Among these were others

[54] Ibid., p. 14.

[55] N., Benjamin and S. Devarajan, "Oil Revenues and Economic Policy in Cameroon:
Results from a Computable General Equilibrium Model", World Bank Policy research
Working Paper No. 745, Washington DC, 1989.

[56] Ahidjo, *As Told by Ahmadou Ahidjo*, p.54.

[57] Ngwa and Lambi, "An Evaluation of the Upper Nun Valley Authority's Agricultural Innovation", p.51.

[58] Ndongko, *Labour Resistance in Cameroon: Strategies and Labour Resistance in the Agro-Industrial Plantations of the Cameroon Development Corporation*, African Studies Centre, Leiden, 1993, p.16.

created to encourage and promote cash and food crop production in the country. [59]

Para public institutions were put in place by the Cameroon government in order to work toward the harmonious integration of development activities throughout the country on account of its geographical, historical, socio-cultural and demographic differences. [60] This was aimed at developing resources through projects set up within a coherent framework, modernising and developing rural areas around development poles.[61] The importance of youths in this development process was prime for the fact that external assistance did not meet the cost of development plans. More still, total national savings were too slender to permit any hopes. There was reason therefore to take advantage of the most precious means at Cameroon's disposal, namely the unused labour of the thousands of Cameroonian youths in the rural areas.[62] This labour force was going to measure Cameroonian's efforts and find a solution for the problem of 'disguised unemployment' which was common in the country side. In line with the preceding view President Ahidjo argued as can be seen next "there should be no illusions whatsoever: we are condemned to work for it is work alone that will put an end to our economic dependence".

Numerous problems in respect of planning, technology transfer, and market research did greatly plague state own corporations. Moreso, the large amounts of capital invested were squandered. They were further used as political capital as Management positions were given to reward political friends, regardless of any business skill they might lack. Many unnecessary employees were taken on for political purposes, as patronage. Corrupt practices enriched many in management but bankrupted the businesses. Attempts to privatize many of these enterprises have met with mixed successes. More success has been found in assisting the growth of small and medium-size enterprises producing goods for local use. But to a large extent the country still depends on the purchase abroad of industrial goods. Large-scale and significant exceptions to this have taken place with respect to refined

---

[59] Ibid.

[60] The Ministry of Planning and Territorial Development, *what you Should Know about the IIIRD Plan*, Temporary Edition, Yaoundé, No Date, p.79.

[61] Ibid.

[62] Ahidjo, *As Told by Ahmadou Ahidjo,* p.58.

petroleum products, cement, fabric and finished clothing, beverages, and aluminum.

It was in line with the foregoing, relating to state corporations that the provisions of presidential Decree No. 87/1141 of 20th August 1987, was implemented, fixing remunerations and perquisites of staff in state and mixed investment corporations.[63] To this end, the salary scale of the public service was applied to all civil servants on secondment and casual bonuses, housing, touring, overtime, duty-post allowances, reimbursement of medical expenses, fuel allocation and vehicles were either cut down or suspended. Under the Agricultural sub-sector, a programme was earmarked covering the North West Region, for instance, designed to reduce post-harvest loses with assistance from the United Nations Development Programme (UNDP).[64] It undertook sensitization campaigns and assured those sufficient quantities of improved seeds were placed at the disposal of farmers in good time.

Farmers were further drilled on the use of modern methods of production.[65] In this way, a new system jointly financed by the state with USAID and European Economic Community (EEC) assistance ensured that fertilizers reached farmers in sufficient quantities and on time. This was in a way to reduce government expenditures in this direction, hardly ever being below 800 million francs CFA yearly, leading to a privatization of the fertilizer supply and distribution system.[66] In spite of these efforts made by the state to solve the problems of state corporations, the commission charged with rehabilitating public corporations still identified WADA as unproductive and thus to be liquidated.[67] Meanwhile, the buying power of government institutions dropped dramatically as they had to cope with budget cuts. The pace of economic reform did not pick up significantly until 2000. Some major para-state companies were privatized, and others such as the national phone company: Cameroon

---

[63] Kum, "The Socio-Economic Impact of the Liquidation of the Wum Area Development Authority", p.61.

[64] Interview with Johnson Ndarikwu Gabuin, Former Director of WADA before Liquidation, 78 Years, Bamenda, 28th August 2010

[65] Présidence de la République, *Crise économique : Réponse du Cameroun*, Cabinet Civil, 1989, p.17.

[66] Ibid., p.18.

[67] Interview with Joseph Ntangsi, Ex-Co- Director of the Wum Area Development Authority (WADA), 1970-1972, Former Representative of the *KFW (*German Development Bank) Yaoundé, 65 Years, Yaoundé, 3rd August 2010.

Telecommunications (CAMTEL) failed to attract private investors. The ailing national airline (CAMAIR) has since ceased operations.

Conclusion

Chapter four has examined Cameroon's early development drive, intimating that it was based on attaining its economic sovereignty, perceived as the final stage for her independence, faced enormous challenges. Government instituted the planned development precept, to be executed through Five Years Economic and Social development plans; Planned Liberalism; Regional Planning, Balanced Development, Self-reliance Development, Food Self-sufficiency, Agro-Industrialisation; Operation Green Revolution and Agro-pastoral Shows. These early economic development strides faced enormous challenges, ranging from agricultural oriented constraints (poor cultivation technics, inadequate inputs and poor or no financing of projects); the petroleum debacle that greatly worked down on agricultural production and state corporations' drain, where a lot of money was borrowed and invested on them. These parastatals turned out to be unproductive, culminating in the economic crisis that broke out in the mid-1980s.

CHAPTER FIVE
THE ECONOMIC CRISIS AND RESPONSES

Introduction

The economic crisis broke out in Cameroon in 1986. For a better understanding what provoked it and how this evolved. chapter four gave a pride of place to the factors that constrained the country's economic development policies predating the crisis. Indeed, the pre-crisis situation, which corresponds to the period from 1960 to 1986, made agriculture the mainstay of the Cameroonian economy and allowed Cameroon to record real growth thanks to the development of the oil sector.[1] It can be understood that some of these difficulties were directly related to the reasons why Cameroon was greatly affected by the crisis. The chapter therefore lays deep emphasis on the contextual setting within which the economic crisis emerged and evolved, its outbreak, notwithstanding the various domestic and external efforts employed, to overcome the crisis.

I- Context

In the 1960s, Cameroon lacked vital economic structures and basic social amenities.[2] The few existing were sparsely distributed over different parts of the country, resulting in an undesirable socio-economic relationship between rural and urban settings. This state of affairs urged most youths to drift to towns for greener pastures. The government of Cameroon embarked on seeking solutions to this trend, in order to enable an adjusted development of all the regions of the country.[3] Principles for the country's rapid and balanced economic development were embedded in President Ahmadou Ahidjo's values of economic sovereignty, capitalist socialism, planned liberalism, self-reliant development and others. He held that economic development was not necessary without complete national sovereignty.[4]

---

[1] Moudio, "The dynamics of food security policy in Cameroon (2008-2019)", pp 12-43.

[2] Ndongko, "A Comparative Analysis of French and British Investment Policies in Cameroon", *Pan African Journal,* Vol. VII, No.2, 1974, pp.145-171.

[3] Kum, "The Socio-Economic Impact of the Liquidation of the Wum Area Development Authority", p.20.

[4] Ahidjo, *The Political Philosophy of Ahmadou Ahidjo*, p.87.

President Ahmadou Ahidjo intimated that Cameroon's autonomy was not complete so long as the economic dependence characteristic of underdevelopment remained. Therefore, complete sovereignty entailed economic sovereignty, which to him could only be, through the influence of what he termed African Socialism. This to him was perceived as social justice that could be obtained through modern technical means by concerting internal effort and foreign aid in a coherent and realistic plan.[5] The ultimate intension of this principle was to ensure balanced development in the necessary stability. Applying such a philosophy was undertaking reconversion, adaptation and not the systematic destruction of existing structures. African socialism was thus a mix of realities as it had to borrow its techniques from abroad and graft on African heritage.[6] It was therefore characterised by Africa's community spirit, respect for spiritual values and the central place of man.

Hence, principles of development like planned liberalism, self-reliant development and a series of Five-Year Development Plans were crafted following the framework of African socialism. Under planned liberalism, the state permitted a free market, managed natural resources and oriented foreign investment towards the common interest.[7] It also partnered with foreign entities to set up various parastatals providing jobs to the populations and youths in particular. By self-reliance, economic development depended largely on the natural, human and financial resources available within the country, while development plans through special projects were to target various aspects of socio-economic life under three main spheres: agriculture, industry and transport. Economic missions were dispatched to friendly nations, to muster financial and technical support. The prevailing political mood at the time was one of optimism that the country would attain self-sustained growth.[8]

The idea of a regional development policy through Five Years Development Plans was to harmonize development in the country. The central aim was to eliminate socio-economic disparities between the various regions thereby integrating their economies.[9] As such, two

[5] Ibid., p.53.

[6] Ibid.

[7] Dongmo, "The Green Revolution and Food Self-sufficiency", p. 1.

[8] Kum and Kum, "Understanding Agro-pastoral Shows in a Planned Economy", pp.770-778.

[9] Fanso, *History for Secondary Schools and Colleges, vol. 2*, p. 170.

medium plans were put in place between 1960 and 1971 aimed at doubling the real per capita income of the country by 1980.[10] It is observed that during the first plan (1960-1965), external financing constituted 72 percent investments of both agricultural and infrastructural sectors.[11] Strategies aimed at tackling rural development with emphasis on self-reliance and regional development were elaborated. This was not only because 85 percent of the population lived in rural areas, but because regional and national development could not be accomplished without a wider examination, planning, management, and utilisation of rural areas.[12] It was by this that Government increased funding for rural development projects. This effort could be seen beginning from the Second Five Year Development Plan.

This saw the second plan (1966-1971) allotted a stunning 26,758 billion francs CFA to rural development and actually investing 18,650 billion francs CFA on rural production.[13] The 1971-1976 plan invested 25,545 billion francs CFA on rural development, amounting to 9.2 percent of its planned investments.[14] The 1976-1981 plan on its part witnessed a phenomenal increase in its rural development budget, with a whopping 108.9 billion francs CFA.[15] Development Plans were principally out to create and extend existing plantations and agro-industrial structures. Projects and programmes under these plans ranged from sectorial through integrated to regional agro-industrial structures.

It is argued that although President Ahidjo resigned at a time when the economic crisis was about to broke out in Cameroon, many Cameroonians, blame its outburst on President Biya. [16] Corruption, bad planning, mismanagement and the use of government money to enrich government personalities and serve patronage purposes were important causes of the crisis. But the economic crisis was partly the result of international economic conditions and the weak, brittle, and dependent economy that Biya inherited on coming to office.[17] The infamous African drought of the 1980s caused export crop production to decrease

---

[10] Ndongko, *Planning for Economic Development in a Federal State,* pp.130-131.
[11] M.D. Tambi, "Economic Growth, Crisis, and Recovery in Cameroon: A Literature Review", *International Journal of Industrial Distribution & Business 6-1*, 2015, p.6.
[12] Ahidjo, *The Political Philosophy of Ahmadou Ahidjo*, p.55.
[13] Ndongko, "The Tracing of Economic Development in Cameroon".
[14] Ibid.
[15] Ibid.
[16] Ibid.
[17] Kum, "TheWum area Development Authority (WADA)", pp.259-260.

at a time when prices for coffee, cocoa, and other agricultural exports were in decline. More significant was the decline in prices and demand in world petroleum markets. Cameroon's income, dependent on exports, dropped rapidly. For a short period, this loss of revenue was covered by drawing on reserves built up in the first years of petroleum exports.[18] Table 5 recapitulates Camerron's economic performance from 1961 to 1985, demonstrating annual macroeconomic indicators within the period.

Table 5: Trends in Some Macroeconomic indicators for Cameroon, 1960 – 1985

No.	Period/indicators	GNP (consumer price level (index 1980 =100))	Consumer Price Index (average annual rate of change	GDP (average annual rate of change in real per capita terms	Rate of Inflation (average annual rate of change)
1.	1965-1975	4,8	8,6	53,3	5.6
2.	1976-1985	8,7	6,5	121,7	10.2

Source: Mbu Daniel Tambi, "Economic Growth, Crisis, and Recovery in Cameroon: A Literature Review", International Journal of Industrial Distribution & Business 6-1 (2015) 5-15, p.7.

Table 5 demonstrates Cameroon's annual macroeconomic indicators, between 1960 and 1985, earmarking that they were generally satisfactory. Petroleum funds that were used to finance development were quickly exhausted, and by 1987 the government admitted that the country faced an economic crisis. Cameroon had become a debtor nation. Budget cuts were necessary, and the ripple effects of this have been felt throughout the economy. The country's major agricultural products at the time were: coffee, cocoa, rubber, bananas, and timber.[19] While major industrial products were among others: petroleum and aluminium, food and beverages, consumer goods, textiles, and ship repair.[20] Exports were predominantly primary products such as: petroleum, lumber, coffee, and cotton, though aluminium and refined petroleum products were also important. Imports were mainly industrial

[18] Kum, "Refitting Economic Sustainability in Cameroon". pp. 184-185.

[19] LeVine, *The Cameroon Federal Republic*, pp.166-167.

[20] DeLancey et al., *Historical Dictionary of the Republic of Cameroon*, p. 11.

products such as machinery and motor vehicles, but food and fuel were also significant. Major export recipients were Spain, Italy, France, and South Korea; imports come from France, Nigeria, China, and Belgium. Tourism plays a small role, well below its potential.[21]

The foregoing, coupled with the discovery of oil in the late 1970s, ensued immense growth, based primarily on agriculture and exportation of raw materials such as cocoa, coffee and cotton and diversified with petroleum production, lumbering, some basic industries and services. The economy grew at a whopping 7 percent rate per annum from then to the mid process, the state adopted models that were neither endocentric, appropriate, nor based on the needs of the plurality of its population. Consequently, the most blatant remnants of her experiments were abandoned projects, dysfunctional machinery and a visibly dissatisfied population. The forgoing impelled an endemic economic crisis on the country with adverse effects on its economy.

It is pertinent to note that these problems resulted to inflation, triggered by expansionary fiscal policies and depreciation of the French Franc's value. Added to the foregoing was the lax macroeconomic management. Besides, a coup attempt was also experienced in April 1984, which turned out to be a prelude to the decline that followed shortly, as it caused an increase in military spending, in order to ensure military and political stability.[22] It was also caused by gross corruption as many civil servants and politicians became embezzlers of the state funds, notwithstanding, widespread custom fraud, paralysed the economy; tax evasion, especially by prominent politicians led to a drop in state revenue.[23] Opponents of the government tended to believe that the cause of the crisis was political, especially the absence of shrewd economic management under the new leadership. Others argued that an overvalued currency was to blame. The country got entrenched into a staid economic crunch, especially after the 1985-1986 budgetary year, leading to a 40 percent fall in real GDP by 1987.[24]

---

[21] Ibid.

[22] Interview with Fondo.

[23] Takor and Kum, "Incubation of the Economic Crisis", p.55.

[24] DeLancey et al., *Historical Dictionary of the Republic of Cameroon.*

II- Crisis Outbreak

The economic crisis broke out in Cameroon in 1986. The period from the mid-1980s to the turn of the century was characterized by structural difficulties, falling revenues, trade imbalances, and rising costs in the production and supply of goods and services.[25] Despite the several years of economic prosperity, three major factors accounted for the deterioration of the economic and financial situation of Cameroon: the persistent and concomitant fall of the US dollar and the prices of export products such as oil, cocoa, coffee and cotton; the associated appreciation of the effective real exchange rate against the US dollar and the decline in the country's oil output. In the words of President Paul Biya, "all our export commodities fell at the same time."[26] The government portrayed the cause of the crisis as largely external: the falling value of exports and especially the precipitate decline of the price of petroleum on the world market.

It is worthy of note that most Cameroon's development projects were instituted within its planned development scheme, but this objective was not attained.[27] Their deficits were a great drain on the resources of the public sector through various subsidies, new capital contributions charged to the investment budget, and state guarantees to loans and debt servicing.[28] In order to arrest this situation, a programme of rational management in the public and semi-public sectors was drawn up with a view to reducing the pressure exerted on the state budget, thereby improving on their performances.

To meet this vision, deductions were made on the state's budget during the 1986/87 financial year; from 850 billion francs CFA to 650 billion francs CFA in 1987/88 and to 600 billion francs CFA in the 1988/89 fiscal year.[29] During this difficult period of Cameroon's economy, a commission charged with rehabilitating unproductive state corporations was put in place with the responsibility of identifying those corporations that were either to be maintained, privatized or liquidated. Under pressure from the International Monetary Fund (IMF), the World Bank, and aid-giving countries, Cameroon was forced

---

[25] Ibid., p.141.

[26] Ibid.

[27] Ahidjo, *Fondements et perspectives du Cameroun nouveau,* Saint Lambert, 1976, p.43.

[28] Ibid.

[29] Fanso, *History for Secondary Schools and Colleges*, p.170.

to accept structural adjustment programs. In return for financial assistance, the government was required to undertake stringent economic restraints and important political reforms.[30]

An evaluation during this period shows that the country's economy experienced a brutal drop in revenue from the exportation of its primary and petroleum products. This drop was estimated at about 329 billion francs CFA, being 8.2 percent of the GDP. Economic activities shrank in several sectors particularly construction and public works, cash crops, retail trade and oil. This led to a fall in revenue and budgetary balance. External and internal borrowing as well as external arrears essentially financed the budget deficit and the country's debt increased sharply. Furthermore, investments dropped by more than 70 percent between 1986 and 1993 and consumption per head fell by nearly 40 percent. State enterprises faced serious problems of payments of arrears, due to external creditors and domestic suppliers as well as failures to reimburse debts to domestic banks. Many banks became undercapitalised, poorly managed and only marginally profitable.

The situation worsened before and after the highly contested October 1992 presidential elections, when serious confrontations occurred between the government and the opposition. The result was that the government became financially handicapped and unable to honour its financial commitments including its payroll. It can therefore be argued from the forgoing that the crisis resulted in an imbalance in macro-economic accounts, and in particular public finances Thus, despite the high development prospects of the early 1980s the country remained poor with economic gains incapable of improving the living conditions of a majority of its citizens. Faced with this quandary, the Cameroon's trade partners, particularly France, Germany, and the United States under the banner of the IMF offered help, but the government backed at their condition of strict cost cutting suggestions and rather instituted internal measures, based on Economic Stabilisation, due to its severe political consequences on the country.[31]

---

[30] DeLancey et al., *Historical Dictionary of the Republic of Cameroon*, p. 13.
[31] Ibid., pp.140-141.

III- Intramural Retorts

The Government of Cameroon did thus embark on redressing the economic crisis in her own way. There was a drastic reduction in the budgetary allocations for each ministry and the Ministry of Stabilization and Plan was set up in 1987 to redress the crisis. Government decided to lay-off workers so as to equally reduce state expenditure. Some ministries like Education, Public Service and Trade and Industries laid-off some of their workers.[32] The government also embarked on the reduction of fringe benefits like family allowance and house allowance to state workers formerly enjoyed by civil servants. There was drastic reduction in salaries for most civil servants while the government encouraged voluntary retirement as well as those were due retirement to quit; the government carried out a strict control of diplomatic missions abroad as it drastically reduced allowances and other facilities to the country's embassy staff.

For the first time since independence the budget of the country for 1987-1988 was reduced, by 18 percent. High-powered delegations of the Cameroon People's Democratic Movement (CPDM) were sent to the provinces to explain the draconian steps announced by the head of state, including forced retirement of many civil servants; curtailing electricity, telephone, and housing facilities granted to top-level civil servants; sale of many administrative vehicles; a change in the official working schedule in a bid to bring about higher productivity; the dissolution or privatization of unproductive parastatal enterprises; and closure of certain costly economic missions in various Cameroon embassies abroad.[33] The government of Cameroon professed a determination to foster urgent economic growth and job creation, and there was a decided uptick in interest in the mining sector and infrastructure development.[34] Although the international community considered the Cameroon approach bold, it was not successful in bringing corrupt officials to trial.[35]

In reducing domestic costs, the government of Cameroon, slashed public expenditures on education, road infrastructure, extension services, rural water supply, electrification, and health services. Part of the

---

[32] Takor and Kum, "Incubation of the Economic Crisis", p.p.60-61-

[33] Ibid., pp.141-142.

[34] CIA World Factbook (January 2012) U.S. Dept. of State Country Background Notes (January 2012) http://www.cia.gov/library/ppublications/the -world-factbook/

[35] Ibid.

government vehicle fleet was sold; civil servants due retirement were forced into retirement; official working schedules were changed, economic missions in foreign embassies from Cameroon were closed, with all casual bonuses, housing, touring, overtime, duty-post allowances, reimbursement of medical expenses, fuel allocations and vehicles to civil servants were either cut or suspended.[36] It was in this regard that reductions were made on the state budget during that same period as can be seen outlined in the previous section.[37]

The 1987-1988 budget reduced government's spending by 18 percent and this was the first time in the country's history that its budget decreased. The reduction in standards of living and influence of the state in the economy did not seem to make the situation any better. Economic indicators did not stop emitting negative signals. From 1985 to 1988, real export earnings fell by two third.[38] A commission charged with rehabilitating unproductive state corporations was equally put in place in 1986, with the responsibility of identifying those that were a drain to state coffers.[39] In this light, a host of them were either to be maintained, privatized or closed down, depending on the commission's reports. It is essential to note here that this commission was politically inclined as many auspicious enterprises like WADA and others were unjustifiably closed down.[40] All these did not curb the crisis and the state had to opt for peripheral assistance. A continues decrease in revenue induced a 40 percent drop in consumption per Cameroonian with the outbreak of the crisis. .[41] The investment rate decreased tremendously during that same period, with rising strains in the country's treasuries. Moreover, armed robbery and theft from banks and government services increased.[42]

Cameroon's external debts incurred, increased from less than half to more than three quarters of its GDP between 1984-1985 and from 1985 to 1988, the country's real export earnings fell by two third, urging her to adopt an IMF supported program in September 1988, through the

---

36 Awung and Atanga, "Economic Crisis and Multi-Party Politics in Cameroon", p.110.

37 Fanso, *History for Secondary Schools and Colleges vol. 2*, p.170.

38 Tambi, "Economic Growth, Crisis, and Recovery in Cameroon", pp.5-15.

39 Kum, "The Socio-Economic Impact of the Liquidation of WADA", p.61.

40 J.C. Kangkolo, 78 years, Former Secretary of State for Interior for West Cameroon, Wum, 23rd November 2012.

41 Tambi, "Economic Growth, Crisis, and Recovery in Cameroon", pp.5-15.

42 DeLancey et al.., *Historical Dictionary of the Republic of Cameroon*, p.142.

signing of an aid package of 150 million dollars in October that same year.[43] The agreement led to a structural adjustment loan from the World Bank as well as assistance from various countries. In May 1989, the World Bank approved an initial structural adjustment loan, to be disbursed in three phases.[44]

The government used this assistance to reduce its then balance of payment deficit and honour its foreign debts. It also initiated internal squeezes and freezes on the national economy by equating salaries of workers in public service with those in parastatal institutions and by eliminating any salary increase at the time.[45] In addition, government froze all new employment for the next few years. Eventually, as commodity prices began to rise (especially petroleum) and with the devaluation of the CFA franc in 1994, the economy reversed and conditions improved.[46] A continues decrease in revenue induced a 40 percent drop in consumption per Cameroonian between the years 1985-1986 and 1992-1993. External debts incurred increased from less than half to more than three quarters of the GDP between 1984-1985 and 1992-1993. The foregoing measures met with international approval, although violent crime rose as a result. Cameroon's plan also failed to reign in corruption.

IV- Structural Measures

In the 1980s and 1990s, Cameroon's economy suffered from a combination of external shocks, including falling oil prices and declining terms of trade, as well as internal challenges, including corruption, mismanagement, and political instability. All these coupled with the outbreak of the economic crisis, led to various macroeconomic imbalances and it became apparent that its emergency strategies solely based on internal adjustments would not be sufficient to shift its economy back to a sustained growth recovery path. This was evident as Cameroon's Economic and Stabilisation Plan failed to yield expected results.

This plan failed because of endemic corruption in the administration and lack of appropriate control mechanisms to ensure that government

---

43 Ibid.

44 Kum, "Refitting Economic Sustainability in Cameroon", p.185.

45 Ibid.

46 Ibid.

efforts were enforced. Hence, government was forced to implement structural adjustment programs by October 1988, which involved liberalizing the economy, reducing government spending, and privatizing state-owned enterprises. These policies were supported by international financial institutions such as the World Bank and IMF. The IMF provided an aid package worth of 150 million US dollars while the World Bank approved an initial structural adjustment loan, to be disbursed in three phases from the World Bank in 1989.

A) Reducing Budget Deficits

As dictated by the Structural Adjustment Programme, Cameroon sharply cut public investment expenditures before later cutting government consumption, followed by privatisation, liquidation of public companies and reduction in size of the public sector. All these measures are believed to have had devastating effects on the economy. To reverse Cameroon's downward trend on the economy, government attempted in the late 1980s and early 1990s to stimulate the economy with the help of a strategy, based only on domestic adjustments measures.[47] These reforms constituted of reducing budget deficits by augmenting tax rates; cutting salaries and subsidies to public enterprises; and restoring external competitiveness by reducing domestic costs and restructuring public enterprises. These programs were essentially concerned with policies whose objectives were to reduce the budget deficit through an increase in tax rates, cuts in the payroll and subsidies to public enterprises. The restoration of external competitiveness was centred on the reduction of the costs of factors of production and restructuring of public enterprises.

There was a sharp decline in the National Budget especially as the 1987/1988 financial budget dropped almost by 80 percent.[48] As far as tackling this was concerned, it was announced in the Finance Law of 1987/8, promulgated in June 1987, that the Cameroon government would reduce its costs and cut public expenditure.[49] The government undertook a series of reform programmes: in September 1988, November 1991 and March 1994 with the IMF and between 1989 and 1994 with the World Bank. The persistent weakness in the market for raw

---

[47] Ibid

[48] Mokake, *Basic Facts on the History of Cameroon Since 1884*.

[49] Tchoungui et al., "Case Study for Cameroon", In D. Reed (ed), *Structural Adjustment, the Environment and Sustainable Development*, p.40.

materials and its effects on public revenue, frustrated attempts to halt the deterioration of economic and financial situations, manifested in a build-up of outstanding government debts and lack of liquidity in its payment system.[50] In view of the increase in the nominal value of the CFA franc, the measures taken were too late and weak.

Problems caused by the preceding situation were aggravated by a sharp drop in Cameroon's terms of trade. Thus, the tradeable goods sector suffered a cost-price squeeze, public revenue fell, domestic arrears built up quickly and the banking system became worse with solvency problems.[51] The machinery for the collection of statistical data also diminished, with no data on the balance of payments as at 1987 and no price index by 1990. There were breaks in monetarily, due to the reorganisation of banks, as the data provided by them, were not sufficiently audited.[52] For instance, data on disbursement and redemption of foreign debts was consistent in general, while that on interest due or paid wasn't. Apart from that of the central administration, no financial statements existed on the dealings of the non-financial public sector in Cameroon.[53]

All these strangleholds made the stabilisation process on the reduction of budget deficits unsuccessful in Cameroon. The investment rate decreased from 27 percent to less than 11 percent of the GDP between 1988 and 1993, leading to rising tensions in the country's treasuries. It was this situation among others that urged the government of Cameroon, to opt for salary cuts in the civil service in 1993. Since then, the country concentrated on paying off its international debt and further restricting public salaries and pay rises to civil servants.

B) Salary cuts and Subsidies slashes to Public Enterprises

Faced with increasing budget deficits during the period of the economic crisis, salaries of civil servants became irregular in Cameroon. The government introduced drastic cuts on civil servants' salaries of about 50 percent in January 1993.[54] These were slashed twice that same year and as workers were increasingly retrenched, many were

---

[50] Ibid.

[51] Interview with Fondo.

[52] ADBG, *Cameroon: Structural Adjustment Programme II (SAPII),* 2002, p.12.

[53] Tchoungui et al., "Case Study for Cameroon", p.41.

[54] Fambon, "Pro Poor Growth in Cameroon", p.102.

compelled to opt for voluntary retirement.[55] These measures were excruciating.[56] In fact, the new government came on that same year decided to tackle salaries, considered to be the main reason for loss of competitiveness and budgetary deficits in the country. Salaries and allowances were cut and 4,000 unfilled positions (*postes fantômes*) were eliminated.[57]

Added to the foregoing, was the freezing of recruitment and salary increment of public sector workers, with net annual savings of 60 billion francs CFA made, representing some 2 percent of GDP.[58] Out station allowances and housing policies were strictly reviewed. The government also decided to reduce its staff abroad on diplomatic mission, reducing their fringe benefits. Civil service salaries cuts were equally extended to decentralised agencies. [59]This measure barely sufficed to rescue the budget for 1993/1994, but subsequently led to a considerable deterioration of socio-economic conditions of civil servants.[60] Between 1992 and 1995, the real wage of government workers dropped tremendously.

To compensate the foregoing situation, many civil servants took second jobs or undertook to improve on their wages by taking bribes.[61] All these gave Cameroon a very bad image that in 1998 and 1999, Transparency International named it the most corrupt of respectively 85 and 99 countries, based on a survey of people's attitudes.[62] A slight improvement was observed in 2000 and it moved up to the seventh from the bottommost. It is also obvious that corruption was spurred by inefficient administration, coupled with long and complex procedures that made the quality of services to citizens and businesses almost

---

[55] Mokake, *Basic Facts on the History of Cameroon Since 1884*.

[56] P. Konings, "The Post-colonial State and Economic and Political Reforms in Cameroon", in A. E., Fernandez Jilberto, and A. Mommen (eds), *Liberalization in the Developing World: Institutional and Economic Changes in Latin America, Africa and Asia*, London and New York, Routledge, pp.244-264.

[57] Tchoungui et al., *Structural Adjustment and Sustainable Development in Cameroon*, p.48.

[58] Kum, "Refitting Economic Sustainability in Cameroon", pp.182-183.

[59] Ibid.

[60] Norrington-Davies, "Climate Change Financing and Aid Effectiveness", p.2.

[61] OECD, *Cameroon-OECD/AfDB*, 2002, https://www.oecd.org/countries/cameroon, retrieved on the 14/03/2017.

[62] Tambi, "Economic Growth, Crisis, and Recovery in Cameroon", p.9.

impossible.[63] Many businessmen did not perceive taxes, but administrative bottlenecks as main obstacles to their activities.[64] More still, the need of public administration users were not adequately taken into account and certain values such as professional conscience, honesty, moral integrity, attendance and punctuality were not sufficiently disseminated. Lack of transparency in behaviour as well as manner of rendering public service was therefore deplored for effective controls and follow ups.[65]

As concerns measures towards cutting subventions to state owned corporations, it was realised these scored so incompatible results in many sectors of the economy, with regards to the means put at their disposal. They did not also attain the objectives set by the various Five Years Development Plans. Their deficits were a great drain of resources to the public sector through various subsidies, new capital contributions charged to the investment budget, and state guarantees to loans and debt servicing.[66] A programme of rational management in public and semi-public sectors was drawn up with a view to reducing the pressure exerted on the state budget and improving on their performances.[67] They had to implement the provisions of Decree No. 87/1141 of 20th August 1987, fixing remunerations and perquisites of staff in state and mixed investment corporations, that had been introduced by the state.[68]

B) Restructuring of Public Enterprises

The trends in the forgoing section urged as to that a series of efforts be made to restructure state corporations. Between 1990 and 1992, the proportion of the total population and number of undernourished Cameroonians were 33 percent and 4 million, respectively.[69] The "Ghost Town" operations of 1991 which caused a lot of social unrest and insecurity in the country, discouraged both local and foreign

---

[63] ADBG, *Cameroon: Country Governance Profile*, Country Operations Department, Central and West Regions, 2004, p.1.
[64] OECD, *Cameroon-OECD/AfDB*, p.79.
[65] ADBG, *Cameroon: Country Governance Profile,* p.vii.
[66] Présidence de la République, *Crise économique : Réponse du Cameroun*, Cabinet Civil, Yaoundé, 1989, p.14.
[67] Gabuin, Former Director of the Wum Area Development Authority (WADA).
[68] Kum, "The Socio-Economic Impact of the Liquidation of WADA", p.61.
[69] Moudio, "The dynamics of food security policy in Cameroon (2008-2019)", pp 12-43.

investors.[70] There was thus rampant capital flight which reduced the amount of capital in circulation; over consumption of foreign goods helped to destroy home based industries while state revenue declined as a result of the smuggling of cheap goods from Nigeria and other neighbouring countries; the inexperience of managing multiparty politics by the state led to extravagance, at the expense of government revenue; the devaluation of the franc CFA in 1994 made it difficult for many small scale industries to import foreign goods; the SAP imposed by the IMF and World Bank on Cameroon, led to an increase in fuel prices, closure of so many firms and industries leading to high rate of unemployment.[71]

The foregoing, led to the restructuring of public and semi-public enterprises, staff redundancies and increased unemployment. Unemployment ran very high at the time, from university graduates to first school leavers; there was equally widespread poverty in both urban and rural settings; a decline in the standard of living especially among civil servants, notwithstanding the per capita income of the country that was low with a decline in economic growth.[72] It was not therefore possible to restore competitiveness as the government had intended, given that domestic prices (salaries and producer prices) had displayed significant downward rigidities.[73] Many commercial enterprises like the Cameroon Bank and the SCB were closed down while heavy industries like CELLUCAM and many small-scale enterprises crumbled.

D) Stabilisation of Public Finances

The World Bank loan was for reforms geared towards improving the banking sector, administration, para-public enterprises and deregulation of trade and marketing organizations for raw agricultural materials, notwithstanding the control, thereby reducing government expenditures. These policies, based on the "macroeconomic model", formed the core of the different agreements on adjustment actions that were to be taken by the government. These covered two main areas: stabilisation of the public finances and stimulation of the economy. Nevertheless, the two structural adjustment programs concluded by the Government

---

[70] Interview with Fondo.

[71] Moudio, "The dynamics of food security policy in Cameroon (2008-2019)", pp 12-43.

[72] Ibid.

[73] ADBG, *Cameroon: Structural Adjustment Programme II (SAPII)*, p.11.

in 1994 and 1995 with the IMF as standby arrangements did not work well as had been envisaged.[74]

From 1994, new economic policies based on monetary adjustments were put in place leading to a gradual change in trends. Remarkable changes were made at the level of exportation as well as on the general scenario of government's finances. The government however continued to suffer from the inability to cope with internal and external pressure coming from debts that could not be paid. Relations with foreign partners also turned into a stalemate especially with the devaluation of the franc CFA against the French franc in January 1994 affecting the country as it did of other African states in the monetary association. The intended boost in exports did thus fail to fully materialize. Hit hard by the crisis, conventional agricultural export production could not respond quickly.[75] For Tchoungi et al add that this was more so, because the balance of payments deficit was funded by an increase in foreign debts and repatriation of external bank assets.[76]

Taking into account the relatively slow response of production mechanisms, SAP measures gave priority to actions based on demand, although the programmes chosen incorporated important measures regulating domestic supply.[77] The economic model chosen for the stabilisation of finances was essentially based on demand, in recognition of the fact that the crisis had been sufficiently exacerbated by external constraints. This urged the economy to be divided into the private, petroleum and government sectors, aimed at strengthening regional monetary policies, by providing support for the reform of indirect monetary policy instruments to allow interest rates to reflect market conditions. The programme was also out to facilitate the development of a strong financial market, as well as strengthen the control of commercial banks.[78]

These developments, led to a gradual change in development trends, remarkable of which was exportation and general setup of Cameroon's budget. With this, the state concentrated on reimbursing its international debt, further restricting salary increases to civil servants. However, by spring 1994 only two of the three phases of the SAP had

---

[74] Kum, "Refitting Economic Sustainability in Cameroon", p.186.
[75] Ibid.
[76] Tchoungui et al., *Structural Adjustment and Sustainable Development in Cameroon*", p.41.
[77] Ibid.
[78] Ibid.

been executed, because of the sluggish pace of the reform. This made Cameroon to be termed one of the most disappointing "adjusters".[79] In 1996, the IMF proceeded to instituting a staff-monitoring program, as a sign of its lack of confidence in the government. In spite of implementing this, the budget deficit remained a source of disagreement between the government and Bretton Wood institutions.[80] It can however be maintained that the economic crisis and SAP policies introduced, boosted the indispensability of the informal sector, which employed about 3/4 of the urban workforce and sizeable number of skilled labour in the country.[81]

By the end of 1996, the government of Cameroon had reached four agreements with the IMF, all of which failed due to its inability to meet agreed terms. There was balance of payment deficits being funded by an increase in foreign debts and repatriation of external bank assets.[82] The service of external debts continued to weigh heavily on public funds due to the deviation of resources meant for indispensable intervention by the state in executing its missions in justice and security sectors, notwithstanding the maintenance, rehabilitation and amelioration of infrastructures. The intended boost in exports further failed to fully materialize due to the slow responses to modern agricultural techniques. This was due to the centralized control of the economic system by the state. There was also little or no social dialogue between the state and civil society actors.

In all, all attempts to solve the problem of internal and external debts failed completely. It was only later in August 1997 that the government was able to come to terms with the IMF, after successfully going through a reference program followed up by that institution. This made Cameroon to remain indebted to external creditors of a whopping 9 billion US dollars, representing 229 percent of its GDP and 369 percent of export goods and services during the period ending December

---

[79] S. Bertelsmann, "Cameroon Country Report", p.12.

[80] African Development Bank Group (ADBG), *Cameroon: Structural Adjustment Programme II (SAPII) Project Performance Evaluation Report (PPER)*, Operations Evaluation Department (OPEV), 2002, p.13.

[81] OECD, Cameroon-OECD/AfDB.

[82] Tchoungui et al., "Case Study for Cameroon", In Reed (ed), *Structural Adjustment, the Environment and Sustainable Development*, pp.53-81.

1997.[83] Sikod summarises this impasse in the following statement: "as of December 31 1997, Cameroon owed external creditors 9 billion US dollars, representing 229 percent of the GNP and 369 percent of export of goods and services".[84]

Nonetheless, the government of Cameroon had come to terms with the IMF in August 1997, after successfully going through a reference program, orchestrated by a replacement of Prime Minister Achidi Achu by Mafany Musonge on the 19th September 1996.[85] This change of government turned situations around for the country and accelerated the implementation of reforms, resulting in the 5 percent annual growth performance recorded in 1997.[86] This permitted the government to sign a fifth letter of intent with the IMF. Musonge's government made appreciable efforts in respecting this letter.[87] The mean annual growth of the country's GDP stood at 4.5 percent, while inflation, measured by homes' final price consumption was redressed to less than 1 percent.[88] Success on the macroeconomic scale did not however lead to an improvement of the living conditions of Cameroonians.

Despite all efforts put in by the state in the foregoing regard, the country, remained one of IMF's "bad pupils," as none of the four programmes negotiated, were completed by 1997.[89] Living standards had dropped considerably during the ten years over which Cameroon experienced the economic crisis. Social services, provided by the state during this period got seriously affected. Road infrastructures also degraded, because maintenance and construction of new ones had totally stopped. Water and electrification programs experienced serious drawbacks especially in rural areas.[90] SAP measures such as cutting

---

[83] S. Fondo, "The Completion point of the HIPC Initiative: what it means for the Cameroon Economy, A Presentation at Hilton, Sponsored by the British Council, 2006, p.4.".

[84] Ibid.

[85] Fondo Economist, 77 Years, Economist, University of Yaoundé II, 13th October 2014.

[86] S. Fambon, "Pro Poor Growth in Cameroon", *STATISTIKA*, University of Yaoundé II, Yaoundé, Cameroon, 2017, p. 103.

[87] Interview with Fondo.

[88] Economy of Cameroon, "Economy of Cameroon: Exports, Imports, Agriculture," no date, in www.cameroon-tour.com/economy/index.html, Retrieved on the 24th August 2015.

[89] OECD, Cameroon-OECD/AfDB, p.76.

[90] Awung and Atanga, "Economic Crisis and Multi-Party Politics in Cameroon"? p.111.

down of the civil service workforce from 180,000 to 120,000 persons and privatizing important corporations such as the CDC, *Société de Development du Coton du Nord (SODECOTON)* and others were not effectively met.[91] The government continued to suffer from its inability to cope with the payment of internal and external debts. However, Cameroon's economy had recovered by the early 2000s.[92]

E) Privatisation of Public and Para-public Establishments

The Cameroon government had created a series of public and para-public institutions before the outbreak of the World Economic Crisis. Many were unproductive during that period and a great drain to the country's resources. CELLUCAM for instance, had been created in 1974, notwithstanding an Austrian paper manufacturer, whose purpose was to manufacture paper in Cameroon, with a massive public investment (120 billion francs CFA).[93] The factory was ready for production in early 1982. Due to a series of industrial accidents, almost no production was done in 1983 and the company was on the verge of bankruptcy.

In fact, the company was poorly conceived from the start and turned out to be a financial disaster. This was the biggest public investment at the time and the typical example of a white elephant in Cameroon.[94] The state had also invested massively in a refinery, *Société Nationale de Raffinage* (SONARA). Although warned by international donors that such a project would not be profitable, the refinery opened in May 1981. Fuel prices, set by the state, were increased to allow SONARA to survive two months after its opening, thus penalising the Cameroonian economy.[95]

In 1984, a new investment code was adopted with the main objective of stimulating economic growth.[96] Between 1982 and 1985 three new important industries were set up. These were, the *Société Industrielle des Tabacs du Cameroun* (SITABAC) producing cigarettes, a new brewery, the *Société Internationale de Brasseries* (SIB) and *Supermont*,

---

[91] Ibid.

[92] Interview with Fondo

[93] Wikipedia, Planned Liberalism, https://en.wikipedia.org/wiki/planned_liberalism, consulted on the 13th March 2023

[94] Ibid.

[95] Ibid.

[96] Mokake, *Basic Facts on Cameroon History from 1884*, p. 159.

producing mineral water.[97] When the first signs of the economic crisis began in 1987, President Biya decided to adhere to the SAP as a measure of taking Cameroon out of the crisis. But this instead brought about a lot of unemployment and many people to live in misery. This was because of the excessive interest rates attached to the loans obtained from the IMF which Cameroon could not afford to pay.[98]

DeLancy et al. intimated that there was considerable pressure for the government to privatize the parastatals, turning them over to private enterprise.[99] Cameroon under president Paul Biya, increasingly turned to the privatisation of state-owned corporations, to stimulate its economy.[100] Cameroon's development efforts were all together managed through a series of Five years development plans until the outbreak of the economic crisis and implementation of Structural Adjustment Programs (SAPs) in the late 1980s.[101] These plans were six in number and spanned from 1960-1990, but the country's underlining economic principle did not change during period of their operation.[102]

In an attempt to handle the economic crisis, the government with instructions from the World Bank and the IMF decided to privatize some state corporations like HEVECAM, CAMSHIP, CAMAIR, INTELCAM and even the CDC.[103] Parastatals were earmarked in Cameroon as a way of fostering and guiding industrial development in desirable directions. With the economic crisis of the mid-1980s and intervention of Bretton Woods institutions and various donor nations, there was pressure on African governments to turn these over to private ownership, in a process, termed privatization.[104] Many parastatals were badly managed, poorly planned, overstaffed, with immense corrupt practices. It was assumed that private ownership would lead to rational management and profitability. The SAP I program called for a reduction in the role of the state on economic policy. This program was

---

[97] Ibid.

[98] Ibid.

[99] DeLancey et al. *Historical Dictionary of the Republic of Cameroon*, p. 308.

[100] Wikipedia, Planned Liberalism, https://en.wikipedia.org/wiki/planned_liberalism

[101] M. M. Ntangsi, *A Balance Sheet of Economic Development Experience in Cameroon*, NT, NH, 2008, pp. 35-39.

[102] A.A. Nwana, "The North West Development Authority (NWDA/MIDENO), in the Socio-Economic Development of the North West Region of Cameroon, 1981-2019", PhD Dissertation in History, the University of Bamenda, 2022 p.3.

[103] Interview with Ntangsi

[104] DeLancey et al., *Historical Dictionary of the Republic of Cameroon*, p.317.

implemented up to December 1993, with little successes, because government showed little commitment in implementing reforms such as: privatization and retrenchment of civil servants as a measure to downsizing the civil service.

According to the privatization reform, the Cameroon government had to disinvest itself from most parastatals; this meant that it would lose grip of this sector of the economy.[105] The little successes on reform were probably because this coincided with the political transition in the country and devaluation of the franc CFA in the Franc Zone. Given that government was so preoccupied with the political situation, the country remained very unstable, with adverse effects on its economy. It was this situation among others that urged the government to opt for salary cuts in 1993.[106] Two salary reductions were implemented and the state failed to pay civil servants for two months that same year. There was the closure of unprofitable banks like the Cameroon Bank. There was also the launching of the "Operation Antelope", as a computerized way of controlling civil service pay roll, as it was shocking to discover that well over 20.000 absentee workers were still receiving salaries.[107]

The Government of Cameroon, carried out two privatization programmes in 1990 and 1994 which targeted 30 enterprises with a series of delays. Pressure to divest began to grow in the mid-1980s, and the first sale took place in 1990. The list of planned divestments included most of the well-known companies in the country like CAMAIR, CAMSHIP, *la Regie des Chemin de Fer du Cameroun* (REGIFERCAM) the railroad in transport; HEVEACAM, SODECOTON, SOCOPALM, CDC and CAMSUCO in agriculture; *Société National /%* (SONEL), INTELCAM, *Société National des Eaux du Cameroun (SNEC)*, and Société des Transport Urbains du Cameroun (SOTUC) in public utilities; and the Port of Douala were among those frequently mentioned. Some 60 to 70 companies were planned to be liquidated and 25 or more sold.[108]

SAP II planned to make up for the delays in these two programmes through finalizing the restructuring process of structures like the CDC, SOCAPALM, SODECOTON, CAMAIR, CAMSUCO and others. It

---

105 African Development Bank Group (ADBG), *Cameroon: Structural Adjustment Programme II (SAPII)*, p.11.

106 F. T. Niba, former Programme Coordinator for the Tikar Development Project and Ex-Chief of Section for Planning, Evaluation and Training, 55 Years, Magba, 18 July 2004.

107 Idem.

108 DeLancey et al., *Historical Dictionary of the Republic of Cameroon*, p.317.

further intended to speed up and expand the scope of implementation of the privatization programme and restructure enterprises still under the State portfolio. Thus, new regulatory frameworks were adopted to enable private sector participation in the water (SNEC), electricity (SONEL) and telecommunications (INTELCAM) sectors.[109] In spite the results, this aspect, registered significant delays, due to a number of foreseeable constraints.[110]

As far as achievements in the privatisation domain were concerned, CAMSUCO, SOCAPALM and a host of others were privatized between December 1998 and July 2001, although this did not meet government's expectations. Several privatization operations such as CAMTEL (fixed telephone), CDC, SODECOTON, CAMAIR or SNEC turned out to be more complex than initially envisaged and experienced significant delays.[111] In short, the programme for the privatization/ restructuring of public enterprises did make headway, even though most of the actions envisaged were not implemented at the end of SAP II. The Cameroon civil service had not also had the required experience. The remaining privatizations got incorporated into the World Bank SAP III, envisaged to all be completed in June 2002; but the privatization of SNEC, CAMTEL, SODECOTON, CDC and CAMAIR encountered major delays.[112] The case of CAMAIR, was for instance because workers went on strike, when it was sold and then the sale was cancelled, even though the airline later went bankrupt and stopped flying.[113]

The privatization reform led to increased unemployment and even though the situation seemed at times to get better due to the involvement of people in the informal sector, most of such employment was precarious and unstable. This is because the civil society was not encouraged as a significant partner of the state as authorities feared their power will be watered down.[114] It was indicated that some 35 corporations were liquidated, 17 had been restructured, 18 privatized

---

[109] OECD, Cameroon-OECD/AfDB, p.79.

[110] Economy of Cameroon, "Economy of Cameroon: Exports, Imports, Agriculture".

[111] African Development Bank Group (ADBG), *Cameroon: Structural Adjustment Programme II (SAPII),* p.11.

[112] Awung and Atanga, "Economic Crisis and Multi-Party Politics in Cameroon"? pp.111-112.

[113] DeLancey et al., *Historical Dictionary of the Republic of Cameroon,* p. 317.

[114] OECD, Cameroon-OECD/AfDB, p.81.

and 10 more in the process.[115] All these made the economic revival process, an uphill task. Other strategies were put in place such as the creation of a platform for dialogue between the government and private sector, through a ministerial committee enlarged to include the private sector and other frameworks of dialogue.[116] A series of measures were equally launched through the National Employment Fund (NEF) aimed at ensuring transparency in the job market and encouraging unemployed citizens through trainings and workshops on how to create small micro projects. The government also created a national employment and professional observatory in order to ameliorate its knowledge about the job market.[117]

The Denationalisation of the CDC, encountered a different problem; the land on which many of its plantations are located was taken from the inhabitants by the Germans, without proper compensation in the 1880s and 1890s.[118] The Bakweri Land Claims Committee has for many years tried to get a settlement of the issue, and privatization gave it a new opportunity to state its case.[119] In general, government moved slowly with the process. Parastatals were excellent sources of patronage in the country, and many officials become very rich from the management positions they occupied in them. Moreover, the reduction in staff, associated with economic rationalization became politically unpopular and an important factor in the massive unemployment problem the country faces.[120] Also, the sale of these parastatals was not as beneficial as expected. The least successful companies have been the most difficult to sell. In some instances, buyers were willing to take profitable parts of companies and to leave the government stuck with the unprofitable parts. Prices received have been lower than hoped, and more often than desired, foreigners (especially French) have been the purchasers rather than Cameroonians.[121]

---

[115] DeLancey et al., *Historical Dictionary of the Republic of Cameroon*, p.317.
[116] African Development Bank Group (ADBG), *Cameroon: Structural Adjustment Programme II (SAPII)*, p.11.
[117] Economy of Cameroon, "Economy of Cameroon: Exports, Imports, Agriculture".
[118] DeLancey et al., *Historical Dictionary of the Republic of Cameroon*, p.318.
[119] Ibid.
[120] Ibid.
[121] Ibid.

F) Liberalisation and De-regularisation of the Economy

During the period 1997-2000, economic programs implemented by the government included radical economic reforms whose objectives were to enhance the productive potential of the economy: firstly, it was to reinforce the functioning of the market economy notably by privatizing public enterprises and liberalizing markets; and secondly, to improve the environment for the development of the private sector through sector-wide reforms in the areas of energy, forestry, transports, and finance, and to reinforce public administration through the reforms of public services and of the judicial system. [122] These reforms continued during the period 2000-2003, when they were supplemented by policies designed to accelerate the reduction of poverty by developing a poverty reduction strategy and by improving the delivery of social services.

The liberalisation of domestic product markets was aimed at bringing prices in line with world prices and make markets more efficient.[123] Conversely, it completely disorganised the market, as before this, purchases were made at regular market places and dates, decided by authorities, ensuring that transactions were carried out properly. With liberalisation, there were no longer such controls. Exploiting the growers' urgent need for cash, traders paid no attention to established prices, and this led to fraudulent practices, severely reducing the cash crop growers' income, causing them to lose interest in producing.[124] The idea of liberalisation was aimed at restoring competitiveness in the country's economy.

A competitiveness committee setup by decree in December 1997 in this light, resumed in 2000.[125] Its aim was to initiate and reinforce dialogue between the state and private sector and promote productive investments within a concerted framework. This committee succeeded in preparing a plan of action, following a strategic seminar-workshop organized in March 2000, approved by the World Bank. Even if these actions were well conceived to address real issues of the country's economy, it is clear that its implementation was not properly done.

[122] Tchoungui et al., *Structural Adjustment and Sustainable Development*, pp.87-88.
[123] Ibid., p.88.
[124] Interview with Fondo Sikod
[125] African Development Bank Group (ADBG), *Cameroon: Structural Adjustment Programme II (SAPII)*, p.9.

Problems were largely underestimated, while some actions were programmed even though the requisite financing for their implementation was not available.[126] This soon proved to not meet concerns of the private sector, since it didn't meet the government's poverty reduction strategy and goal for robust and sustainable growth. Despite its difficulties, the government made noteworthy efforts with resounding results.

IV- National Management Mechanisms

Africa's institutional fragility has most often been based on poor planning or weak policy implementation. In this backdrop, more attention is focused on how future decision makers will be and the people they will choose to help in formulating and implementing policy than on major policy orientations and sustainability. President Biya's political philosophy was for instance, based on community and freedom, rooted in the culture and vision of Cameroon at the time.[127] It was at the service of man and social justice, designed to spur equality and greater humanness. In this process, government's vision sought to lead Cameroonians from their ethnic cultures into a national one, characterized by tolerance, freedom, and sharing. [128]

Although the Cameroon's economy performed satisfactorily well from 1997, with a growth rate of more than 4 percent a year and low inflation, it did suffer from weak institutions and persistent corruption, that nevertheless hampered development projects. This was so much that much time and resources were spent on solving problems of governance, specially making good use of the debt remission obtained under the HIPC initiative. However, the economic crisis boosted the importance of the informal sector, which employed about 3/4 of the urban workforce and a sizeable number of skilled people in the Cameroon.[129]

Following Cameroon's institutional weaknesses, a National Governance and Anti-Corruption Programme (NGP) was formulated in 1996, although only formally approved by the head of state in 2000.[130] The

---

[126] Ibid.
[127] DeLancey et al., *Historical Dictionary of the Republic of Cameroon*, p. 107.
[128] Ibid.
[129] OECD, Cameroon-OECD/AfDB, 2002, https://www.oecd.org/countries/cameroon, retrieved 14/03/2017
[130] Ibid.

National Anti-Corruption Observatory (NAO) was chaired by the Prime minister with units established in ministries. Several reforms improved transparency, including the one, involving the system of handling state procurement contracts.[131] However, the programme did generally enclose a strategy based on: accountability or the obligation to render account, transparency, stakeholder participation, reform of the legal system and judicial frame work, including the defence of human rights and fight against corruption. With the help of international funding bodies, public finances were stabilized in Cameroon although amid severe governance problems. The limited results so far obtained were especially due to the meagre resources for combating corruption.[132] Despite the continuous spread of President Biya's rigour and moralisation concept, standards kept falling as can be seen in the forthcoming citation:

> This key slogan of the Paul Biya presidency is based on the idea that the Cameroonians could attain higher goals and objectives with a greater sense of purpose and dedication. According to the head of state, "rigor and moralization" signifies the struggle against tribalism, sectarianism, clientelism, provocation, and intoxication. Consequently, moralization becomes a permanent endeavour against laxity, fraud, diversion of public resources, corruption, favouritism, and arbitrary action. The slogan was immensely popular in the early stages of the Biya presidency. It was applied in multiple practical cases, mentioned in all public speeches at all levels in the country, and served as the demarcation line between the Ahmadou Ahidjo and Biya regimes. Over time, the public has become very cynical with respect to the "rigor and moralization" concept, as the Biya regime has become known as even more corrupt than its predecessor.[133]

At the political level the separation of power was assured at the executive, legislative and Judiciary. This was to ensure accountability and transparency. In practice however, there was a marked pre-eminence of the executive over the other organs. The predominance of the ruling party in parliament from the 1990s following the introduction of multiparty politics in Cameroon did so weigh on the effectiveness of legislature to control government action. Political weaknesses were equally noted in the organization of presidential and parliamentary elections, despite efforts made by the government, at inviting national and international observers. This let-down was blamed on the failure of the government to put in place the constitutional council provided for

---

[131] Ibid

[132] ADB, *Cameroon: Country Governance Profile*, Country operations Department, Central and West Regions, September 2004, p.viii

[133] DeLancey et al., *Historical Dictionary of the Republic of Cameroon*, p. 330.

by the 1996 constitution, as this was thought would have a major role in strengthening democracy and political transparency.

The legal system of the country was seen more as a threat to freedom than a defender of it. In fact, its credibility did not generally respect its own ethics. The principles that governed its independence were not usually respected. The weaknesses of the judicial system were many. Corruption was an established fact as the rules of law were many at times deliberately ignored. Attachments applied to some enterprises constituted handicaps for the development of private national and foreign investments. Judicial delays did disconcert persons awaiting trial, giving rise to disparaging remarks about justice.[134] The discriminatory suspension of enforcement of court decisions was also fraught with consequences. Lastly, the management of human rights gives violations by traditional chiefdoms and military authorities.

Regarding budget preparations and control, it should be noted that the then legislative framework in the country was unsuitable because it did not take into account the notions of objective and outcome, based on macroeconomic planning. It was in this light that a new legislative outline was necessary for adoption by parliament to meet these requirements. On the whole, Cameroon's budget preparation process was carried out properly by the Ministry of Finance and Budget (MINFIB) in collaboration with the *Ministère de l'Economie, de la Planification et de l'Aménagement du territoire* (MINEPAT).[135] Nevertheless, some lapses relating to weak institutional capacities of these institutions somewhat undermined the efficiency of the system. The investment budget was also important to point out that authorities had abandoned the system of management of capital expenditure by multi-annual programme authorizations, though provided for by the ordinance of 1962.[136]

Despite all efforts put in by the state of Cameroon in mid-1996, its budgetary situation remained low. But figures began changing in 1996-1997 with the advent of a new government and drafting of a new programme aimed at consolidating the benefits of devaluation, fighting poverty and creating favourable conditions for the private sector. The new political direction led to a notable improvement in state finances,

---

134 ADB, *Cameroon: Country Governance Profile*, Country operations Department, Central and West Regions, September 2004, p.viii

135 Ibid.

136 Kain Marius, 70 Years, Pioneer Clerk of WADA, Wum, 26th November, 2006.

despite the low price of oil and substantial debt servicing. The budget was also helped by major structural reforms in 1994, such as the TCA turnover tax, introduced as part of the 1993 tax and Customs reforms, replaced in 1999 by the Value Added Tax (VAT). This boosted tax revenue and tax transparency in the non-oil sector. Openness about oil revenues was helped by annual audits of the *Société National d'Hydrocabule* (SNH). In 1999-2000, higher oil prices produced a budget surplus and VAT revenue reached 4 percent of the GDP, which was high compared to that in other Sub-Sahara African countries at the time.[137]

It was obvious that an inefficient administration, with long and complex procedures would be incapable of offering quality services to citizens and businesses.[138] Many businessmen did not perceive taxes as the main obstacles to their activities but administrative bottlenecks, leading to investment risks.[139] Public resources, when poorly controlled and not managed transparently, led to significant budget deficits in Cameroon, impacting its balance of macroeconomic aggregates. Certain standards such as professional ethics, trustworthiness, moral integrity, attendance and punctuality were equally not sufficiently disseminated. Lack of transparency in behaviour as well as in the manner of rendering public service was therefore deplored. [140]

Administratively, the Constitution and General Rules and Regulations of the public service define accountability by civil servants and state employees. Such accountability, however, was not fully exercised, given the administration's poor performance. However, many reforms were undertaken within the framework of the implementation of the NGAP in order to improve the institutional framework, human resources and procedures. But the civil service remained deprived of its managers and resources. Corruption also became endemic in the sector, aggravated by the loss of purchasing power of Cameroonians after the 1994 devaluation. In fact, between 1992 and 1995, the real wage of government workers dropped by 75-80 percent.[141]

---

[137] Ibid

[138] ADB, *Cameroon: Country Governance Profile*, Country operations Department, Central and West Regions, September 2004, p.1.

[139] OECD, Cameroon-OECD/AfDB, 2002, https://www.oecd.org/countries/cameroon, retrieved 14/03/2017.

[140] ADB, *Cameroon: Country Governance Profile*, Country operations Department, Central and West Regions, September 2004, p.vii.

[141] Ibid.

Institutional failings were also as a result of very poor organisation of the civil society and concentration of power at the centre. Despite the 10000 or so officially approved Non-Governmental Organisations (NGOs) in Cameroon, there was no one that represented them. This was partly because of the nominal nature of many of them, which were therefore not very active. However, civil society was not encouraged as a substantial partner to the state because the authorities feared their power will be watered down. At the same time, decentralization, which officially started with the January 1996 local elections, was being obstructed by problems with transferring funds and by lack of trained people. The Central authorities also retained substantial power to intervene and replace mayors elected by government representatives and even postponed local elections just like that due in January 2001.[142]

The restructuring of enterprises of public and private sectors which led to the closure of some companies on the one hand and the freezing of recruitment in the public service on the other hand led to increasing unemployment in Cameroon. The situation seemed at times to get better due to an involvement of people in the informal sector, yet most of such employment was precarious and unstable. Other strategies were put in place such as the creation of a platform for dialogue between the government and private sectors through a ministerial committee enlarged to include the private sector and other frameworks.[143] A series of measures were equally launched through the National Employment Fund (NEF), aimed at ensuring transparency in the job market and encouraging unemployed citizens through trainings and workshops on how to create small micro projects. The government also created a national employment and professional observatory in order to ameliorate its knowledge about the job market.[144]

V- Village Development Associations (VDCs)

Still in order to boost its economic ordeal during the period of the crisis, the government of Cameroon laid deep emphasis on the importance and reconsideration of Village Development Associations (VDAs) in the

142 OECD, Cameroon-OECD/AfDB, 2002, https://www.oecd.org/countries/cameroon.

143 Ibid.

144 "Economy of Cameroon: exports, Imports, Agriculture", in Cameroon-tour.com/economy/index.html, Retrieved on the 24th August 2015.

country's revival process. This development initiative had developed within the ambit of Cameroon's Self-reliant development drive during the early 1970s and gained grounds mostly in the Grassfields region of the country. Generally, one of those very principal elements that characterised the customs and traditions of the people of Cameroon was communalism, especially in the aforementioned region. Before European imperialism, genuine community labour participation could be seen in the construction and maintenance of palaces, village to farm roads, inter village roads, and shrines in the country. [145]

The British Colonial Authority introduced the system of 'Indirect Rule', which was intended to be a continuum of the "old order". Through this, the place of the traditional authority was strengthened in the then British Cameroon. The British, ruling the people through traditional authority was because traditional authorities had the capacity to rally their inhabitants for local development. This privileged position enjoyed by traditional authorities in the British Cameroon did not obtain in French Cameroon where the policy of 'assimilation' prevailed. In the former British Cameroon where the chiefs retained significant political and economic autonomy, numerous local associations emerged than was, in the Francophone part of the country.[146] Moreover, local development approaches in both parts of Cameroon were different even in appellation; 'community development' and *'action Communautaire'* respectively[147] prior to independence in 1960. The traditional hierarchical institutions with chiefs at the helm were a heritage of British colonial rule. Geschiere observed that in the adjacent part of the former French Colony - Bamileké part of the Western Grassfields - such associations were relatively strong as well.[148]

It is no surprise therefore that Village Community Projects (VCPs) realised through local participation were quite common, well managed,

[145] Interview with Fanso

[146] P. Geschier, *Culture: Pandora's Box?* Paper presented at the conference "Good Governance for Africa: Whose Governance?" organised by the University of Limburg and ECDPM, Maastricht, 23–24 November 1995.

[147] E. Yensu, Balanced Rural Development in Cameroon within a Democratic Context. In: P. Nkwi and F. Nyamnjoh (eds.), *Regional Balance and National Integration in Cameroon. Lessons Learned and the Uncertain Future.* ICASSRT monograph 1, African Studies Centre, Leiden, The Netherlands, 1997.

[148] Ibid.

and effective in this part of Cameroon.[149] Although the post-independence period witnessed an increase in local participation, mostly in the execution of the country's Concept of Self-Reliance, government initiated and sponsored projects, the 1990s saw an unprecedented avalanche of self-reliant development projects through enthusiastic and committed local participation in the country.[150] The economic crisis of the 1980s as mentioned earlier, caused serious economic problems in rural areas and Cameroon government, under pressure from structural adjustment programs and related influences, diverted much of its technical and financial support to rural development.[151] This turning point in development and decisiveness of VDA from the 1980's was a partial response to the economic crisis that hit the country and the stringent fine-tuning measures, later implemented in 1990 following the prescriptions of the World Bank and IMF.

It was in this regard of the prescriptions laid by the MIF and World Bank that Cameroon government authorized communities to form and or strengthen VDAs' activities as community agents to lead self-help initiatives.[152] While many villages formed these associations, they often did not know how to use them within the context for which they were instituted. The concept of self-reliance was already well known in Anglophone Cameroon, and many of its initiatives grew into fruition, supported by local elites and by those living in urban areas and abroad. Funds were occasionally contributed or levies were charged to finance water, education, electrification, and similar local developments.[153] Substantial assets come through remittances from community members living and working abroad. This enabled local populations to exploit to their advantage, resources that could otherwise lie dormant, thereby perpetuating the ignorance and poverty of their communities, by making use of the under-utilised labour alongside funds raised for community development to be enhanced.[154]

---

[149] C. C. Fonchingong & L. N. Fonjong, The Concept of Self-Reliance in Community Development Initiatives in the Cameroon Grassfields, *Nordic Journal of African Studies,* 12(2), 2003, p. 200.
[150] Ibid.
[151] DeLancey et al., *Historical Dictionary of the Republic of Cameroon*, p.388.
[152] Ibid., p.389.
[153] Fonchingong & Fonjong, The Concept of Self-Reliance in Community Development Initiatives, p.199.
[154] Ibid.

It is worthy of note that, VDAs were popular developments in the North West and West Regions of Cameroon because of their centralised systems of governance. For the North West Region, there were Village Development Associations such as the: Esu Development Association (ECUDA) emanating from the Esu Development Committee (EDC), Mankon Cultural and Development Association (MACUDA), Aghem Cultural Development Association (ACADA), Njinikom Area Development Association (NADA), Kuk Cultural and Development Association (KCUDA) and a host of others. They incarnated democratic structures that worked in collaboration with committees and subcommittees, depending on the nature of the project. These structures equally worked in partnership with NGOs such as the Swiss Association for International Development (SAID). This structure was an ardent partner in self-reliant development in the Cameroon Grassfields. Their intervention in pipe borne water schemes, road rehabilitation and development of water catchments in collaboration with diverse communities was so remarkable. NGOs further worked with other grassroots structures in the maintenance of pipelines, digging of trenches, supplying sand, stones and laying of pipes for distribution of water to quarters within various localities in the region.

Conclusion

This chapter laid deep emphasis on the contextual setting within which the economic crisis emerged notwithstanding the various domestic and external efforts that were employed by both the Cameroon government, IMF and World Bank, to overcome the crisis. Economic misfortunes during the mid-1980s nonetheless led to criticism of the planned development philosophy due to poor governmental judgment at guiding private foreign investments, the pervasive corruption paralyzing bureaucratic structures, the overheated process of industrialisation and ill-advised government backing of certain foreign investors. Analysis of agricultural policies in Cameroon since 1960 shows that government investments boosted the agricultural sector. However, the inadequacy of these policies and constraints resulting from the destabilizing effects of Structural Adjustment Programs (SAP) inevitably led to strikes all over the country. The mid-1980s' economic crisis that shook Cameroon resulted in the country's withdrawal from specific sectors of activity. Because of its international economic status at the time, Cameroon was compelled by the Bretton Woods institutions to adopt the Structural Adjustment Programs (SAPs) to get its economy back on track.

CHAPTER SIX
THE HEAVILY INDEBTED POOR COUNTRIES INITIATIVE (HIPC) AND COMPLETION POINT EXPECTATIONS

Introduction

Chapter six focuses on Cameroon's admission into the HIPC initiative, the decision and completion points and prospects for its economic development goals. The HIPC initiative was instituted by the IMF and World Bank to assist emerging economies grow economically. This was a poverty reduction strategy adopted in the early 2000s, aimed at improving social welfare. Before her admission into the HIPC initiative Cameroon's economy was characterized by failure in its five-year plans; decline in agricultural production; relative food and economic crisis. President Paul Biya was thus forced to adopt and set up a multitude of reforms under the aegis of the IMF and World Bank. These reforms were to be part of Cameroon's general strategy for reducing poverty, improving its regulatory and economic framework for participatory management of natural resources. They intended to reduce poverty and improve food security by diversifying the economy, developing rural areas and agricultural sector, strengthening the private sector, etc. Cameroon therefore went through a long period of readjustment with successive reforms. The implementation of these reforms led to its attainment of the decision and finally completion point of the HIPC initiative in 2006 which enabled a significant cancellation of the country's debt as shall be seen subsequently.

I. From Preliminaries to the Decision Point

Despite, the IMF/World Bank disaffection with the implementation of the structural adjustment program in Cameroon, it went ahead to admit the country to the Highly Indebted Poor Countries (HIPC) Initiative, during the last quarter of 2000. [1] When the economic crisis broke out in the world and Cameroon in particular, the government carried out some stabilization and structural adjustment programmes which led to the discontinuation of its medium and long-term

---

[1] Awung and Atanga, "Economic Crisis and Multi-Party Politics in Cameroon", p. 110.

initiatives. As Cameroon's economy declined in the 1980s and 1990s, the IMF, the World Bank, and major aid-giving countries played powerful parts in pressuring the government to improve the economy.[2] When the CFA franc, the common currency of Cameroon and 13 other African states was devalued by 50 percent in January 1994 an overall drop in purchasing power of nearly 65 percent of the population occurred.[3]

Cameroonian authorities also tried to cope by borrowing to finance budgetary deficits in the system, unfortunately debt servicing grew rapidly and started crowding out investments.[4] Commodity sub-sectors were liberalized in the first part of 1990s, thus exposing farmers to the vagaries of world market prices. Further, more, as argued by Baye and Fambon, the joint effects of the economic crises and structural adjustment programmes forced many Cameroonians to adopt coping devices such as engaging in two jobs or more, seeking for survival in the informal sector.[5] Also, they engaged in occupational and geographical mobility, changing regional patterns of activities and productivities, and adopting ''behavioural innovations' 'like corruption and other malpractices for survival. These adaptations, improved the pattern of welfare among households in the different regions and sectors of activities in the country. Increased poverty in rural communities induced many young people to migrate to large towns where they expected to find better conditions.[6]

While in towns these young people, ended up in a grid of relatives and friends who initially supported them against the worst hardships; even though some succeed in making ends meet, while others got exposed to unemployment or under-employment, crime and social behaviour, that led to insecurity problems to other city dwellers.[7] It is even estimated that, nearly 4 out of every ten Cameroonians by 2001 were living with an annual income below the poverty line of CFAF

---

[2] OECD, Cameroon-OECD/AfDB, p.79.

[3] CIA World Factbook U.S. Dept. of State Country Background Notes (January 2012) http://www.cia.gov/library/ppublications/the -world-factbook/.

[4] Mbanga, and Sikod, The impact of debts and debt service payment on investment in Cameroon. Nairobi, Kenya: Final report submitted to AERC, 2002.

[5] Baye, Fambon, and Sikod, "Globalisation: Institutional changes and poverty in Rural Cameroon". Final Report, Tokyo Japan: FASID, 2002

[6] Baye., and Amongwa, Decomposition of Inequality in the Distribution Living Standard in Cameroon, *African Journal of Economic Policy, 9(2),,* 2002, pp. 51-75.

[7] Ibid.

232.547 (roughly equivalent to US$1 per person, per day or FCFA 19,000 a month).[8] This represented the estimated annual income, necessary for an individual in a city like Yaounde, to buy a 'minimal basket 'of essential food and non-food items. In 2001, eight poor people out of ten were living in the country-side and the incidence of poverty there is more than double the incidence in the cities. [9]

A number of projects had been put in place such as the Agricultural Sector Adjustment Plan (ASAP) in 1994, the National Participative Development Program (NPDP), the New Agricultural Policy (NAP). There was also the establishment of the National Agricultural Extension and Research Program (NAERP), the sectoral strategy for animal husbandry, fisheries, and animal industries, the Poverty Reduction Strategy Document (PRSD), and the Rural Sector Development Strategy Document (RSDSD). Their objective was precisely to improve rural producers' access to financial markets and promoting the management of natural resources to create an effective environment-friendly system in Cameroon.

After numerous failures in sufficiently revamping Cameroon's economy, the HIPC Initiative was put in place in 1996 under the Multilateral Debt Relief Initiative (MDRI), coordinated by the Bretton Woods institutions, and other multilateral, bilateral and commercial creditors, to ensure that the poorest countries in the world were not overwhelmed by unsustainable debt burdens.[10] This programme thus reduced debts of countries meeting strict criteria. Cameroon got admitted into it even though not initially planned. The procedure went through two major qualifying steps based on an interim relief at a decision point and finally the completion point that provided reforms, which increased the country's ownership of its economic development policy.

From the foregoing, an accelerated Structural Adjustment Plan was put in place with the full support of the IMF, for an economic and financial program, to be realized within a period of 3 years, (1st July 1997 to 30th June 2000). The execution of this program came alongside a voluntary action staged by the government of Cameroon, to portray a

[8] PRSP (2003). Cameroon: Poverty Reduction Strategy. Paper IMF Country Report, International Monetary Fund, Retrieved July 30, 2006, from http://www.imf.org/external/country/cmr/index.htm

[9] Baye., and Amongwa, Decomposition of Inequality in the Distribution Living Standard in Cameroon, pp.50-75

[10] OECD, Cameroon-OECD/AfDB, p.79.

better image and credibility of itself abroad; by paying back about 5 billion US dollars of debts owed.[11] It also went ahead to closely associate with the private and public sectors, towards the evaluation of a three-year economic and technical program as well as negotiating a financial agreement with the IMF.[12] The first milestone was to be the decision point at which the World Bank and the IMF would formally determine whether the country was eligible for the debt relief.[13] Countries at this point, met stringent qualifications, including income thresholds. The international community then committed a level of debt relief for the country.

Still in line with reforms, the 1994, turnover tax TCA, was replaced in 1999 by the VAT, to boost tax revenues and tax transparency in the non-oil sector. Openness about oil revenues was helped by annual audits of the SNH.[14] In 1999/2000, higher oil prices produced a budget surplus and VAT revenue reached 4 percent of the GDP.[15] This financial and economic program was satisfactorily executed with support from the IMF through its structural adjustment facility, the World Bank through a 3rd loan for structural adjustments, the European Union (EU), the African Development Bank (ADB) and other creditors.[16] It is been sustained that between 1990 and 2001, the proportion of Cameroonians living on less than 1 US dollar per day and less than 2 US dollars per day represented 33.4 percent and 64.4 percent of the total population respectively.[17]These moves led to a better adhesion of economic operators and civil society to policies of adjustment and reform.

The IMF provided financial assistance, technical advice and monitored efforts geared toward reducing the proportion of Cameroon's population, living in poverty and facilitating long-term growth in the country's economy.[18] The execution of this program came alongside

---

[11] African Development Bank Group, Cameroon: Review of the Bank Assistance to the Multisector, 1996-2004, Operations Evaluation Department (OPEV), 2008, p.9.

[12] Ibid.

[13] The World Bank, "Heavily Indebted Poor Country (HIPC) Initiative", www.worldbank.org/en/topic/debt/brief/hipc, retrieved on 18th November 2018.

[14] African Development Bank Group (ADBG), *Cameroon: Structural Adjustment Programme II (SAPII),* p.14.

[15] OECD, Cameroon-OECD/AfDB, p.76.

[16] Tchoungui et al., *Structural Adjustment and Sustainable Development*, pp. 49-50.

[17] OECD, Cameroon-OECD/AfDB, p.79.

[18] Ibid.

the voluntary action staged by the government to portray a better image and credibility of Cameroon abroad; by paying back about 5 billion US dollars of its external debts owed. The government also went ahead to closely associate with the private and public sector, in evaluating a three-year economic and technical program as well as negotiating a financial agreement with the IMF. These moves led to a better adhesion of economic operators and the civil society to adjustment policies and reform.

The financial and economic program for the period stretching from 1st July 1997 to 30th June 2000 was satisfactorily executed with the needed support from determinant international bodies like the IMF through its structural adjustment facility, the World Bank through a 3rd loan for structural adjustment, the European Union, the African Development Bank (ADB) and the Paris Club. However, in spite of the agreements of Naples concluded with the Paris Club in Paris in 1997, the service of external debts still continued to weigh heavily on public funds due to the deviation of resources meant for indispensable intervention by the state in the execution of its regular missions in favour of social sectors like (justice and security) and in the domain of maintenance, rehabilitation and amelioration of infrastructure.

From 1996-1997 to 1999-2000, the mean annual growth of the GDP stood at 4.5 percent and inflation measured by the index of the final price of consumption by homes was redressed to less than 1 percent.[19] The situation with public finance greatly improved, thanks to a better mobilization of funds and a rationalization of national expenses. Success on the macroeconomic scale did not necessarily mean an amelioration of living conditions among Cameroonians. In effect, living standards dropped considerably during the ten years over which Cameroon experienced the economic crisis. The availability of social services provided by the state were seriously affected during this period and very little could be done at the time. Road infrastructure also degraded seriously due to lack of maintenance. The construction of new roads was totally stopped. Water and electrification programs also experienced serious drawbacks especially in rural areas due to lack of financing.

[19]"Economy of Cameroon: exports, imports, agriculture", in Cameroon-tour.com/ economy/index.html, Retrieved on the 24th August 2015.

However, the good performance registered during the execution of the three-year financial plan of 1997-2000 concretely enabled a macroeconomic stability as well as the long-needed bases for a sustainable economic growth.[20] Cameroon's economy had mostly recovered by the early 2000s.[21] This was because the IMF had contributed through the HIPC Initiative in reducing its international debt glitches. In the long-term she and the IMF cooperated in the Poverty Reduction and Growth Facility (PRGF) project despite, the world economic crisis that occurred during the first decade of the 21st century and shortly afterward.[22] After these first three years, the eligibility of Cameroon to the alignment, reinforced by the HIPC initiative was decided upon in May 2000 by the administrative council of the IMF and the World Bank opened up new perspectives of development for the country.[23]

It was as a result of the preceding matter that Cameroon reached the decision point in October 2000, enabling her to benefit from the Heavily Indebted Poor Countries (HIPC) initiative, thanks to efforts put in by its government.[24] By this, bilateral donors, forgave substantial amounts of debt even before the "completion point" was reached and also in spite of the country's failing annual growth rate, since its admission into the programme. After publishing this, the Board of Executive Directors of the International Development association (IDA) and the IMF agreed that the amount of debt relief committed at the decision point for Cameroon would be 1,260 million US dollars in net present value (NPV) terms.[25] This was calculated to bring the NPV of debt to the equivalent of 150 percent of exports on the basis of end-June 1999 data. This relief represented a reduction of 26.9 percent of the debt as of end-

---

[20] Ibid

[21] Delancey et al., *Historical Dictionary of the Republic of Cameroon*,209.

[22] Ibid.

[23] African Development Bank Group (ADBG), *Cameroon: Review of the Bank Assistance to the Multisector, 1996-2004*, Operations Evaluation Department (OPEV), 2008, p.3.

[24] Awung and Atanga, "Economic Crisis and Multi-Party Politics in Cameroon", p. 110. (The HIPC decision point is when countries under IMF and World Bank programs initiate reform to benefit from debt relief. When these countries deepened their reform by drawing up poverty reduction strategy papers, they reach completion point).

[25] International Monetary Fund (IMF), "Cameroon: Enhanced Heavily Indebted Poor Countries (HIPC) Initiative, Completion Point Document and Multilateral Debt Relief Initiative (MDRI)," IMF Country Report No. 06/190, 2006, p.5.

June 1999 after a traditional relief and reduction of 25 percent in the nominal value of the debt service over time.[26]

More still, the Boards of IDA and IMF concurred to provide Cameroon with interim debt relief until it reached the floating completion point. Interim assistance under the enhanced HIPC Initiative was also granted by the African Development Bank Group (AfDB), the European Union, and the Paris Club group of creditors (through flow postponement on Cologne terms).[27] Executive Directors had determined that the completion point would be reached when Cameroon complied with the conditions laid down in the decision point document. Even though the IMF and World Bank's intervention never led to positive outcomes for nations needing its assistance, there was no doubt that this helped countries like India to progress as can be seen following:

> Accordingly, India enacted a range of industrial policy reforms, including: de-licensing; encouragement of foreign direct investment (albeit only into joint ventures); opening of India's equity markets to foreign institutional investors; increased access to international capital markets for Indian-based firms; devaluation and convertibility of India's currency; reduction of restrictions on exports; and severe reductions in import tariffs and quantitative controls on imports. In fact, India's average tariffs fell from more than 87 percent in 1990 to 43 percent in 1996, while the standard deviation of tariffs dropped by about 30 percent during the same period.[28]

The good performance registered in Cameroon at the time, enabled a macroeconomic stability as well as the long-needed bases for a sustainable economic growth, which permitted her to reach the decision point in October 2000.[29] It was then admitted into the Heavily Indebted Poor Countries (HIPC) Initiative and benefitted from an interim debt relief from its creditors in October that same year. This opened up new perspectives of development for the country. Interim debt relief assistance was used in accordance with the criteria set forth at the decision point. The government of Cameroon, agreed to: establish a special Treasury account at the Bank of Central African States (BEAC) where the budgetary savings from HIPC relief would be deposited;

[26] Ibid

[27] Ibid.

[28] Stephen Ezell and Robert Atkinson, the Indian Economy at a Crossroads, The Information Technology & Innovation Foundation (ITI F), 2014, p.18.

[29] African Development Bank Group, Cameroon: Review of the Bank Assistance to the Multisector, 1996-2004, Operations Evaluation Department (OPEV), 2008, p.3.

establish a monitoring committee (HIPC Consultative Committee) comprised of representatives from the donor community and civil society; and accept and disseminate technical and financial audits to ensure effective use of these resources in the form of the delivery of goods and services.[30]

The special account was opened at BEAC, with the sum of 213 billion francs CFA for the execution of poverty alleviation projects.[31] The government started to make required deposits in this account including resources on account of HIPC Initiative debt service relief, from official bilateral creditors. In 2003/2004, the government fell behind in depositing HIPC relief funds into the account but later caught up with the deposits, clearing the arrears by 2006.[32] Her economic recovery was driven by increased investment in the oil and gas sector, as well as the expansion of the agricultural and service sectors. The government of Cameroon further implemented foreign investment friendly policies, improving the business environment, and reducing poverty, notwithstanding those promoting regional integration, including the creation of the Economic and Monetary Community of Central Africa (CEMAC) and the African Union (AU).

As concerns the HIPC Consultative Committee, it was established in October 2002. It initially provided guidance for the selection of good projects that could be suitable for the use of HIPC funds, including a percentage, earmarked for civil society projects. In 2003, the government of Cameroon, adopted a budget nomenclature which allowed the identification of poverty-related programs and projects.[33] Delays had occurred in the execution of HIPC-funded projects due to problems in putting the HIPC Consultative Committee in place, preparing high quality projects and establishing transparent disbursement procedure. Execution rates of HIPC-financed projects were thus low in 2003 and 2004.[34] Steps were taken, to improve the programming and execution

---

[30] International Monetary Fund (IMF), "Cameroon: Enhanced Heavily Indebted Poor Countries (HIPC) Initiative, Completion Point Document', p.14.

[31] N. Kini, "Cameroon: Implications of the HIPC Completion Point", 2006, http://www.postnewsline.com/2006/05/implications_of.htmlmore, 20th November 2018.

[32] International Monetary Fund (IMF), "Cameroon: Enhanced Heavily Indebted Poor Countries (HIPC) Initiative, Completion Point Document," p.14.

[33] Ibid.

[34] Ibid.

of HIPC-financed projects including streamlining disbursement procedures, strengthening the capacity of the national consultative committee, and putting in place an information system for monitoring projects' implementation. As a result, the execution rate increased from 25 percent in 2003 to almost 100 percent in 2005. HIPC projects were targeted at improving public services delivery in areas ranging from education (construction and rehabilitation of schools, recruitment of temporary teachers), health care (including improving immunizations and combating malaria and HIV/AIDS), social development (including literacy projects), urban sanitation, rural development (including rural infrastructure), and justice.[35]

Two technical and financial audit reports covering the use of HIPC resources respectively during July 2001–December 2003 and January-December 2004 were produced, discussed with the Consultative Committee and made accessible to the public.[36] The audits found that some projects were implemented without prior approval by the HIPC Consultative Committee and that part of the HIPC spending did not observe proper public procurement and execution procedures (e.g., spending without prior commitment orders).[37] The government is implementing the recommendations of the audits focused on improving the management of HIPC resources by line ministries and on compliance with proper procurement and public spending procedures and the government took actions to address these problems.[38] Emphasis was laid on improving the procedures for formulating project proposals and establishing a control unit within the HIPC Consultative Committee to strengthen the monitoring of project implementation. Again, special projects coordinators were nominated in line with different ministries, to supervise the implementation of HIPC projects. The Consultative Committee also encouraged the engrossment of local communities and NGOs in the execution of HIPC projects.[39] For example, 350 local associations and communities were intricate in road maintenance

[35] Interview with Sikod.
[36] Idem.
[37] International Monetary Fund (IMF), "Cameroon: Enhanced Heavily Indebted Poor Countries (HIPC) Initiative, Completion Point Document', p.14.
[38] Ibid.
[39] Interview with Sikod.

projects. This raft of measures, paid off and the execution rate for HIPC projects, including capital projects, gradually picked up. [40]

The HIPC debt relief grants were computed at the decision point, assuming that Cameroon would reach the completion point by April 2003 and .like in other developing countries, the country was expected to deepen reforms which would take her to the HIPC completion point that same year and guarantee full and irrevocable reduction in debt available under the HIPC initiative.[41] These reforms constituted of preparing and implementing poverty reduction strategy, maintaining a stable macroeconomic environment, setting up mechanism to ensure efficient and transparent use of interim debt relief gained from reaching the decision point, and strengthening public expenditure management. IDA in pursuance of this engagement, delivered interim assistance in the amount of US$60 million in NPV terms through March 2003 and the IMF granted interim debt relief of US$14.6 million in NPV terms as of end 2005. Total assistance during the interim period amounted to US$201 million in NPV terms. [42]

This nevertheless failed to implement some aspects of the reforms, leading to an increase of the country's fiscal deficit before the 2004 elections.[43] Since the structural adjustment program relied on market forces to stimulate the economy, it was definitely at discrepancy with the regime in power's objective, as it entailed, plummeting the size of government and consequent loss of the source of political patronage. The privatization process equally called on the state to disinvest itself from most parastatals, which meant it was going to lose control of some important sectors of the economy.[44]

The SAP resulted to the impoverishment of most Cameroonians, led to the emergence of a new class of nouveau riches and reduced the capacity of the state to act independently. Notwithstanding it's constant attempts at undermining the programme's reforms, Cameroon recorded

---

[40] International Monetary Fund (IMF), "Cameroon: Enhanced Heavily Indebted Poor Countries (HIPC) Initiative, Completion Point Document," p.15.

[41] Awung and Atanga, "Economic Crisis and Multi-Party Politics in Cameroon", p. 110.

[42] International Monetary Fund (IMF), "Cameroon: Enhanced Heavily Indebted Poor Countries (HIPC) Initiative, Completion Point Document and Multilateral Debt Relief Initiative (MDRI)," IMF Country Report No. 06/190, 2006, p.13.

[43] Awung and Atanga, "Economic Crisis and Multi-Party Politics in Cameroon", p.112.

[44] Interview with Sikod

some striking achievement: the devaluation of the CFA franc led to resumption of growth, the export of commodities was liberalized, the banking and financial sector was cleaned-up and restructured, making political interference more difficult, new and more liberal labour and investment codes were enacted. Moreover, the privatization process albeit haltingly, progressed; while competition was allowed in certain sectors that had previously been monopolized by the state such as the telecommunications and audio-visual sectors.[45] With a net present value (NPV) of debt of 353 percent of export goods and services, a scheduled debt ratio of debt-service to government revenue of 94 percent, Cameroon gained admission into the HIPCI-2 alongside many other African countries[46].

In order to overcome the adverse impact of poor governance and corruption on socio-economic development, the Cameroon government adopted the National Governance Program (PNG) in 2000 to support sustainable growth, poverty reduction, and social inclusion. It established anti-corruption institutions such as the National Anti-Corruption Observatory, a permanent watchdog body in the education sector; anti-corruption units in all ministries and some public agencies, and positions of inspector-general in ministries to liaise with the anti-corruption units in fighting corruption. It also established a regulatory agency to oversee public procurement; imposed and published sanctions for violations of public procurement rules in the Public Procurement Journal.

To improve public financial management, government implemented reforms in budget preparation and execution, and reinforced budget management information systems. Together with reforms in the forestry, maritime, air and road transport sectors, these measures represent a major departure from the earlier decades. The PRSP was endorsed by the IDA and IMF Boards in July 2003 as a credible framework for concessional assistance. This program was adopted to run up to 2015. The reforms under the PNG resulted in more openness in the economy and, inspired by the PRSP, a greater participation of the civil society in public affairs. A National Governance and Anti-Corruption Programme (NGAP), was put in place that same year,

[45] Awung and Atanga, "Economic Crisis and Multi-Party Politics in Cameroon"., p.113

[46] Takor and Kum, "Incubation of the Economic Crisis in Post-Colonial Cameroon", pp.54-65.

charged with rendering accounts, transparency, stakeholder participation, reform of the legal system and judicial frameworks, including the defence of human rights and fight against corruption.[47] After achieving this milestone, the government had to make more sacrifices in order to attain the completion point, for more sustainable benefits.

II- Completion Point

The completion point was the period after which countries that registered under the HIPC initiative received the balance of debt relief that the international community committed them to, at the end of the decision point.[48] To reach this point and graduate from the programme, each listed country had to meet certain reforms and take concrete steps to reduce poverty.[49] After the decision point, Cameroon used a large part of the resources previously allocated to external debt payments, to finance key sectors such as education, health and infrastructure. This supported her efforts towards meeting goals that were setup in its Poverty Reduction Strategy Paper (PRSP), adopted in August 2000.[50] The strategy included policies aimed at improving access to education, healthcare, and social protection programs. Important economic and social progress was achieved between both points. Despite these achievements, much of the country's population still lived in poverty. There was thus need for more sacrifices, if greater gains were to be made in terms of reducing poverty and meeting UN Millennium Development Goals (MDGs).

A post-decision point programme Structural Adjustment Credit (SACIII) was initiated, focused primarily on macro-economic stabilization, poverty reduction, and good governance.[51] This program was based on the interim Poverty Reduction Strategy Paper of 2000, supported by the IMF, through a new 2000-2004 PRGF, SAC III, and by the World Bank.[52] This reform program was out to develop a stable, sound and efficient financial sector, boost public confidence in the

[47] Interview with Fondo Sikod.
[48] Idem.
[49] Kini, "Cameroon: Implications of the HIPC Completion Point".
[50] International Monetary Fund (IMF), *Cameroon: Poverty Reduction Strategy Paper,* Country Report No. 10/257, Publication Services, Washington, D.C, 2010, p. 13.
[51] Kini, "Cameroon: Implications of the HIPC Completion Point".
[52] African Development Bank Group, *Cameroon: Review of the Bank Assistance to the Multisector*, p.21.

financial system, and increase its capacity to finance productive economic activity. Internal and external imbalances were gradually eliminated despite budget slippages in 2004. As such some state-owned banks and insurance systems were restructured. To begin with, the *Banque International du Cameroun pour l'Epargne et le Credit (BICEC)* and *Société Camerounaise d'Assurance et de Reassurance* (SOCAR) were privatized, while the *Compagnie National de Reassurance* (CNR) was closed down.

The Banks' restructuring process, attracted solvent and profitable ones into Cameroon. These new banks met international prudential standards, despite the shortcomings in country's governance system. After benefitting from the process, Cameroon deepened reforms, to enable it reach the HIPC completion point and guarantee a full and permanent reduction in the debt available under the initiative. As such, reforms such as the poverty reduction strategy, maintaining a stable microeconomic environment, setting up mechanisms to ensure the efficient and transparent use of the interim debt relief reforms and consolidation of public expenditure management, were prepared and implemented.[53]

Nevertheless, government failed to implement some of the programme's components and this led to an increase in its fiscal deficit in 2004. Meeting these important challenges, required the government to make good use of the resources freed up by the debt relief; improve conditions to boost private investments and growth, enhance governance and reduce corruption, notwithstanding the strict monitoring of the use of debt relief resources. [54] To begin with, Cameroon's quality and timeliness of fiscal reporting improved. Monthly fiscal data produced within each month of the reporting period and was consistent on a commitment and cash basis. [55] It began publishing monthly budget execution monitoring documents on a regular basis beginning from mid-2005.[56] The accounting and budget nomenclatures were

---

[53] J., Ntangsi, Former country Representative of the *KFW (*German Development Bank), 65 Years, Yaoundé, 3rd August 2010.

[54] A. Bio-Tchane, "Cameroon's Post-Debt Relief Challenges", 2006, www.cameroon-info.net/article/cameroons-post-debt-relief-chanlenges-96834.html, retrieved on the 20th November 2018.

[55] International Monetary Fund (IMF), "Cameroon: Enhanced Heavily Indebted Poor Countries (HIPC) Initiative, p.25.

[56] Ibid.

harmonized in order to facilitate the preparation of financial accounts.[57] Given the reduced role of the state in the economy, the private sector became the engine of growth and this led to a macroeconomic stability in the country.[58] The government failed to meet the conditions of the first four IMF programs and a three-year Poverty Reduction and Growth Facility (PRGF) was thus approved by the IMF in October 2005.[59] The Audit Chamber became operational in the beginning of 2006.Table 6 below, the poverty situation of Cameroon by 2007

Table 6: Poverty index between 1996 and 2007

Milieu	1996	2001	2007
National	0.416	0.404	0.390
Urban	0.419	0.407	0.352
Rural	0.344	0.332	0.322

Source: IMF, "Cameroon: Poverty Reduction Strategy Paper", p.38.

It was within the foregoing facility that the National Food Security Program (NFSP) was put in place under the supervision of the ministry of agriculture and rural development (MINADER). Even though Cameroon did not negotiate any new IMF program, she nevertheless continued cooperation with the Fund under Article IV of its consultations. The full implementation of the HIPC and MDRI Initiatives reduced Cameroons stock debt from 5.7 billion US dollars in 2005 to 525 million in 2006. [60] In 2006 alone, debt service relief was estimated at 128 million US dollars. This progress made under SAP III helped Cameroon to reach the completion point in May 2006.[61] This meant that the country was going to benefit from a 1400 billion Francs CFA debt cancellation of its bilateral and multilateral debt over a period of 10 years. Table 7 is the country's stock of debt at completion point. Table 8 on the other hand, presents Cameroon's public external debt in US dollars, between 2004 and 2005.

---

[57] Ibid.

[58] Bio-Tchane, "Cameroon's Post-Debt Relief Challenges",.

[59] Ibid.

[60] International Monetary Fund (IMF), *Cameroon: Poverty Reduction Strategy Paper*, p.34.

[61] Bertelsmann, "Cameroon Country Report", p.12.

Table 7: Cameroon: Stock of Debt Relief under MDRI and HIPC at Completion Point (In US million dollars)

Organization	MDRI	HIPC	Total
IMF	213	34	247
IDA	721	165	886
AfDB	190	2	192
Total	1,124	201	1,325

Source: International Monetary Fund (IMF), "Cameroon: Enhanced Heavily Indebted Poor Countries (HIPC) Initiative, Completion Point Document and Multilateral Debt Relief Initiative (MDRI)," IMF Country Report No. 06/190, 2006, p.53.

Table 8: Public External Debt (In U.S. million dollars)

Year	2004	2005
Multilateral	**2,056**	**1847**
World Bank	1,194	1112
AfDB	331	310
IMF	318	272
Other	213	530
Bilateral	**4696**	**3977**
Paris Club	4560	3914
Non-Paris Club	136	63
Commercial	233	376
Grand Total	6984	6200

Source: International Monetary Fund (IMF), "Cameroon: Enhanced Heavily Indebted Poor Countries (HIPC) Initiative, Completion Point Document and Multilateral Debt Relief Initiative (MDRI)," IMF Country Report No. 06/190, 2006, p.65.

Table 8 demonstrates that Cameroon's multilateral public external debt stood at 2, 056 US million dollars in 2004 and 1847 in 2005. Its Bilateral debt on the other hand stood at 4696 US million dollars in 2004 and 3977 in 2005. There was some real GDP growth following government reforms and the reaching of the completion point of the Heavily Indebted Poor Countries (HIPC) debt relief program in 2006.[62] This occurred because most completion point triggers had been reached, including satisfactory implementation of the poverty reduction

[62] Kum, "Refitting Economic Sustainability in Cameroon", p. 192.

strategy, maintenance of macroeconomic stability, social sector and structural reforms, and actions to improve governance and reduce corruption.[63] Nonetheless, that related to making the regulatory framework in the water sector operational was not fully implemented and the Cameroon government, decided to follow the advice from the World Bank, that the sector should be regulated through a lease contract, with the private operator that will manage the provision of water rather than through the creation of a water agency.[64] The regulatory framework was then instituted and had to go operational once the selected operator and the leased were signed.

Significant developments in the minerals and mining sector, including diversification away from the then dependence on petroleum, appeared to be under way. Initially, the sharp rise in the world price of petroleum brought a brief burst of growth; in the same way, the drop in petroleum prices accompanied by a world economic crisis have caused severe contraction in Cameroon's economy. The boom-and-bust was repeated. Slow-moving structural reforms, the short supply of electricity needed for industrial growth, riots, and a view of government as corrupt and lacking transparency hindered growth. Adding to this was the world economic crisis that began a year after reaching the completion point. Several projected foreign investment programs were curtailed, particularly in the mining sector.[65] Timber, aluminium, cotton, rubber, transport, bananas, and tourism were negatively affected. Unemployment was, by one estimate, at a 30 percent level.

Some successes had been recorded especially in the domain of the development of agribusiness, processing agricultural products for domestic use or export. A significant progress had also been made in extending the road, rail, and air services. Telephone facilities increased but were for the most part out of date and in poor repair. Cell phone use witnessed phenomenal increases in recent years. National radio broadcasting covered the entire country, and television was also available in most areas by 2006. With the construction of large-scale hydroelectric projects in the coastal region and in the north, the country multiplied several times its electricity-generating capabilities. However, supply

[63] International Monetary Fund (IMF), "Cameroon: Enhanced Heavily Indebted Poor Countries (HIPC) Initiative, Completion Point Document and Multilateral Debt Relief Initiative (MDRI)," IMF Country Report No. 06/190, 2006, p.3.

[64] Ibid.

[65] DeLancey et al., *Historical Dictionary of the Republic of Cameroon*, p. 14.

remained well below demand, and electricity shortages became a major impediment to development. There was thus to, after the completion point, beep these sectors up in order for it to meet the purpose for which substantial amounts of their debts were pardoned.

The most important success in infrastructure building was in the education sector. Relative to many African countries, Cameroon had a high proportion of children in school as far as at the time of independence, but shortages of appropriately trained men and women became a major restraint on growth and development.[66] Tremendous growth in facilities and number of staff and students took place thereafter, but the country faced a serious brain drain with many of its most highly educated persons departing for work in South Africa, Western Europe, and North America. The economy presented major problems for the Biya government, a factor that exacerbated it to respect the IMF and World Bank conditionalities.[67]

III- Post HIPC Initiative Expectations

Cameroon's economic policies underwent significant changes between 1960 and 2006. These economic policies were shaped by a variety of factors, including changes in the global economic environment, natural its resource endowments, and socio-political developments. From independence to the outbreak of the economic crisis, Cameroon's economic development policies geared towards promoting economic growth, reducing poverty, and improving social welfare in the country. While progress was made, the country still faced significant economic challenges, including abject poverty, corruption, human rights abuses, limited access to economic opportunities, inequality, a lack of economic diversification and others that made the country admitted into the IMF and World Bank HIPC initiative, to merit that a substantial fraction of its debts be forgiven. Cameroon's HIPC initiatives' completion point did thus presage a new economic dawn for a country that was loaded with heavy external debt burden. Over 65 billion francs CFA of the country's external debt was cancelled every year for over a period of 10 years. Reaching the completion point of the HIPC initiative did not however mean economic self-sufficiency, but a bridge for more sacrifices to building a vibrant economy.

---

66 Ahidjo, *Contribution to National Construction*, pp. 57-61.

67 DeLancy et al., *Historical Dictionary of the Republic of Cameroon*, p.13.

Cameroon had to continue to fuel efforts in the fight against corruption, good management of public finances, reinforcing judicial transparency; continuing to strengthen the legal system; speedily implementing the Extractive Industries' Transparency Initiative (EITI) for the oil sector; strengthening the public procurement system and further enhancing budget transparency, through the publication of quarterly information.[68] Cameroon was equally to continually make positive contributions towards poverty reduction. The foregoing was aimed at ensuring economic growth and maintaining its new status-quo.[69] Government had to narrow excessive borrowing to finance spending, considering its unsustainability. It therefore had to live within its means in the post-completion era, to maximize growth.

The IMF Poverty Reduction and Growth Facility further advised on gradual increase of non-oil revenues to make up for future declines.[70] Maximising the effectiveness of debt relief and stimulating economic growth depended critically on government's ability to continue to make tangible progress in its efforts to improve on the foregoing domains. It is therefore with regards to the foregoing that it was necessary for the state to pursue its development goals, forestalling that, no national nor international programme or policy be geared toward discouraging food crop production. In this regard, a strategy like Cameroon's agro-industry, implemented to assist the green revolution needed to be sufficiently activated to serve as a viable alternative for petroleum and cash crops that served as the country's main sources of export income. By so doing, it needed to actually place emphasis on food crop production and transformation which had proven to be a viable source of income and means of feeding the country's population and beyond.

For a significant sustainable food production to be maintained in Cameroon, farmers under the foregoing strategy had to be provided access to improved agricultural inputs (seed, fertilizers and chemicals, services, and rewarding markets), to be complemented by some of the most detrimental footraces (transport and credit facilities) to an efficient agricultural system. [71] There was also need for the involvement of a

---

[68] Bio-Tchane, "Cameroon's Post-Debt Relief Challenges."

[69] African Development Bank Group, *Cameroon: Review of the Bank Assistance to the Multisector*, p.21.

[70] Ibid.

[71] Reinnier Kazé , Waiting on the green revolution in Cameroon, 16 July 2015 https://www.theafricareport.com/2772/waiting-on-the-green-revolution-in-cameroon/

strong private sector in Cameroon's green revolution approach. This was essential in that this was going to serve as a network for improved input supplies and technologies; farmers' training; the provision of market information; output marketing opportunities; promotion of agricultural cooperatives; commercial banks for agro-loans and machineries dealers for farm implements, wherever smallholder farmers were found in the country. [72]

Again, establishing business connections between both parties, was going to work toward a win-win solution in which farmers could gain access to factors of production and markets for their crops. This sector could also offer indispensable advice to farmers about the use of farm inputs, techniques and participate in other activities, such as grain milling, vegetable oil extraction, and aggregation thereby creating jobs and wealth for local populations.[73] These are hoped were not only going to help improve agricultural productivity, but enhance the socio-economic and political stability in the country.

Given that Agriculture is a key sector of Cameroon's economy, and the government has over the years implemented policies aimed at promoting the development of the sector which have often produced mixed results (positive and negative). These strategies include the distribution of improved seed varieties, the provision of training and technical support to farmers, and the construction of irrigation systems to support year-round farming. It has within this dispensation, dedicated its emphasis on food crops production especially during the economic recovery period, remaining almost entirely the responsibility of women, while men concentrated on cash crops. Food crop cultivation, was done, using crude tools like: hoes, sticks and cutlasses which was a great hurdle to the process. [74] Improving on agricultural techniques would enhance youth unemployment in Cameroon, which is a major challenge.

---

[72] S. Roy, "Investing in the Private Sector the Way Forward for African Agriculture", 2012 https://www.agribusinessglobal.com/markets/africa-middle-east/investing-in-the-private-sector-the-way-forward-for-african-agriculture/, Consulted on the 12th March 2021

[73] Jennifer Blanke, *How to make the green revolution a reality in Africa*, The African Development Bank Group, 31-Aug-2017, https://www.afdb.org/en/news-and-events/how-to-make-the-green-revolution-a-reality-in-africa-17294, consulted on the 12th March 2021

[74] Kazé, "Waiting on the Green Revolution in Cameroon".

Many young people are unable to find work, and those who do often work in low-paid and insecure jobs.

SAP achievements could not be dented, given that immense efforts had been put in to better the situation, although they remained unsustainable. For these efforts to be viable it was necessary for Cameroonians to be increasingly exhilarated into the modern farming methods propounded by Cameroon's agricultural development policies cum, SAP, HIPC initiative and others and also, engage in large scale food and cash crop production. Women needed to be as much as possible urged to refrain from subsistent farming and encouraged to farm for sale and become income earners. The men who regarded agriculture as mainly for the women needed to be lured into taking great interest in it as a viable way of livelihood. In fact, there was to be an unavoidable desire by both to adhere to the use of modern agricultural facilities such as fertilizers, chemicals, draught animals, tractions, extension programmes and high yielding seed species to have the country's agriculture revolutionised, thereby kindling in them the desire for farming as a business. [75]

Climate change that has most often worked against agricultural productivity due to extreme weather conditions needed to be paid adequate attention in Cameroon's quest for economic development. This needed to be mitigated through concepts like the FAO's climate smart agriculture.[76] The model could enable that food security challenges be addressed, through increased productivity and funding from partners, climate adaptation and alleviation practices. By this, the state and other development stake-holders in Cameroon needed to ensure that there was equally the adoption of appropriate technologies, supportive policy frameworks, and public investments, in order to develop and implement effective risk-sharing patterns. Such could enable them, set up a climate smart agriculture agenda with highly competent staff to ensure that all activities in the agriculture space were fully climate proof and climate smart.[77]

One of the problems of Cameroon's economic development endeavors during the period of study, was the poor follow-up of projects that were implemented by the state. Government's follow up of most investment projects was undertaken without reference to their initial

[75] Kum, "Wum Area Development Authority (WADA)", p. 283.

[76] Blanke, *how to make the green revolution a reality in Africa.*

[77] Ibid.

objectives, but rather focused on the decisions of foreign private and public investors especially from France. Generally, besides the inability to follow up most of the investment projects earmarked as stipulated, Cameroon's planning mechanism as a whole, failed because the law establishing FIDES elaborated the scheme for Cameroon as an autonomous entity whose particular problems were to be resolved without taking specific considerations. On the whole therefore, five years development plans were merely parts of the overall metropolitan French plans where much attention was focused on the decisions of foreign private and public investors. This outright intervention of foreign experts worked down on Cameroon's adequate follow-up of projects. There is therefore need for Cameroon to nationalise its development endeavours.

Conclusion

The first two decades of Cameroon's economy were marked by instantaneous growth, owed to its economic development policies and oil proceeds. These however became unsustainable due to colossal mismanagement, corruption, misappropriation, embezzlement and poor follow-up of government initiatives. The government endorsed some exigent measures to curb the crisis and improve its economy in what was termed: Economic and Stabilisation Plan. This plan was built on cutting down government overheads, but failed to achieve the expected results. After numerous failures in sufficiently revamping Cameroon's economy the Heavily Indebted Poor Countries (HIPC) Initiative was put in place in 1996 under the Multilateral Debt Relief Initiative (MDRI), coordinated by the IMF, World Bank and others, to ensure that the poorest countries in the world were not overwhelmed by unsustainable debt burdens. Despite the Cameroon government's constant attempts to undermine SAP policies, it recorded some noteworthy results, leading it to reach the decision point in 2000 under the SAP II programme and "completion point" in 2006, under the SAP III programme. It argued that the completion point was just an opportunity for more sacrifices and efforts to be made by Cameroon for sustained growth. It is in this regard that the second part of the chapter laid emphasis on prospects for Cameroon's economy development efforts.

GENERAL CONCLUSION

Chapter one was dedicated to examining the contextual setting of Cameroon's economic development policies. This chapter was logically divided into the period of the German protectorate that ended with the outbreak of WWI, ensuing to the League of Nations mandates, ending with WWII, resulting to the UN trusteeship. The later periods were both animated by Britain and France. It laid deep emphasis on the organisation of colonial economies in the British and French Cameroons, with emphasis on the different economic development patterns each of both European administrations employed for their economic gains. The chapter began by generally examining the motives of European colonisation especially the Germans and their economic development patterns in Cameroon. It continued with both the mandates and trusteeship periods in both British and French Cameroons, emphasizing on their economic development strategies in the territory, during these periods. The chapter further brings out both the strengths and weaknesses of France's economic development strides in its part of the territory during the trusteeship period. It ends with the independence and reunification struggles in territories in 1960 and 1961.

Chapter two examined early post-independence economic development groundworks. It laid emphasis on Cameroon's utmost desire to attain its economic sovereignty, through a series of mechanisms, ranging from development planning, African socialism, planned liberalisms, the institution of development management institutions and others. During this period, policies aimed at promoting industrialization, expanding infrastructure, and improving social welfare, including the creation of schools, hospitals, and other public amenities, were implemented. The chapter equally gave a pride of place to how development was funded in Cameroon during early independence period, based on both internal and external sources, notwithstanding its foreign policy orientations.

Cameroon's debt trap entanglements were equally examined in the chapter notwithstanding some of the efforts that were employed to save it from the predicament. The chapter has further laid emphasis on the regional planning mechanism that Cameroon instituted during the second five years development plan period and withing its planned liberalism precept. The fundamental basis of this development model was traced, notwithstanding the distribution of investments among the six economic and administrative regions: Northern Region, South-

Centre region, Littoral Region, West Cameroon Region, Western and Eastern Regions. After its succinct appraisal, the chapter concluded with the concept of balanced development with the context of the country's economic trends. Between the 1960s and 1970s, Cameroon's economy experienced rapid growth, urged by its rich natural resources, including oil, gas, timber, and agricultural products.

Chapter three highlighted Cameroon's agricultural development strategies during the period before the outbreak of the economic crisis. It has expounded why and how Cameroon's planned development scheme, initially laid emphasis on industrial development, but endorsed agricultural development in the early 1970s. The chapter unfastened with the early post-independence efforts, employed, to enhance the country's agricultural economy. Aside that were the country's self-reliance development model, fashioned to subordinate its international economic relations to domestic development objectives, depending principally on local efforts and labour. It has demonstrated that this gave rise to the country's Food self-sufficiency drive: to ensure a sustainable production of food for local consumption and sale to its neighbours, notwithstanding the Agro-industry strategy, Operation Green Revolution and Agro-pastoral shows were instituted in Cameroon. All the foregoing, in a bit to meet the agricultural development needs of the country, before the outbreak of the economic crisis in 1986. The chapter argues that although Cameroon's policy makers made tremendous inroads in its agricultural policies, they met with immense drawbacks. Chapter four shall focus on the country's Economic development drawbacks, before 1986.

Cameroon's early development drive was based on attaining its economic sovereignty, perceived as the final stage for her independence, faced enormous challenges. Government instituted the planned development precept, to be executed through Five Years Economic and Social development plans; Planned Liberalism; Regional Planning, Balanced Development, Self-reliance Development, Food Self-sufficiency, Agro-Industrialisation; Operation Green Revolution and Agro-pastoral Shows. These early economic development strides faced enormous challenges, ranging from agricultural oriented constraints (poor cultivation technics, inadequate inputs and poor or no financing of projects); the petroleum debacle that greatly worked down on agricultural production and state corporations' drain, where a lot of money was borrowed and invested on them. These parastatals turned out to be unproductive, culminating in the economic crisis that broke out in the mid-1980s.

Cameroon's economy suffered from a combination of external shocks, including falling oil prices and declining terms of trade, as well as internal challenges, including corruption, mismanagement, and political instability between the 1980s and 1990s. Government was forced to implement structural adjustment programs, which involved liberalizing the economy, reducing government spending, and privatizing state-owned enterprises. This chapter laid deep emphasis on the contextual setting within which the economic crisis emerged notwithstanding the various domestic and external efforts that were employed by both the Cameroon government, IMF and World Bank, to overcome the crisis. Economic misfortunes during the mid-1980s nonetheless led to criticism of the planned development philosophy due to poor governmental judgment at guiding private foreign investments, the pervasive corruption paralyzing bureaucratic structures, the overheated process of industrialisation and ill-advised government backing of certain foreign investors.

Analysis of agricultural policies in Cameroon since 1960 shows that government investments boosted the agricultural sector. However, the inadequacy of these policies and constraints resulting from the destabilizing effects of Structural Adjustment Programs (SAP) inevitably led to strikes all over the country. The mid-1980s' economic crisis that shook Cameroon resulted in the country's withdrawal from specific sectors of activity. Because of its international economic status at the time, Cameroon was compelled by the Bretton Woods institutions to adopt the Structural Adjustment Programs (SAPs) to get its economy back on track.

The first two decades of Cameroon's economy were marked by instantaneous growth, owed to its economic development policies and oil proceeds. These however became unsustainable due to colossal mismanagement, corruption, misappropriation, embezzlement and poor follow-up of government initiatives. The government endorsed some exigent measures to curb the crisis and improve its economy in what was termed: Economic and Stabilisation Plan. This plan was built on cutting down government overheads, but failed to achieve the expected results. After numerous failures in sufficiently revamping Cameroon's economy the Heavily Indebted Poor Countries (HIPC) Initiative was put in place in 1996 under the Multilateral Debt Relief Initiative (MDRI), coordinated by the IMF, World Bank and others, to ensure that the poorest countries in the world were not overwhelmed by unsustainable debt burdens. Despite the Cameroon government's constant attempts to undermine SAP policies, it recorded some noteworthy results, leading to reaching the decision point in 2000 under the SAP II programme and "completion point" in 2006, under the SAP III programme. It argued that the completion point was just an opportunity for more sacrifices and efforts to be made by Cameroon for sustained growth. It is in this regard that the second part of the chapter laid emphasis on prospects for Cameroon's economic development efforts.

SOURCES CONSULTED

Books

African Development Bank Group (ADBG), *Cameroon: Review of the Bank Assistance to the Multisector, 1996-2004*, Operations Evaluation Department (OPEV), 2008.

African Development Bank Group (ADBG), *Cameroon: Structural Adjustment Programme II (SAPII) Project Performance Evaluation Report (PPER)*, Operations Evaluation Department (OPEV), 2002.

Ahidjo, A., *Anthologies des Discours du President Ahidjo, 1973-1978,* (II), Dakar, NEA, 1980.

Ahidjo, A., *As Told by Ahmadou Ahidjo*, Paul Bory, Monaco, 1968.

Ahidjo, A., *Contribution to National Construction,* Paris, Présence Africaine, 1964.

Ahidjo, A., *Fondements et perspectives du Cameroun,* Paris, Saint Lambert, 1976.

Ahidjo, A., Recueil *des discours Présidentielle de 1973-1978,* Centre de propagande Economique, Paris, 1978.

Ahidjo, A., *The Political Philosophy of Ahmadou Ahidjo,* Paul Bory, Monte Carlo, 1968.

Anderson, P., and Lorch, R.P., *Agricultural Growth is the Key to Poverty Alleviation in Low Income Developing Countries*, In the Unfinished Agenda: Perspectives on overcoming Poverty and Environmental Degradation, Washington D.C, 2001.

Anyanwu, C., *Community development. The Nigerian perspective.* Ibadan: Gabesther Educational Publishers, 1992.

Ardener, E., et al. *Plantation and Village in the Cameroons: Some Economic and Social Studies*, Oxford University Press, United Kingdom, 1960.

Ardener, S. G., *Eye-Witnesses to the Annexation of Cameroon, 1883-1889*, Ministry of Primary Education and West Cameroon antiquities Commission, Buea, 1968.

Barkindo, B., Omolewa, M., and Babalola, G., *Colonial Economy and underdevelopment of Africa and the Wider world 3: Africa since the scramble*, Longman Nigeria, 1994.

Bilsorrow, E., and Delargy, F., *The Impact of Rural Development Projects in Demographic Behaviour*, New York, UNFPA, 1985.

Brunel, S., *La Coopération Nord-Sud,* Paris, Presses Universitaires de France, 1997.

Cheradame, A., *La colonisation et les colonies Allemands,* Paris, 1905.

Commissariat Général à l'Information, *Le chemin de fer Trans camerounaise*, Paris, Société Presse Associée, 1969.

Cornevin, R., *Histoire de la Colonisation Allemande*, Paris, PUF, 1969.

Delancy, M. D., et al., *Historical Dictionary of the Republic of Cameroon*, Fourth Edition, the Scarecrow Press, Inc. Lanham, Maryland, 2010.

Djeudo, A. B., Advanced *Human, Economic and Regional Geography (Area Studies): Concepts and case studies in a World of Development Contrast A4 in I Volume,* Success Education Publishers Limbe, Cameroon, 2008.

Douya, E., *Cotton Supply Response in Cameroon*, Dakar, Senegal, CODESRIA., 2008.

Eyongetah, T. and Brain, R. *A History of the Cameroons,* London, Longman, 1974.

Eyongetah, T., Brain, R., and Palmer, R., *A History of Cameroon (New Edition),* Longman Group, UK, 1987.

Ezell, S., and Atkinson, R., The *Indian Economy at a Crossroads*, The Information Technology & Innovation Foundation (ITI F), 2014.

Fanso V. G.,*Cameroon History for Secondary Schools and Colleges, vol.2, The Colonial and Post-Colonial Periods*, London, Macmillan Publishers, 1989.

Fanso, V. G., *Cameroon History for Secondary Schools and Colleges, from prehistoric Times to the twenty-first century (revised and updated combined edition),* Team Work Press, Bamkika'ay, Kumbo. 2017.

Friedman, J., and Alonso, W. (eds), *Regional Development and Planning*, Cambridge, 1964.

Galtung, J., et al. (eds.), *Self-Reliance: a Strategy for Development*. London: Bogle L'Ouverture publications, 1980.

Gardinier, D. E., *Cameroon-United Nations Challenge to French Policy*, London Institute of Race Relations, Oxford University Press, 1963.

Ghari, D., et al., *The Basic Needs Approach to Development: Some Issues Regarding Concepts and Methodology*. Geneva: ILO Publication 1980.

Jackson, S., and Ghosh, P. K. (eds), *Appropriate Technology in Third World Development,* London, Greenwood Press, 1984.

Jean-Yves, M., *Social differentiation and regional disparities: educational development in Cameroon,* ORSTOM, Paris, 2008.

Jequier, N., *Appropriate Technology: Problems and Promises*, Paris, OECD, 1976.

Kibaya, J.F.M., *L'information stratégique agricole en Afrique : L'échec de la vulgarisation*, Harmattan, Paris, 2006.

Krause, W., *Economic Development the Under-Developed World and American Interest,* San Francisco, Wards Worth, 1961.

LeVine, V.T., *The Cameroon Federal Republic*, Cornell University Press, Ithaca and London, 1971.

Meier, G. M., *Problems of Cooperation for Development*, New York, Oxford University Press, 1974.

Mokake, J. N., *Basic Facts on Cameroon History*, Cure Series Publishers, Limbe, 2008.

Moon, T.P., *Imperialism and World Politics*, New York, 1940.

Mveng, E., *Histoire du Cameroun*, Paris, Présence Africaine, 1963.

Ndongko, W. A., *Planning for Economic Development in a Federal State: The Case of Cameroon, 1960-1971*, Munchen, Welt Form Verlage, 1975.

Ndongko, W. A., *Regional Development Policy in Cameroon*, the Faculty of Law and Economics, University of Yaoundé, 1975.

Ndongko, W.A., *Labour Resistance in Cameroon: Strategies and Labour Resistance in the Agro-Industrial Plantations of the Cameroon Development Corporation*, African Studies Centre, Leiden, 1993.

Ndongko, W.A., *Regional Economic Planning in Cameroon*, Research Report No. 21, the Scandinavian institute of African Studies, Uppsala, Sweeden, 1974.

Ngango, G., *Les investissements D'origine extérieur en Afrique noire Francophone : Statut et incidence sur le développent*, Paris, Présence Africain, 1973.

Ngoh, V. J., "The Political Evolution of Cameroon", 1884-1961, PhD thesis, Portland State University, 1979.

Ngoh, V. J., *The World since 1919: A Short History,* Pioneer Publishers, Yaoundé, 1989.

Norrington-Davies, G., Climate Change Financing and Aid Effectiveness: Cameroon Case Study, OECD, March 2011.

Ntangsi, M. M., *A Balance Sheet of Economic Development Experience in Cameroon*, NT, NH, 2008.

Philippe, H., *Analyse du sous-développement en Afrique noire : l'exemple de l'économie du Cameroun,* Paris presses universitaires de France, 1968.

Piel, G., *Technology and Economic Development,* USA, Alfred A. Knofe, 1963.

Rudin, H. H., *Germans in the Cameroons 1884-1914*, New York, 1969.

Sandbrook, R., *The Politics of Africa's Economic Stagnation. United Kingdom*, Cambridge University Press, 1985.

SCET Cameroun, *Projet de Développement Rural intègre du département de la Menchum,* Vol. 3, Direction des études et projets, MINAGRI, Yaoundé, 1982.

Seitz, J., *The Politics of Development,* New York, Basil Blackwell Inc, 1988.

Présidence de la République, *Crise économique : Réponse du Cameroun*, Cabinet Civil, 1989.

Renonim, P., *Le Traite de paix de Versailles,* Paris, Flammarion, 1969.

Societe d'Etudes pour le Développement Économique et Social, *Rapport pour les possibilités de développement industriel du Cameroun*, Paris, La Société, 1960.

Takang, B. S., *An Illustrated History of Cameroon Since 1800: A Digest for Advance Level Students*, Book House, Yaounde, 2013.

Tamekamta, A. Z., and J. K. Menkene, J.K. (eds.), *L'urgence d'une révolution agricole au Cameroun*, Paris, L'Harmattan, 2013.

Tchoungui R., et al., *Structural Adjustment and Sustainable Development in Cameroon*, Overseas Development Institute, London, 1995.

The Ministry of Planning and Territorial Development, *What you Should Know about the IIIRD Plan*, Temporary Edition, Yaoundé, No Date.

Wallstein, I., World *Systems Analysis*, Durtham NC, Duke University Press, 2004.

Welch Jr., C. E., *Dream of Unity: Pan-Africanism and Political Unification in West Africa*, Cornell University Press, Ithaca, New York, 1966.

Wood, S.H., *World Affairs: 1900 to Present Day*, Longman Group Ltd, 1978.

Zuvekas, C., *Economic Development: An Introduction,* London, Macmillan, 1979.

Articles and Book Chapters

Agbor-Tabi, P., "German Colonialism in Africa: Domestic Pressure or Governmental Policy?" in *Cameroon Review of International Studies*, Vol 2, No. 1, 1985, pp.10-25.

Awung, W.J., and Atanga, M., "Economic Crisis and Multi-Party Politics in Cameroon, Cameroon *Journal on Democracy and Human Rights*, Vol.5 No. 1, 2011, pp 94-124.

Baye, M., and Amongwa, F., 'Decomposition of Inequality in the Distribution Living Standard in Cameroon," *African Journal of Economic Policy, 9(2),,* 2002, pp. 51-75.

Bederman S.H., and DeLancey, M.W., "The Cameroon Development Corporation, 1947-1977", Kofele-Kale, N., *An African Experiment in Nation Building: The Bilingual Cameroon Republic since Reunification*, Westview Press, Boulder, Colorado, 198, pp. 251-278.

Benjamin, N., and Devarajan, S., "Oil Revenues and Economic Policy in Cameroon: Results from a Computable General Equilibrium Model", *World Bank Policy research Working Paper No. 745,* Washington DC, 1985, pp.1-48.

Bret, A. E., "Adjustment and the State: Problem of Administrative Reform", IDS Bulletin, 19(4): 4, 1988, pp. 4-11.

Bustin, E., "The Congo", Carter, G. M., *Five African States, Responses to Diversity: the Congo, Dahomey, the Cameroon Federal Republic, the Rhodesians and Nyasaland south Africa*, Cornell University Press, Ithaca, New York,1963, pp.9-144.

Daka A., et al., "Public Agrarian Policies and Food Security in Cameroon: Problems and Challenges towards Agricultural Development", *European Journal of Humanities and Social Sciences, Vol* 1, Issue 4, July 2021, pp.22-28.

Dawson, N., et al., "Green Revolution in Sub-Saharan Africa: Implications of Imposed Innovation for the Well-being of Smallholders", *World Development*, Vol. 78, 2016, pp. 204-218.

EDIAFRIC, "République du Cameroun : Mémento de L'économie Africain", *numéro spécial du bulletin de L'Afrique noire* No. 456, Paris, 1967, pp. 17-52.

Fambon, S., "Pro Poor Growth in Cameroon", *STATISTIKA*, University of Yaoundé II, Yaoundé, Cameroon, 2017, pp.97-109.

Fonchingong, C. C., and Fonjong, L. N., "The Concept of Self-Reliance in Community Development Initiatives in the Cameroon Grassfields," *Nordic Journal of African Studies* 12(2),2003, pp.196–219.

Fonjong, L. N., "Changing Fortunes of Government Policies and its Implications", *Nordic Journal of African Studies*, 2004, pp. 13-29.

Henry, P. M., "The United Nations and the Problem of African Development", *International Organization,* XVI, No. 2, (Spring 1962), pp. 362-374.

Jua, N., "State, Oil and Accumulation," in Geschiere P. and Konings, P. (eds.), *Pathways to Accumulation in Cameroon*, Leiden, ASC, KARTHALA, 1993, pp.131-159.

Konings, P., "The Post-colonial State and Economic and Political Reforms in Cameroon", in Fernandez Jilberto A.E., and Mommen, A.(eds), *Liberalization in the Developing World: Institutional and Economic Changes in Latin America, Africa and Asia*, London and New York, Routledge, pp.244-264.

Kum, G. F. and Kum, J. K., "Understanding Agro-pastoral Shows in a Planned Economy (1973-1987): the Case of Cameroon", Scholars Journal of Arts, Humanities and Social Sciences, pp. 773-774.

Kum, G. F., "Drives and Prospects of Agriculture in Vocational Training During the period of the Germans in Cameroon", Njock Nyobe, I. S., and Nzogue, J.P. (eds.) *Le Cameroun sous Domination Européen: Entre Rencontre, Partages et Conflictualités,* 1884-1914, Editions Ifrikaya, 2018, pp. 159-170.

Kum, G. F., "The Operation Green Revolution 1973-1986: Sustaining Cameroon's Planned Development Precept, *World Journal of Education and Humanities*, Vol. 3, No. 2, 2021, pp. 63-78.

Kum, G.F., "Refitting Economic Sustainability in Cameroon (1986-2006): Retorts of a Miscarried State", *Annals of the Faculty of Arts, Letters and Social Sciences,* the University of Yaoundé I, No.20, New Series, 2018, pp. 177-197.

Le Vine, V.T., "The Cameroon Federal Republic", G. M. Carter (ed.), *Five African States, Responses to Diversity,* Cornell University Press, Ithaca, New York,1963, pp.

Mbouri Mbak, H., "La production alimentaire au Cameroun," in *Traité sur la sécurité alimentaire au Cameroun*, Areion Publishing., Paris : Areion Publishing, 2002.

Mbu, E., "An Imperial Presidency: A Study of Presidential Power in Cameroon", Kofele-Kale, *An African Experiment in Nation Building: The Bilingual Cameroon Republic Since Reunification*, pp.133-187.

Moudio, J.M., "The dynamics of food security policy in Cameroon (2008-2019)", *American Journal of Public Policy and Administration,* Vol.6, Issue 1, 2021, pp 12-43.

Ndongko, W. A., "A Comparative Analysis of French and British Investment Policies in Cameroon", *Pan African Journal,* Vol. VII, No.2, 1974, pp.145-171.

Ndongko, W. A., "Regional Economic Planning in Cameroon", *Intereconics*, No. 5, 1974, pp.154-157.

Ndongko, W. A., "The Political Economy of Regional Economic Development in Cameroon", N. Kofele-Kale, N., An African Experiment in Nation Building: The Bilingual Cameroon Republic since Reunification, Westview Press, Boulder, Colorado, 1980, pp. 227-250.

Ndongko, W. A., "The Tracing of Economic Development in Cameroon", *Africa Development*, Vol.11. No.3, 1977, pp.66-87.

Ngwa A. C and Lambi, C. M., "An Evaluation of the Upper Nun Valley Authority's Agricultural Innovation in the Ndop Plain (Cameroon) since 1970", *Epassa Moto* vol. 4, No. 1, 2009, pp.50-67.

Okafor, F.C., "Integrated Rural Development Planning in Nigeria: A Spatial Dimension", *Cahier d'Etudes Africaine*, Vol., No.2, 1986, pp.83-95.

Oyono, D., "L'Allemagne et le statut international du Cameroun 1919-1939 », *Revue Camerounaise des Relations Internationales,* Vol. 2, No 1, Berlin, 1985, pp. 106-134

Pingali, P., et al., "Changing Donor Trends in Assistance to Agricultural Research and Development in Africa South of the Sahara", in Lynam, J., et al. (eds.) *Agricultural Research in Africa: Investing in Future Harvests*, The International Food Policy Research Institute (IFPRI), Washington, DC, 2016, pp. 139-170.

Preiswerk, R. "Sources of Resisting to Local Self-Reliance", Galtung, J., et al. (eds.), *Self-Reliance: a Strategy for Development*. London: Bogle L'Ouverture publications, 1980.

Toenniessen, G., Adesina, A. and Devries, J., "Building an Alliance for a Green Revolution in Africa", *Annals of the New York Academy of Sciences,* 2008, pp.233–242

Takor, N. K., and Kum, G. F., "Incubation of the Economic Crisis in Post-Colonial Cameroon 1960-1987: An Experience in State Capitalism", *International Journal of Humanities Social Sciences and Education (IJHSSE)*, Volume 5, Issue 8, August 2018, pp.54-65.

Tambi, M.D., "Economic Growth, Crisis, and Recovery in Cameroon: A Literature Review", *International Journal of Industrial Distribution & Business 6-1*, 2015, pp. 5-15.

Tchoungui, R., et al., "Case Study for Cameroon", In Reed D. (ed), *Structural Adjustment, the Environment and Sustainable Development*, London, UK: Earthscan Publications, 1996, pp.53-81.

The Farmers Voice, "Agro-Pastoral Show 2010: Ebolowa says, "Yes we can", *The Farmers Voice*, Bafoussam, 16th March 2010, pp. 2-6.

Yensu, E., "Balanced Rural Development in Cameroon within a Democratic Context", In: Nkwi, P., and Nyamnjoh, F. (eds.), *Regional Balance and National Integration in Cameroon. Lessons Learned and the Uncertain Future*. ICASSRT monograph 1, African Studies Centre, Leiden, The Netherlands, 1997.

Theses and Dissertations

Abéna Etoundi, M.J., "La planification économique au Cameroun : aperçu historique (1960-2000)", Thèse de Doctorat/Ph. D en Histoire, Université de Yaoundé I, octobre 2010.

Chia, M. P., "WADA and the Rural Development of Menchum Division: A Case study of Bum Area," Maitrise in Geography, the University of Yaoundé I, 1988.

Kum, G. F., "The Socio-Economic Impact of the Liquidation of the Wum Area Development Authority (WADA) on Wum Central Sub-Division 1989- 2004" Maîtrise Dissertation, Department of History, University of Yaoundé I, 2004.

Kum, G. F., "Wum Area Development Authority (WADA), 1965-1994, Implantation, Economic and Social Conversions in Menchum Division", Doctorat/PhD in History, University of Yaounde I, Cameroon.

Mboudou, A. M., "Le financement du développement au Cameroun", Thèse de Doctorat de 3éme Cycle, Sciences Economiques, Université de Yaoundé, 1981.

Mbuh, K. E., "Canadian Financial and Technical Assistance to Cameroon (1962-2006)," Masters Dissertation, Department of History, University of Dschang, 2010.

Nwana, A.A., "The North West Development Authority (NWDA/MIDENO), in the Socio-Economic Development of the North West Region of Cameroon, 1981-2019", PhD Dissertation in History, the University of Bamenda, 2022.

Takang, S. B., "The Cameroon Development Corporation, 1946-2020: Political and Socio-Economic Mutations, PhD thesis, Department of History and Archaeology, University of Bamenda, 2023.

Yuh, P.C., "Wum Area Development Authority (WADA): Catalysis for Rural Development", B.A. Dissertation, International School of Journalism, University of Yaoundé, 1977.

Policy Papers

African Development Bank (ADB) *Cameroon: Country Governance Profile*, Country operations Department, Central and West Regions, September 2004.

Baye, M., Fambon,, S., and Sikod, F., "Globalisation: Institutional changes and poverty in Rural Cameroon". Final Report, Tokyo Japan: FASID, 2002.

Benjamin, N., and Devarajan, S., "Oil Revenues and Economic Policy in Cameroon: Results from a Computable General Equilibrium Model", *World Bank Policy research Working Paper No. 745,* Washington DC, 1985.

Collint, D., Hansen, C.W., and Wingender, A., "Two Blades of Grass: The Impact of the Green Revolution", Centre for the Study of African Economies (CSAE) Working Paper WPS/2016-30.

Fondo, S., "The Completion point of the HIPC Initiative: what it means for the Cameroon Economy", A Presentation at Hilton, Sponsored by the British Council, 2006."

Gauthier, B., and Zeufack, A., *Governance and Oil Revenues in Cameroon*, London, OxCarre Research Paper 38, October 2009.

Geschier, P., *Culture: Pandora's Box?* Paper presented at the conference "Good Governance for Africa: Whose Governance?" organised by the University of Limburg and ECDPM, Maastricht, 23–24 November 1995.

International Monetary Fund (IMF), "Cameroon: Enhanced Heavily Indebted Poor Countries (HIPC) Initiative, Completion Point Document and Multilateral Debt Relief Initiative (MDRI)," IMF Country Report No. 06/190, 2006.

International Monetary Fund (IMF), *Cameroon: Poverty Reduction Strategy Paper,* Country Report No. 10/257, Publication Services, Washington, D.C, 2010.

Jua, N., *Economic Management in Neo-Colonial States: A Case Study of Cameroon*, Research Report No. 38, African Studies Centre, Leiden, Netherlands, 1990.

Internet Sources

"Economy of Cameroon: exports, Imports, Agriculture", in Cameroon-tour.com/economy/index.html, Retrieved on the 24th August 2015.

Amin, A. A. (ed.), *Developing a Sustainable Economy in Cameroon*, https://books.google.cm/books/about/Developing_a_Sustainable_Economy_in_Came.html?i =0yewbFW06aYC&redir_esc=y, consulted on the 30th January 2023.

Bamou, E., and Masters, W.A., Distortions to Agricultural Incentives in Cameroon, Paper 42, December 2007, p.9, https://www.researchgate.net/publication/228618483, consulted on the 07th March 2021.

Bertelsmann, S., Cameroon *Country Report, BTI*, 2012, in http://www.bti-project.org, retrieved on 20/07/2013.

Blanke, J., *How to make the Green Revolution a Reality in Africa*, The African Development Bank Group, 31-Aug-2017, https://www.afdb.org/en/news-and-events/how-to-make-the-green-revolution-a-reality-in-africa-17294 , consulted on the 12th March 2021

Chauleur, P. "Un libéralisme planifié » pour associer le secteur privé aux efforts de développement", https://www.monde-diplomatique.fr/1976/08/CHAULEUR/33871, Retrieved on 03, November 2023.

CIA World Factbook, U.S. Dept. of State Country Background Notes (January 2012) http://www.cia.gov/library/ppublications/the -world-factbook/

Dongmo, C., "The Green Revolution and Food Self-sufficiency: Cameroon's Land Theory of Economic Development", *Cameroon Link,* June 2008. Retrieved on 7th February 2011, http://www.camerounlink.net/?bnid=83&SessionID=&wid=&tid=&nid=38660&id

Global Forum for Rural advisory Services, https://www.g-fras.org/en/world-wide-extension-study/africa/central-africa/cameroon.html, consulted on the 12th March 2021.

Jennifer Blanke, *How to make the green revolution a reality in Africa*, The African Development Bank Group, 31-Aug-2017, https://www.afdb.org/en/news-and-events/how-to-make-the-green-revolution-a-reality-in-africa-17294, consulted on the 12th March 2021.

Kazé, Reinnier, Waiting on the green revolution in Cameroon, 16 July 2015 https://www.theafricareport.com/2772/waiting-on-the-green-revolution-in-cameroon/

Kini, N., "Cameroon: Implications of the HIPC Completion Point", 2006, http://www.postnewsline.com/2006/05/implications_of.htmlmore, 20th November 2018.

MINADER, "National Strategy for Rice Growing in Cameroon: (Milling) III", 2009, p.5, https://www.jica.go.jp/english/our_work/thematic_issues/agricultural/pdf/cameroon_en.pdf, consulted on the 07th March 2021.

OECD, Cameroon-OECD/AfDB, 2002, https://www.oecd.org/countries/cameroon, retrieved 14/03/2017.

Roy, S., "Investing in the Private Sector the Way Forward for African Agriculture", 2012, https://www.agribusinessglobal.com/markets/africa-middle-east/investing-in-the-private-sector-the-way-forward-for-african-agriculture/, Consulted on the 12th March 2021

The World Bank, "Heavily Indebted Poor Country (HIPC) Initiative", 2018, www.worldbank.org/en/topic/debt/brief/hipc, retrieved on 18th November 2018.

USAID, Annual Review of Agency's Four Priority Areas of Concentration in Cameroon, 1983, https://www.google.com/search?client=firefoxd&q=USAID+Annual+Review+of+Agency%27s+Four+Priority+Areas+of+Concentration+in+Cameroon%2C+1983, Retrieved on 03 October 2023.

Wikipedia, Planned Liberalism, https://en.wikipedia.org/wiki/planned_liberalism, consulted on the 13th March 2023.

Archival Materials

NAB, File no. 1946/2- "An Ordinance to Provide the Establishment of the Corporation known as the Cameroon Development Cooperation" (CDC), 1946.

NAB, File No. 748 QC/a/1966/2, "Agricultural Shows", 1966.

NAB, File No. DVA/J.2/2, (Qb/a 1960), "Five Years Development Plan", 1960.

NAB, File No. PMO 422 (Qb/a 1962/2), "General Economic Situation in West Cameroon Arising from Reunification", 1962.

Interviews

Akwo Martin, 61 Years, Former Extension Farmer WADA, Wum, 20th September 2015

Christopher Agem, 75 years, Former Extension Farmer WADA, Wum, 20th September 2015.

Fondo Sikod, 77 years, Economist University of Yaounde II, Yaoundé, 13th October 2014.

Gabuin Ndarikwi Johsnson, 84 years, Former Directed of WADA, Bamenda, 2016.

Joseph Che Kangkolo, 78 years, Former Secretary of State for Interior for West Cameroons, Wum, 23rd November 2012.

Joseph Ntangsi, 65 years, Former Representative of the *KFW (*German Development Bank) Yaoundé, Yaoundé, 3rd August 2010.

Niba F. T., 55 years, Former Programme Coordinator for the Tikar Development Project and Ex-Chief of Section for Planning, Evaluation and Training for WADA, Magba, 18 July 2004.

INDEX OF NAMES AND CONCEPTS

A

B

C

D

E

I

J

K

L

R

S

Y

Z

Structures éditoriales du groupe L'Harmattan

L'Harmattan Italie
Via degli Artisti, 15
10124 Torino
harmattan.italia@gmail.com

L'Harmattan Hongrie
Kossuth l. u. 14-16.
1053 Budapest
harmattan@harmattan.hu

L'Harmattan Sénégal
10 VDN en face Mermoz
BP 45034 Dakar-Fann
senharmattan@gmail.com

L'Harmattan Cameroun
TSINGA/FECAFOOT
BP 11486 Yaoundé
inkoukam@gmail.com

L'Harmattan Burkina Faso
Achille Somé – tengnule@hotmail.fr

L'Harmattan Guinée
Almamya, rue KA 028 OKB Agency
BP 3470 Conakry
harmattanguinee@yahoo.fr

L'Harmattan RDC
185, avenue Nyangwe
Commune de Lingwala – Kinshasa
matangilamusadila@yahoo.fr

L'Harmattan Congo
219, avenue Nelson Mandela
BP 2874 Brazzaville
harmattan.congo@yahoo.fr

L'Harmattan Mali
ACI 2000 - Immeuble Mgr Jean Marie Cisse
Bureau 10
BP 145 Bamako-Mali
mali@harmattan.fr

L'Harmattan Togo
Djidjole – Lomé
Maison Amela
face EPP BATOME
ddamela@aol.com

L'Harmattan Côte d'Ivoire
Résidence Karl – Cité des Arts
Abidjan-Cocody
03 BP 1588 Abidjan
espace_harmattan.ci@hotmail.fr

Nos librairies en France

Librairie internationale
16, rue des Écoles
75005 Paris
librairie.internationale@harmattan.fr
01 40 46 79 11
www.librairieharmattan.com

Librairie des savoirs
21, rue des Écoles
75005 Paris
librairie.sh@harmattan.fr
01 46 34 13 71
www.librairieharmattansh.com

Librairie Le Lucernaire
53, rue Notre-Dame-des-Champs
75006 Paris
librairie@lucernaire.fr
01 42 22 67 13

www.ingramcontent.com/pod-product-compliance
Lightning Source LLC
Chambersburg PA
CBHW071437230926
51846CB00001B/261
* 9 7 8 2 3 3 6 5 0 5 3 8 1 *